The Compact History of the American Red Cross

CHARLES HURD

Illustrations by **GIL WALKER**

HAWTHORN BOOKS, INC. ✚ *Publishers* ✚ **NEW YORK**

THE
COMPACT HISTORY
OF THE
AMERICAN
RED CROSS

✦ ✦ ✦ ✦ ✦ ✦ ✦

© 1959 by Hawthorn Books, Inc., 70 Fifth Avenue, New York City 11.
Copyright under International and Pan-American Copyright Conventions.
All rights reserved, including the right to reproduce this book, or portions
thereof, in any form, except for inclusion of brief quotations in a review. This
book was manufactured in the United States of America and published simultaneously in Canada by McClelland & Stewart, Ltd., 25 Hollinger Road,
Toronto 16. Library of Congress Catalogue Card Number 59–5616.

FIRST EDITION, MARCH, 1959

ACKNOWLEDGMENTS

The author acknowledges with gratitude permission to quote from the fol-
lowing books: "The American Red Cross, a History," by Foster Rhea
Dulles, © 1950 by The American National Red Cross, and published by
Harper & Brothers; "Angel of the Battlefield," by Ishbel Ross, © 1956 by
Ishbel Ross, and published by Harper & Brothers; "Lanterns on the Levee,"
by William Alexander Percy, © 1941 and published by Alfred A. Knopf,
Inc.; various columns by Roscoe Drummond, appearing in and © by the
New York Herald Tribune; "The American Red Cross in the Great War,"
by Henry P. Davison, © 1921 and published by The Macmillan Company.

MAY 11 '59

The Library of Congress has catalogued this publication as follows:

Hurd, Charles, 1903–
    The compact history of the American Red Cross.
[1st ed.] New York, Hawthorn Books [1959]
    308 p. illus. 23 cm.

    1. Red Cross. U. S. American National Red Cross. i. Title.
                       Full name: Charles Wesley von Bolick Hurd.

HV577.H8   361.506   59–5616 ‡

Library of Congress

Dedicated to
THE RED CROSS VOLUNTEER

Preface

The American Red Cross is a tangible expression of our concern for one another in time of need. It exists to prevent or lighten sufferings from war, natural disaster and disease. In its modern organization the Red Cross is both a potent means for helping the distressed and an expression of the great moral force of man's highest impulses.

Almost every country has a Red Cross society, individually developed to meet that country's needs, but cooperating for humane purposes under international agreements with all others. The American Red Cross, through which we serve, is one of the largest.

As developed over an active life of more than 75 years, the American Red Cross today embraces more than 3,700 local chapters. It has more than 40,000,000 adult and junior contributing members. Approximately 2,000,000 volunteer workers support its services, coordinated and directed by a professional staff that serves both in the United States and throughout the world wherever American armed forces are located.

The history of the Red Cross in America is essentially the story of volunteers, to whom this work is dedicated.

Much of the volunteer and professional work is spectacular, as in the cases of war or major disaster. Much of it is done behind the scenes—quietly, faithfully, efficiently and sometimes at great sacrifice—the commonplace and ordinary jobs.

As an organization, the American Red Cross is unique. Its basic authority is a Congressional charter by which the government charges the organization with specific responsibilities. These are: to provide services and assistance to members of the armed forces, to conduct a disaster preparedness and relief program, and to provide other government-requested assistance in carrying out the terms of the Geneva Conventions. No other organization in the United States has such a charter. The charter is law—the Red Cross must provide the services described in it.

Thus the American Red Cross is an organization whose responsibility is set by our government, but whose funds and workers all are drawn from our private resources.

As a national organization, the Red Cross has the trained machinery and personnel to act as the "good neighbor" wherever disaster beyond the scope of local resources may strike. As an organization of local chapters, it is rooted in the local community "next door" to everyone.

The people of the United States have good reason to be proud of the American Red Cross. It is our own creation and structure. In its heart and being it is ourselves.

—THE AUTHOR

Contents

The
Compact History
of the
American
Red Cross

✛ ✛ ✛ ✛ ✛

1

Birth of the Idea

H OW DID the Red Cross start? One might as well ask how any of the great moral movements in the history of mankind started.

It is sometimes possible to pinpoint events, but none of these started anything. Occasionally individuals have framed concrete ideas out of aspirations, questions, and conclusions that were agitating the minds of many thinkers in their ages. They have given form to ideas, words to thoughts and, most important, activity to ideals.

With those qualifications, one ventures to place in perspective the most widely accepted humanitarian movement of the last hundred years, and to say, "This is how it began." Rather, from the standpoint of the American reader—particularly the millions of Red Cross volunteers—"Here are its two beginnings." Because there were two of them.

First there was the beginning in Europe, coming in 1862 out of the torment of emotions that had wracked a single sensitive man for three introspective years. Second, more than a score of years later, there was the American beginning, through the emotional and yet practical maneuvering of a diminutive, dedicated woman already internationally famous for her battlefield work in the Civil War.

The story, therefore, begins with these two figures—Jean Henri Dunant in Europe and Clara Barton in the United States. That is, they are focal points in the narrative. Perhaps it all actually began when the first manlike creatures long ago carried a hurt compatriot into a sheltering cave and there washed his wounds, brought him food, and helped his family to survive.

II

Europe in the mid-nineteenth century was in many respects actually similar to the storybook conception that pervades our imagination of it. Here was a continent in which—all at the same time—imperialistic wars could be waged, civilians could proceed with their business as usual, and a man on holiday could walk out casually and see the aftermath of a massive battle fought the previous day. This is what happened.

Dunant, a Swiss, in his thirties already a prosperous, widely traveled banker, had gone to Italy for a combined business and pleasure tour of the Lombardy plains. On a spring night he slept at Castiglione della Pieve, but fitfully because of the sound of artillery fire. The noise came from the vicinity of the village of Solferino, then as now a hamlet of less than 1,000 population but destined to be one of history's notable names.

On the following day he and others in the neighborhood went out to see the remains of a battle fought there between an Austrian army on one side and a coalition of French and Sardinians on the other. What they saw was a carnage shocking in any era.

Over the battlefield lay between 30,000 and 40,000 men, many dead but mostly wounded. The exact number of casualties has never been determined. The opposing armies had fought each other to a draw and each side had withdrawn to regroup its living and its supplies. Left behind, after the custom of the times, were the grievously hurt, intermingled across the plains with the dead.

So accustomed was the human mind of the time and place to the battles that had marked two thousand years of this region's history that the wounded were left to die. It was less a hardness of heart perhaps than a feeling of resignation, because what could be done? Leadership was needed where it did not exist.

On this day Dunant felt the urge to leadership, perhaps as a reflex of his organized and organizing mind. Before nightfall he had mustered as many doctors and helpers as possible from the surrounding villages and led them to a crude form of medical relief work on the battlefield.

Had such a thing been done before? Probably thousands of times, but this action by Dunant was so decisive a factor in his own experience that soon the course of the historic regard of nations toward the plight of the wounded in war turned. This change took only three years, because modern man was ready at last to take another step toward civilization of the mind.

In 1862, the outraged man—a brooding figure with his beard and classic nose and deep-set eyes—wrote a small book entitled *Un Souvenir de Solferino*. At his own expense he sent it to leading members of all the governments of Europe, and particularly to the French, German and Austrian emperors, the chief architects of Europe's wars.

The book met its time, because already Napoleon III had begun negotiations with his traditional enemies aimed at preventing another holocaust such as Solferino. There was creeping into the consciousness of the heads of states some small feeling of guilt and revulsion at what their imperial plans cost in human lives.

In an age noted for pamphleteering Dunant's appeal might have been applauded for its humane intent, and thereafter dropped, with some compliments for his call to action to "press forward in a human and truly civilized spirit the attempt to prevent or at least to alleviate, the horrors of war."

Writing the book was all that Dunant could do. He was not a political figure, a member of a distinguished social group or a member of a professional society.

There was in Geneva, however, a distinguished group of scholars who called themselves the Society for Public Benefit. These took up Dunant's cause. They formed a special committee, which Dunant was invited to join, even though he was not then or later a member of the society. He was asked to sit down with Gustave Moynier, president of the society and chairman of the committee, alongside General Guillaume Dufour and the celebrated medical authorities, Drs. Louis Appia and Theodore Maunoir.

These were the hardheaded men of affairs and prestige needed to create the machinery suggested by Dunant. They worked hard and fast. Calling themselves the Committee of Five the group began, as Dr. Maunoir wrote, "to set up an agitation." Dunant was assigned to visit the capitals of Europe, to repeat personally the things he had described in his book and to inflame people's imaginations. His fellow committee members sent out invitations to a conference to be held in Geneva.

The first Geneva conference met in September of 1863, with delegations from sixteen nations including representatives of officialdom, learned societies and welfare organizations. Out of the conference grew two basic tenets: (1) the need for formation of volunteer civilian organizations to render aid to the wounded in wartime; and (2) proclamation of neutrality in wartime for the wounded, for the volunteers going to their assistance, and for the materials and equipment used in this work.

The conference further recommended that the Committee of Five should be renamed the International Committee of the Red Cross, as the recognized link between the national Red Cross Societies to be formed in the future.

The name was derived from a prior recommendation that the flag of the projected organization should be a reverse of the Swiss flag, which consists of a white cross on a red background.

A diplomatic conference to translate resolutions into treaties was called for the following year, also to meet at Geneva.

III

There could hardly have been a worse year than 1864 in which to invite the Government of the United States to participate in a conference dealing with the abstractions of such a subject as formation of an organization to humanize war.

First, a war was raging in the United States which made any European conflict since the time of Emperor Napoleon I seem puny.

Second, the abstractions about which the European powers were talking dealt with matters already put into practical operation to a surprisingly advanced degree in the midst of the Civil War in the United States. The wounded, and those sent to assist them, were receiving much of the consideration which was still a talking point in Europe.

Third, the Government of the United States still was of a mood wanting no part of any commitments to Europe, particularly in the light of activities by some of the principal countries there which gave tacit if not overt aid to the secessionist movement.

Out of courtesy, the Lincoln Administration designated the American Minister to Switzerland as official observer at the conference in 1864; he could watch and perhaps confer, but not by any means commit. The Government also authorized a second observer to attend under the same conditions: Charles S. Bowles, European representative of the American Sanitary Commission.

Why Dr. Bowles?

In the Civil War the Union had already recognized the extreme need for civilian services to back up the small Medical Department of the Army. Thus the Sanitary Commission had been formed. Its membership included thousands of women who gathered bandages, supplies and comforts for the battle-wounded, for distribution through official channels.

The Sanitary Commission supplied countless volunteer nurses for military hospitals and in many other ways operated much as the Red Cross was to do in later wars. This commission was not established to work on the battlefields, as did the lone wolverine Clara Barton, who in 1864 was taking her trains of mule-drawn wagons wherever the fighting raged in Virginia. However, after the Battle of Gettysburg, it did send some agents to the front.

Dr. Bowles cooperated with the International Committee, largely by passing along reports on what the Sanitary Commission was doing. In one speech he said that the commission "has long since met with and overcome the difficulties which some delegates are now predicting and recoiling before." At one point, he appeared to feel that his Government would automatically vote adherence to the proposed agreement.

The Treaty of Geneva officially establishing the Red Cross as the Geneva Convention was signed by representatives of twelve countries on August 22, 1864. The original signatories were Baden, Belgium, Denmark, France, Hesse, Italy, the Netherlands, Portugal, Prussia, Spain, Switzerland and Württemberg. Dr. Bowles carried back to Washington in person a report of what had been done.

Within two years, the Geneva Convention was to be ratified also by Great Britain, Greece, Mecklenburg-Schwerin, Norway, Russia, Sweden and Turkey . . . but not by the United States.

In Washington, the Geneva Convention simply bumped into a combination of circumstances too great to be overcome. Secretary of State William H. Seward was adamant in his stand against any treaty binding the United States to act in concert with foreign governments, par-

ticularly in a period when the activities of the leading powers reflected a shift in political standards to every transient whim of self-interest.

Restudy of the Red Cross question immediately after the Civil War resulted in another negative response, this time by Secretary Seward with the concurrence of the Department of War.

A further try was made in 1866, when what was hoped would become a branch of the Red Cross movement was established in Washington, under the presidency of the noted Dr. Henry W. Bellows, with the formidable title of the American Association for Relief of the Misery of the Battlefields. And still another attempt was made in 1869, after Hamilton Fish had become Secretary of State under President Grant.

In 1872, Dr. Bellows' organization folded up.

But the failure of the organized effort served in a manner not realized at that time to clear the way for the individual who later was to bring it into tangible being. This was Clara Barton—at that moment the most unlikely of all such chosen leaders—who, broken in health and spirits, had sailed in 1869 to Europe on a self-imposed exile that was to last for four long years.

✛ ✛ ✛ ✛ ✛

2

One Woman
and Her Mission

Iɴ 1894, ᴀɴ ᴀʀᴛɪᴄʟᴇ in the *Review of Reviews,* outstanding among serious publications of its time, stated:

> The country has Miss Clara Barton, industrious, indefatigable, persistent and enthusiastic. For 13 years since the United States signed the Geneva Convention the National Red Cross Association in this country has been Miss Clara Barton and Miss Clara Barton has been the National Red Cross Society.

This comment was written when Clara Barton was seventy-three years old and presumably in the twilight of a fantastic career that had made her so well known in so many fields that no specific identification of her appeared any longer in articles about her. It was the twenty-fifth anniversary of her first contact with the Red Cross.

Most elderly men and women of prominence of that age have developed from early promise based on brains or beauty, or both. At least they have shown an early drive or ambition. And very few of them have remaining, at that age, the energy to continue at the same pace for almost a score more years.

What was it that made her what she was?

Clara Barton was a late starter and late finisher, never a sprinter. Everything for which she is noted occurred in a lifetime that found her no more nor less than a politically appointed copy clerk in the Patent Office in Washington, D.C., in the fortieth year of her life. Not only was she in the most anonymous of mediocre jobs but her health was poor and her spirit was broken; and her homeliness and seeming lack of personality would have been insuperable handicaps to most other women.

What type of person was this who, aroused by humane passions in the Civil War, would outstrip and outlive the whole bevy of highly educated, forceful, brilliant, and energetic women leaders who were her contemporaries?

Clara Barton was born December 25, 1821, at North Oxford, Massachusetts, the fifth and last child of Captain and Mrs. Stephen Barton. She was christened Clarissa Harlowe Barton, but the formal names quickly died away from all records except those of the parish clerk. Captain Barton could hardly be classed as a leading figure in his society; he was a normally prosperous New England farmer, able to give his children rudimentary educations before sending them out to work, two at an early age in the local spinning mill. Some accounts credit the Barton family with part ownership of some mills. The Captain apparently found his greatest recompense in life in being an "old soldier." And by that fact he planted a seed that perhaps accounted as much as any other factor for Clara's late but dramatic development.

Clara was Captain Barton's pet, the last and the runt among his litter of five children. And, perhaps because all the rest of his family and friends had become bored to death with his old-soldier tales, she became his favorite audience. Between attending classes at school (which she started at four), riding horseback and doing her share of chores at home, Clara listened with spongelike memory to her father's yarns, which always culminated in the Battle of the Thames where he fought with "Mad Anthony" Wayne and where Chief Tecumseh was slain.

Echoes of the tales came many years later when Clara Barton lived the life of military camp, military headquarters and eventually foreign royal courts. She once boasted, "I never addressed a colonel as captain, got my cavalry on foot or mounted my infantry." Her friends noted with amused and affectionate indulgence another throwback to the old militia captain—Clara Barton loved to wear the jeweled and enameled medals and orders that in later times were showered on her.

Even the horseback riding remained an active asset. Ishbel Ross wrote of her in *Angel of the Battlefield,* "More than once [in the Civil War] she saved her skin on the battlefield by a last-minute dash on horseback when she had stayed to tend the wounded until the Confederates were close at hand."

Clara's girlhood was thoroughly typical of the New England of her day; school and household chores and all the questions about the future faced by a thin and not very strong girl, but one overflowing with vibrant energy—a little girl who rode as well as any adult and who was given her own horse at the age of ten.

But she was plain, and while she cherished friendships she made no romantic attachments. In fact, she never learned to dance. Perhaps her small size made her more self-conscious than she cared to admit. When Clara "grew up," the elevation and breadth were not very marked. She never exceeded five feet in height and never, even in her settled matronly years, topped one hundred pounds in weight.

There was some talk of her following the older children into a job in the local mill. But the plan was abandoned, not because of scruples against sending a girl in her teens to work a twelve-hour, six-day week, but because she was too short to reach the spindles that children's hands were so adept at changing.

Instead, Clara was kept in the public schools, in preparation for about the only career open to a foredoomed spinster not strong enough to do manual work—schoolteaching.

How her father must have worried over this child of his with her small physique and her plain looks—high cheekbones, a very wide mouth and rather heavy businesslike features. These homely handicaps all but nullified the charm in Clara's appearance contributed by luxuriant brown hair, small hands and a tiny waist.

In May of 1839, at the age of seventeen and one-half, Clara Barton stepped into her presumable life career when she won appointment as a school teacher in District School Number 9, a job within living distance of her home.

For a decade this pattern held—teaching in small schools, year after year exerting discipline over pupils much larger and stronger, if

younger, than herself, and developing more and more firmness in her
jaw. In teaching Clara was successful, so much so that in 1849 she
enrolled in the Liberal Institute, at Clinton, New York, to prepare for
a better teaching job. When she left the institute, she organized a new
"liberal school" for children at Bordentown, New Jersey.

During the years at Clinton there was a hint of romantic attachment
in Clara's life, an association with Samuel Ramsey, a divinity student
at Hamilton College. But if romance seemed to be hinted at one time,
it turned into friendship, and in later years Ramsey became one of
Miss Barton's aides in the Red Cross. *Finis* was written to any pre-
suppositions of romantic feelings when finally Clara sued him to recover money she had lent to him.

II

In February, 1854, when she had reached the age of thirty-three, Clara
Barton had to give up schoolteaching because of throat trouble, the
first of a long series of bouts of ill health that were to mark her adult
life. She left Bordentown and went to Washington, D.C., where she
became a copyist in the Patent Office. There she was one of scores of
people with good eyes and penmanship who took to their rooms arm-
fuls of official papers, there to copy the requisite number of forms required by law in each case.

At piece-work rates she was able to earn, she wrote, between $71
and $83 a month—money earned by working late into each night,
leading a monastic existence, and barely eking out a living in the in-
flationary period that marked the national capital in that era.

Life became much more pleasant when Clara's native efficiency and
grit, plus energetic pulling of wires through political friends, won her
an appointment as confidential clerk to the Commissioner of Patents,
Charles Mason. The job gave her a salary of $1,400 a year, short and
regular working hours, and a certain definite position in the Washington hierarchy of bureaucratic levels. There she might well have remained for life but for a change in the Administration in 1857 that
cost Mason his job and Clara her appointment. Way had to be made
for a new crop of patronage appointees. Also, there was a definite
move to oust women from government jobs.

Ill with malaria, dejected and "finished" with Washington, Miss Barton, now thirty-six, returned to North Oxford, where she was enabled to earn a living by the generosity of the new government masters who assigned her copying work that was forwarded by post. Thus almost three years passed, the malaria was overcome, and unexpectedly, in 1860, the press of work bearing down on the Patent Office prompted the regime to invite Clara back to a salaried post.

She jumped at the chance and picked up both her old routine and her old political friendships in short order.

In the relatively small community of Washington, it was possible for an educated woman of dignified bearing to be both a clerk in a bureau and a friend of congressmen and Cabinet members. It was probably easier in many ways for a plain woman than for an attractive one with whom officials might fear involvement. But easy or not for one of her type, Clara Barton capped her own position by winning an invitation to the Inaugural Ball for President Abraham Lincoln. Then she lost the first opportunity to meet her future great friend when a bad cold kept her from attending.

As Clara Barton sniffled her lonely way through the evening of the Inaugural Ball no one, and she least of all, imagined that she would be one of the few persons so closely associated with Lincoln in national fame little more than four years later that upon his assassination the military would rush a special guard to her house.

III

There was to be, however, something less than accident in her meteoric career. It would seem, indeed, that Clara Barton, working from a mixture of selfish and unselfish motives, had seen a driving need for women like herself to lay a groundwork of influence in Washington.

Part of the reason she had been fired two years earlier from her job in the Patent Office was her sex. In 1855 President Franklin Pierce and his Secretary of the Interior, Robert McClelland, had opened a direct move to oust women from government offices. McClelland undertook a personal crusade against the female copyists because of the "obvious impropriety in the mixing of the sexes within the walls of a public office."

Commissioner Mason tried to fight the order, carrying personally the fight to retain his confidential clerk, Miss Barton. McClelland suggested at first a compromise, that Clara be given work to do but away from the office of the Commissioner of Patents. Even that suggested compromise was overcome by Mason, but the growing crusade against women clerks then provided an excuse for patronage reshuffling when the Democratic President James Buchanan was nominated in 1857. Buchanan finally forced the resignation of Commissioner Mason, to replace him with a Democrat, and Clara was finished.

When she returned to Washington two years later, she had a new plan for survival in the seething world of politics where even a clerk's job was political manna to the victorious spoilsmen.

If the life of a Washington clerk was to be her life—and she decided that this would be so—she was going to have behind her every political resource that she could muster. In the following six months she did muster the resources, and in that short period stepped forever out of the clerk's role.

Through a friend, Elvira Stone, she met Senator Henry Wilson, from Massachusetts, and captivated him, less as a woman than as a personality. Soon they were visiting one another almost daily. Without Henry Wilson's backing much of Clara Barton's Civil War achievement might never have occurred.

Perhaps Wilson was no more drawn to Clara Barton than he was angry at her highest superior, Secretary of the Interior Caleb B. Smith, whom he referred to in his first visit with Clara as a "damned old fool." It could be highly valuable to a senator to have a loyal follower in the center of the office of a Cabinet member he despised. And Wilson went a step further to fortify through his own friendships Clara's position and her loyalty to him. As Chairman of the Senate Committee on Military Affairs, he spoke of her to his closest friend, Charles Sumner, Postmaster General in Lincoln's new Cabinet, and Sumner, too, became Clara Barton's friend.

Thus matters stood in April, 1861, when Fort Sumter fell, the Civil War began and President Lincoln issued his call for volunteers. Clara Barton had been back in Washington for five months when she was transformed from an ambitious, self-seeking although hard-working, spinsterish clerk into a tiny bundle of galvanized energy in the Union cause.

If it is true that heroes are born, not made, it also is true that the born heroes spend a lot of energy getting into the spot where they can assert their birthright. So it was with Clara Barton.

The Civil War fired her with an enthusiasm marked from the very first by a sympathy for the men it struck. Before a battle was joined between the forces of the Union and the South she was a marked individualist in finding busy occupation in Washington—particularly in reading to, and writing letters for, the Massachusetts volunteers who came to train and live in quarters in the as yet uncompleted Capitol building.

When the wounded from the First Battle of Bull Run were brought back to Washington in bloody bandages to be racked up on straw ticks in all sorts of makeshift shelters, Clara was there among them, helping as she might. Not that she was alone; most of Washington's women were there, too, fulfilling the traditional nursing role of women behind the lines of wars since the beginning of history.

But this little woman, who combined her ministrations with the long hours of work involved in earning a living, was striking out on a new tack. The battlefield itself was calling to her—the same call that across the ocean had summoned to historic greatness seven years earlier a similar determined woman, but one with more professional equipment to back her ardor. There Florence Nightingale, the nurse, had written another chapter in the emancipation of women on the battlefields in the Crimean War.

For almost a year, Clara Barton was what appears in retrospect to have been perhaps the biggest nuisance in the offices of the bureaucracy of what passed in the early bumbling stages for the Union Government's War Department. Probably more than one of the ranking officials there sighed with relief in March of 1862 when final illness struck old Captain Stephen Barton, then eighty-eight years old. Clara Barton, notified of his condition, hurried home and saw him die. But this dramatic interlude only gave added impetus to her ambition.

"He is journeying home," she wrote of her father. "With this, my highest duties close, and I would fain be allowed to go and administer comfort to our brave men who peril life and limb in defence of the priceless boon the fathers so dearly won."

That letter, with its Victorian turn of phrase, was not the outpouring of an emotional woman caught up in the mawkish sentiment of frustration. It was a note from one already a leading agitator for her cause, and it was written to—and received seriously by—Governor John A. Andrew of Massachusetts. He knew Clara well by then.

The first year of war had made Clara Barton a fairly notable figure in Massachusetts, flying about as she did under the long protective shadow cast by Senator Wilson. She had written hundreds of letters telling Massachusetts of the "comfort needs" she solicited for its men summoned to the war. She had made an earlier trip home marked by a small-sized lecture tour to whip up fire for her cause.

In fact, she was a one-woman crusade, eager to do a job but notably eager likewise to do it herself; few women appeared then or later among her associates and none ever was invited to be her equal. She would lead or fail.

Her progress seemed more negative and noisy than anything else, but she showed an infinite capacity for at least getting attention from the dominant personalities, such as the Army Surgeon General, Alfred Hitchcock, who, in reply to a letter that Clara prompted Governor Andrew to write, at least recognized her: "I do not think at the present time Miss Barton had better undertake to go to Burnside's Division to act as a nurse."

Clara's sharp reply was that forty young men in that division were former school pupils of hers. She took her case to Major D. H. Rucker, Assistant Quartermaster General, finding him where he sat behind a wicket in a large office handing out orders. Facing him, Clara cried, and he invited her inside. He asked her why in the name of all that counted did she, a woman, want to go to the front?

Clara Barton told him. And she described the supplies that were stacked in her lodgings and that overflowed into a warehouse—all contributed by her backers in Massachusetts who trusted that she personally would see them delivered to the men in the field. Rucker melted and gave her the first military pass she had ever held in her hand—a pass to go to the front in Virginia if his superiors approved. The Major added, "And God bless you."

But Rucker was only a major. His paper was a preliminary, the first step through a dozen offices, culminating in Major General John Pope's lordly command headquarters.

The date was August 12, 1862. Clara Barton finally was free to go to the field, entitled to free transportation by train or steamboat for herself and her voluntarily gathered supplies. As for Clara, she was simply a lone volunteer serving without pay, rank or authority except what she could wheedle or demand.

The great permission came the day after she had written in her diary: "Battle at Culpeper reached us . . . Concluded to go to Culpeper . . . Packed goods." Clara wrote that she removed the hoop from her skirt, put on a plaid jacket and dark skirt, loaded her comfort supplies into a wagon, and alone drove a four-mule team to Cedar Mountain, where she arrived two days later.

She found Brigade Surgeon James L. Dunn surrounded by wounded and all but out of surgical dressings. Of these, Clara had a large supply. Later Surgeon Dunn claimed that he had coined Clara's future title, "Angel of the Battlefield." He recalled, "I thought that night if heaven ever sent out a holy angel, she must be one, her assistance was so timely."

So it started, this Civil War career that continued until the war ended, a career written by one woman wherever the war raged in Virginia—a battle Clara fought with nursing assistance, hot soup and pies prepared on rain-soaked battlefields. And she gathered one by one her principal lieutenants—Mrs. Ada Moreell, Miss Lydie F. Haskell, Miss Almira Fales, to name only a few. Soon she had a small corps gathering the gifts that she carried with her. But she went alone, except for men to drive added wagons.

The die had been cast, and somewhere in the lantern-lit nights of the years that passed so quickly and yet seemed too long, the New England schoolteacher, the Washington clerk, the patronage-conscious government hand—all evaporated in the mists and there emerged that rarest of nature's phenomenons, a *leader* of self-asserted rank who neither held nor needed a commission from authority because the authority had not been invented to give it.

Somewhere in the heart of it lingered the spark that would glow slowly into the Red Cross.

The first lonely drive past unbelieving sentries to Culpeper was the curtain raiser to a score of battlefields, to activities that over the years would finally reach such proportions that the newspapers would devote long dispatches to Clara and her utilization of "mother earth as a kitchen hearth." These dispatches would tell of vast stretches of battle-scarred earth where Clara would turn out, with her now loosely organized but disciplined helpers, 700 loaves of freshly baked bread for a field breakfast for the wounded, 200 gallons of soup, a wash boiler full of whisky sauce for bread puddings.

I have had a barrel of apple sauce made today and given out every spoonful of it with my own hands. I have cooked ten dozen eggs, made cracker toast, cornstarch blanc mange, milk punch, arrowroot, washed hands and faces, put ice on hot heads, mustard on cold feet, written six soldiers' letters home, stood beside three death beds . . .

So it was right up to the Battle of Petersburg and the Siege of Richmond, marking the end of the war, and followed so soon afterward by General Lee's surrender. Clara was at both these final battles, and from them came echoes of responses that were to mark closely her long future road.

One was the chance meeting with a Swiss youth, Jules Golay, a volunteer in the Union Army whom she nursed. The other was a reunion after many years with her brother Stephen who had gone South, and there remained with his property and Confederate friends throughout the Civil War.

Jules Golay recovered, wrote to his family of Clara's motherly ministrations, and in turn it was to be his parents' home in Geneva where Clara first heard of the Red Cross movement in Europe. She met Stephen, by now a Union prisoner and a dying man, watched him die, and went on in later years to make his son and her nephew one of her closest lieutenants in her own American Red Cross movement.

But other years were ahead—arduous and rewarding years.

IV

If the publicity Clara Barton attained in the Civil War enabled her to become the national figure she needed to be in order to make her life work a reality, it must be equally recorded that one humane and often heart-rending chore immediately following the war provided the capstone for her reputation.

It had been glamorous and exciting to tend the wounded on the battlefields of Virginia. She might have stopped there and plunged immediately into the profitable lecture field that beckoned her. But now Clara set for herself a second mission.

She was the first to step forward and volunteer—to insist upon the job—of doing all possible to identify the unknown dead from this bloody, fratricidal war. Grim statistics illustrate the formidability of that task.

The Union forces had recorded 359,528 dead. Of these, only 172,-400 had been identified. Furthermore, even the number of known graves on the battlefields were 43,973 less than the dead. The harassed War Department, plagued by the dual problems of sending back the living soldiers to their homes and with carrying out all sorts of contrary political policies relative to occupation of the lately rebellious areas, had no time to worry about individuals who had passed to other muster rolls.

But Clara Barton insisted that someone should worry. And between the final battle and the ultimate surrender of the Confederate forces she dressed in appropriate clothes lent by friends to call on President Lincoln. Thrice she called, and twice she got soaked in the March rains, but Lincoln was too busy for even her to intrude upon him. It finally was Senator Wilson who acted as her emissary. On March 11, 1865, one week after Clara saw Lincoln at his second inauguration but refrained from making her issue there, a historic letter was delivered to her lodgings:

> To THE FRIENDS OF MISSING PERSONS: Miss Clara Barton has kindly offered to search for the missing prisoners of war. Please address her at Annapolis, giving her name, regiment and company of any missing prisoner.
>
> (Signed) A. LINCOLN.

That was enough. Newspapers throughout the country reported the appeal. The government provided various facilities but no compensation for Clara Barton, and she dove into the work with the help of her old wartime friends, plus the addition of young Jules Golay.

This is not the place to even summarize adequately that phase of Clara Barton's work, an arduous year that culminated in a visit to the wretched Andersonville prison in Georgia that was the most inhumane of all the prisoner-of-war cages, a place where Union soldiers died by the thousands and their bodies were dumped into mass graves. Clara worked through the records, sorted out the bodies and worked to have the spot hallowed as a national cemetery. So it became.

While Lincoln lay in state after his assassination in April, 1865, Clara wrote one hundred letters to families of missing men. A month later President Johnson ordered special printing facilities placed at her disposal. And in 1866 Congress appropriated $15,000 for continuation of the job. In 1869, upon giving a final accounting, Clara Barton's Bureau of Missing Persons had identified more than 20,000 dead who otherwise would have remained anonymous, as well as distributed hundreds of thousands of circulars and letters of inquiry or advice. She had spent $16,759 as well as her time.

But the period had long since passed when Clara needed to borrow clothes for a formal call, or to wonder where she would find the means to support her volunteer work.

This time she heeded the call of the lecture platform, and its rewards were munificent.

From Boston and New York to cities as far west as Des Moines, Iowa, and Madison, Wisconsin, Clara Barton made the lyceum circuit. Hers was a twofold purpose: to take to the public the story of war as she had seen it, and to seek out in every case information that would contribute to her search for the missing dead.

Honest appraisal, and her own background, seem to indicate that money was not the controlling impulse in her lecture tours, but the money was important. Her fees ranged from $50 to $150 an engagement, and the engagements multiplied at such a rate that her progress from city to city often became as rigorous as her battlefield experiences —flood-swollen rivers to ford, freezing nights at railroad junctions, and travel that was at best a hardship in trains as they existed then.

She was more an enthusiastic speaker than a skilled one, but she had the gift of turning a phrase. Talking of Fredericksburg, she described "its rocky brow of frowning forts"; she reconstructed South Mountain in a word picture of "stubble hillside and burning September sun"; Antietam in full fury was "a chain of Etnas." And yet she could say, "I am the most timid person on earth. All speech-making terrifies me. First, I have no taste for it, and lastly I hate it."

Nevertheless, she rose to what the public demanded of her, that public which filled halls to hear the little woman variously billed on the garish posters of the day as "Angel of the Battlefield," "Angel of Mercy," "Daughter of the Regiment," or "The Florence Nightingale of America." In Boston she once recorded paying $10.75 for a new hat and spending $2.25 to have her hair specially dressed for a formal evening appearance.

There was stimulus also in the associations which her own fame brought to her. Louisa May Alcott, herself a sometime nurse in Washington during the war; Julia Ward Howe, Lucy Stone, Frances Willard and Susan B. Anthony—all were her friends. Susan Anthony aroused her interest in the Equal Rights movement, but Clara eschewed overactive attention to it. She was too busy and, strange as the observation may seem at the time in the light of her subsequent Red Cross activity, she was never one to plunge too quickly or too deeply into a movement.

Furthermore, she was giving all she had to her own interests—so much so in fact that on a night in the winter of 1868–69 she walked onto a lecture platform in Portland, Maine, looked at the audience facing her, and found speech failing her completely.

She collapsed that night, and entered upon a decade of ill health.

In August of 1869, after months devoted to cleaning up the Missing Persons work, and setting her affairs in order, Clara Barton made a will that in the event of her death would dispose of an estate of $30,000 she had accumulated in the past three years, bought passage for Europe, and sailed on the liner *Caledonia*.

Clara Barton's destination was Geneva, Switzerland, where the parents of Jules Golay—Isaac and Eliza—had insisted she should come to let their climate aid in repairing her ravaged health.

✛ ✛ ✛ ✛ ✛

3

Prelude
to Acceptance

Upon arriving in Geneva in 1869, Clara Barton received two surprises. The first was recognition that here, 4,000 miles from home, she was a personage, a celebrity because of the work she had organized and had done almost alone in the Civil War. The second was to learn about the Red Cross, concerning which she apparently had not heard the least word in Washington.

The latter requires a paragraph or two of explanation, because the Red Cross was already a well-known topic of debate in high official circles in Washington. But in the division of jealous cliques the "Angel of the Battlefield" had been frozen out of the earlier private diplomatic discussions.

Clara Barton was a protégé of the influential Senator Wilson, a friend of Lincoln and Grant, but not so admired by everyone else. On the other side of the fence, among the groups and individuals who did great works and were no more shy than Clara Barton about building their own positions for the sake of their missions, were the leaders of the Sanitary Commission, headed by Dr. Bellows, and Miss Dorothea Dix, a prominent volunteer aide.

The Sanitary Commission was the officially recognized agency in the Civil War to provide nurses for convalescent soldiers brought back from the battles and to gather medical supplies and other contributions for the Army's medical service. Clara Barton knew of this work and applauded it, but the mutual feelings existing between the Sanitary Commission and the one-woman mulecade taken to the battlefields by Clara Barton are understandable.

Now, in 1869, the dedicated advocates of the Red Cross were apparently willing to grasp at straws, or the tiniest wisp of a woman who seemed to have influence in America. There was more in their welcome to Miss Barton than a tribute to her fame or personality. And they were honest about it.

On a clear October day this whole story was unfolded to Clara Barton by a delegation of Swiss, headed by Dr. Appia, who called upon her in the Golay home. They complimented her on her battle-field work as dramatically relayed to Geneva by the younger Golay through his parents. And Clara Barton responded with the almost excessive emotion that now and then broke through her normally cool New England exterior. She was shocked. She found the whole story as incomprehensible to herself as to the Swiss. She looked at the nations already members of the Red Cross and commented:

> Not a civilized people in the world but ourselves missing, and I saw Greece, Spain and Turkey there. I began to fear that in the eyes of the rest of mankind we could not be far from barbarians. This reflection did not furnish a stimulating food for national pride. I grew more and more ashamed.

In this and subsequent talks, the Red Cross became Clara Barton's new life mission. She went on to Corsica to spend the winter, according to plans originally made in the United States, but now her baggage contained a small library of literature on the Red Cross. Primarily she read and reread a small book already dubbed by the French historian Joseph Ernest Renan as "the greatest work of the century"—a translation of *Un Souvenir de Solferino*.

Reading day by day through the hot and sultry hours marking her Corsican winter, Clara Barton achieved complete self-identification with this stirring story and its aftermath—an interest so deep that it made her forget her dyspepsia, her fatigue and worry about the strains imposed upon her frail body through forty-nine extraordinary years.

II

In 1870, tired of Corsica, Clara Barton returned to Switzerland, nursing the aftermath of a bout with malaria. After visiting the Golays at Geneva again, she went to Bern, where she was joined by Judge Joseph Sheldon and his wife, Abby, taking a holiday after Sheldon had paid an annual visit to a factory he owned in England.

Here the outbreak of the Franco-Prussian War found Clara Barton, and here Dr. Appia and his group again called upon Miss Barton, with an invitation to accompany them on their work of mercy in this war. The group went along without Clara, who needed a few more days to mend her health. She followed within a week, almost alone as of old. Her only companion was a Swiss girl, Antoinette Margot, slim, fair and an art student, capable at translating French and German.

When the pair started for Strasbourg, Antoinette took without realizing it a far longer step, one of constant attendance on Clara Barton that would last for years.

Traveling by train and by coach, breasting the flood of refugees from the battle zones, Clara and Antoinette reached Mülhausen, where they were not permitted to go near the wounded, and then Strasbourg, which was not yet under siege. Here occurred another small incident showing the depth and breadth of the background Clara Barton's war work had created for herself, and for her newly adopted movement.

In Strasbourg were an American consul and vice consul, who would have been only anonymous, harassed officials to any other Americans, but not to Clara. The consul was Felix C. M. Petard, a Civil War surgeon, and the vice consul a former Civil War chaplain, both old friends. Dr. Petard had a covey of stranded tourists on his hands. He turned them over to Clara to shepherd, which suited her perfectly as she wanted to get to Huguenau. She reached Huguenau, another battlefield, but again was not permitted near the wounded so she went to Brumath to await Fate's next move. There Fate moved.

Messengers found Clara and delivered a letter sent by Louise, Grand Duchess of Baden, inviting her to come for a visit and take part in the Red Cross work. Grand Duchess Louise was probably the most prominent European aristocrat actively dedicated to Red Cross work. Herself a tiny but regal woman, a noted philanthropist and daughter of the Prussian King, William I, soon to become German Emperor, she immediately became a fast friend to Clara, and a lifelong one.

Clara Barton already had written to the American ambassador in Paris, Elihu B. Washburne, offering her humane services to the French. But in her view of service, it mattered not at all that the first acceptance of her came from the German side, where Dr. Appia had recommended her to Grand Duchess Louise. There was a job to be done and, after touring several of the Duchess's palaces, already turned into hospitals, and discussing plans for civilian aid, she accepted the offer and Louise's hospitality.

Her visit continued through several weeks—while the Grand Duke of Baden commanded the German forces submitting Strasbourg to siege—until September when news of the capitulation of the city prompted Clara to request permission to go to the aid of the civilian population there.

For forty days, while the Grand Duchess Louise collected relief clothes and provisions for the conquered city, Clara supervised distribution of them. Finally she improvised a system of using local women to make, alter and mend the indiscriminately gathered clothing and other articles. And in the course of succoring a city, the erstwhile schoolteacher and battlefield nurse became the intimate of Louise; the friend on a perfectly equal level of Count Bismarck and his Countess, while the Iron Chancellor served as Governor General of conquered Alsace; and, on the other hand, of a French officer, Bergmann, who headed a French relief committee and naturally despised the German invaders.

The year 1870 passed into 1871. Clara regained her health. She went on to direct relief work at Metz, which had been so shattered by a German siege that the residents had eaten their horses, and some said their pets, before surrendering. She had a hand in distributing relief there sent by America through a commission headed by her old friend, General Burnside, but Burnside and his group were not cordial enough to give Clara official position among themselves. In American official eyes Clara was still on the fringe of things.

Clara Barton went to Paris and viewed the shuttered city occupied by its conquerors. She pitied it, but perhaps because of earlier and more satisfying experiences with the Germans, the conquerors, she spoke her mind:

"Germany is more like us. There is a fixedness of purpose in her people, her anchor goes to the bottom. France swings in the water, and changes with every whipping wind."

But Clara set up headquarters in Paris, and launched her own relief program. Horace Greeley printed an appeal for funds to aid her work. Senator Henry Wilson, touring Europe, visited her. Edmund Dwight, a famous Boston lawyer, collected bounty for her works. But when the work in Paris was finished, Clara returned to Karlsruhe, to spend the Christmas that was her fiftieth birthday with other German friends, the Zimmermans, and to go on to visit again with the Grand Duke and Duchess of Baden.

Then came the depression that always followed buoyant times of busy strain, and this time affliction of the eyes that came near to blindness. Clara retreated with Antoinette to England, where she spent a miserable year, aimlessly and pessimistically waiting, half paralyzed, with her eyes bandaged. Only twelve months after her gay Christmas at Karlsruhe she was in London, a physical wreck, hardly cheered at all by the visits of friends who mustered around her.

In October, 1873, after four years in Europe, Clara sailed for America, to nurse her broken health in solitude in the family home at North Oxford, Massachusetts. Nothing now was farther from her mind than a crusade on behalf of the Red Cross.

Four more years would pass—years of illness and fitful recoveries, a long siege in a sanitarium at Dansville, New York, and finally establishment of a home there by Clara—before the Red Cross idea and Clara, with restored health, would come together again.

Then in 1877 came news of impending war between Russia and Turkey. The spark reminded Clara Barton of the Red Cross and she picked up its cause. She wrote to Dr. Appia: "Like the old war horse that has rested long in quiet pastures I recognize the bugle note that calls me to my place, and, though I may not do what I once could, I am come to offer what I may."

Dr. Appia replied with a long account of progress in European development and appreciation of the Red Cross, and sent a batch of literature on it. "And now, my worthy friend," he enjoined her, "go on courageously with faith and hope. The cause is good; let us defend it everywhere and let us be firm in upholding the banner of charity. It will be ever the surest means of combating the principles of war."

Close after this letter came another from M. Gustave Moynier, president of the International Committee, enclosing a letter commending Clara Barton to the President of the United States as representative of the Red Cross.

By this time Horace Greeley was dead, and Henry Wilson too. But Clara Barton journeyed back to Washington and found herself still capable of making new friends, rallying other formidable names to her banner.

How bright the prospects looked then, as rosy perhaps as the flaming red color of the Red Cross banner itself. But that was the curtain-raising atmosphere of false hope preceding a long battle indeed. The 1877 endeavor turned out to be only a flicker of hope, quickly extinguished.

III

Equally sure of her way around Washington, when there was a challenging job to be done, and with health fully restored by the tonic of activity, Clara Barton called upon President Harrison with her extraordinary credentials from M. Moynier. The President received her courteously and with sympathy. He suggested that she proceed to lay the cause before other members of the Cabinet. Most of them were equally affable.

But only one member of the Cabinet counted, in this Administration where the President believed firmly in deputizing his authority to the men chosen as his responsible assistants. That focal point for all things dealing with international commitments was the Department of State. The Secretary of State was W. M. Evarts, and the Assistant Secretary was Frederic W. Seward, son of the Secretary of State who had studied the same proposal advanced by Dr. Bellows in 1866.

Assistant Secretary Seward got out the files of comment left by his father, and subsequent ones from the State Department regime under Hamilton Fish. His reply, which neither Secretary Evarts nor the President saw fit to overrule, was firmly in the negative.

"It is all settled," Mr. Seward told Miss Barton at their final interview. "It will never be considered again."

Few prophecies by men in responsible public office have been more incorrect. But for the moment the ruling collapsed the hopes of the

Red Cross for an official foothold in America and the ambitions of Miss Barton as well.

With such backing and prestige, both for the idea and for its spokesman, the question immediately arises as to what made the establishment of the American Red Cross such a profound achievement, almost a revolutionary thing. The answer is that there was a great deal more than the chartering of a relief agency involved, that from its very start the Red Cross was a symbol of principle and debate much broader than its field of operations.

In the century that had elapsed between the Revolution and 1877, American political thinking was dominated to the point of obsession by a fear of entangling alliances with foreign countries. Among political leaders this was not a matter of party debate; it was virtually unanimous. The whole Red Cross idea ran head on into this stone wall. However respected Miss Barton and her associates might be, however great might be the respect also accorded to the *idea* behind the Red Cross, still it was "foreign." Thus adherence to the Red Cross Convention meant that the United States was binding itself to do something in concert with other countries.

Each national Red Cross Society—even those in Iron Curtain countries today—carries official status. In other words, it exists on the basis of a pledge by the country involved to respect Red Cross neutrality in time of war and to uphold the standards of the Red Cross.

For the United States to join the Red Cross required that the President sign, and that Congress ratify, a treaty of cooperation in Red Cross matters with the other nations that already had adopted the Geneva Red Cross Convention. Thereafter, the Red Cross would be in a position to seek a charter from Congress and thus become the truly national organization that was anticipated.

But the stumbling block was that "entangling alliance" business involved in the necessary treaty.

Clara Barton accepted defeat in 1877, but only defeat as in a battle, not in a campaign. While writing, talking, agitating—discussing strategy with such old master campaigners among her friends as General Phil Sheridan—she awaited patiently another sort of political climate.

This came with the election in 1880 of President Garfield, and with his choice of James G. Blaine as Secretary of State. Then Clara Barton

and her American coterie of Red Cross friends moved fast indeed. The
activity started with a telegram of congratulations from Clara to Garfield on his election. Immediately after his inauguration in March of
1881, she was again on the White House doorstep, with the four-
year-old letter from M. Moynier.

Never had prospects looked brighter. Now there was no tedium of
interminable interviews and explanations. With Administration support, Congress seemed destined to fall into line. It was only a matter
of time, and the mists of legalistic clouds hovering over the "entangling alliance" bugaboo seemed to have been dissipated.

Now was the time to take the big step of establishing the nucleus
of a formal organization to hoist the Red Cross banner the minute
authorization to act as a quasi-official arm of the government was
granted.

Boldly and confidently Clara Barton called together her coterie of
friends, for a meeting at her residence at a time which is officially
inscribed as the founding date of the American National Red Cross.

✛   ✛   ✛   ✛   ✛

4

First Steps

On May 21, 1881, a small group of persons met in an inconspicuous house in Washington, D.C., to organize "the greatest venture of voluntary service in the world."

Miss Barton opened this important meeting with a review of the long fight already waged by her for recognition of the Red Cross idea. She passed briefly over the frustrations, going on to spark anew the enthusiasm of her handful of followers, and to launch an idea different from but supplementary to the European Red Cross pattern.

Her keen judgment had made her aware that something more than the European war-assistance program was needed to spark American enthusiasm. At this meeting Miss Barton broached the "something else."

Why not, she asked her co-workers, stress equally the need for a peacetime organization to assist victims of natural disasters to recover from such onslaughts?

The new idea more than anything else accounted for eventual acceptance of the Red Cross by the American government. But it opened also a new field of battle for the tough-minded Clara Barton —open battle with the leaders of the very Red Cross whose cause she espoused.

But was any crusade ever easy? Crusades, even the ones of highest intent, are essentially battles for change, battles against the *status quo*.

Crusaders always find the *status quo* well organized, well accepted and
well defended. *Status quo* breeds organization. On the contrary, no
crusade is ever well organized at the start. To have a crusade there
must be followers gathered from rebels against the *status quo*. Rebels
are notably individuals. To organize them takes time and energy. Clara
Barton never doubted that she lacked either. She thrust forth her new
idea, that of a Red Cross as a continuing, ever present relief organization.

In its development, that conception was to put the American Red
Cross next door to anyone in the United States, who might face otherwise overwhelming ruin at the hands of flood, wind or fire.

It is quite probable that this new addition of a humane activity,
apparently incorporated in her plans at this last moment by Miss
Barton, can be credited for the present stature of the American Red
Cross.

The meeting adopted Miss Barton's constitution for the founding
of a society to become a member of "The Red Cross of the International Conventions of Geneva," of which Miss Barton then was
designated "American Representative."

II

There were many individuals who felt that it was humiliating that
the American organization should have to embark on this great venture as a branch of a foreign group. Perhaps Clara Barton shared
the feeling, but if so she did not show it.

The important thing was that there existed an instrument to fill a
void in America's fast-developing national consciousness, a means by
which the great and open heart of America could at last be set up
as an organized guide for the hand representing its resources and
strength.

No "great names" were present at the meeting in Miss Barton's
modest house at 1326 I Street. But their presence was not needed.
Already the struggling idea had won acceptance by many impressive
leaders—among them Robert T. Lincoln, Secretary of War under
Garfield and son of the President, who had backed Clara Barton
mightily in her Civil War work. Lincoln won over his wealthy friend
George Pullman.

Clara was backed, too, by a firm little band of nationally known newspaper correspondents who seemed to see in Clara Barton and the Red Cross idea an inevitable step toward what later would be called America's "manifest destiny." The writers included Walter P. Phillips, George Kennan and Colonel Richard J. Hinton, all giants in a day of thought-inducing personal journalism. These were the "second generation" of Clara Barton's newspaper friends, the successors of the great Civil War correspondents, Horace Greeley and Charles A. Dana.

And as Clara Barton set forth her plan, her old friends were watching her work from Europe. Moynier's last letter to Clara Barton had assured her, "I await with complete confidence the result of your sympathetic endeavors."

Then the cruelest of all blows struck the country, and the newly inspired Red Cross movement.

On July 2, President Garfield was shot by the assassin, Charles J. Guiteau. The President died in September.

Once more the political work must be started all over again, first with the new President, Chester A. Arthur, and later with the Secretary of State who succeeded Blaine, Frederick T. Frelinghuysen. Miss Barton bearded the political lions, rounded up old Civil War friends, and bombarded Congress with letters. At the same time Walter Phillips, who was correspondent for the Associated Press, handled the national publicity.

In the meantime Clara Barton moved to organize as a beginning a local Washington Chapter of the Red Cross. In October the forming group obtained from the government of the District of Columbia a charter, and that very fall it put into practice its avowed purpose.

When fires ravaged forests in Michigan, scattering destruction over a wide area, affecting hundreds of families, and creating needs beyond the scope of local resources, the infant Red Cross went to the rescue.

The fires occurred in September. Before winter grasped this remote country in its grip, the Red Cross had raised and distributed $80,000 for immediate relief and the rehabilitation work which is so much more important. And, in passing, the first chapter taught others how to organize and operate.

On March 16, 1882, Congress ratified the international treaty covering the Red Cross. By this date, the Red Cross movement had ceased to be an individual promotion; ratification had hinged upon active work by a literal "Who's Who" of American leadership—politicians, educators, physicians and humanitarians. But the light of conflict had never shifted a moment from the five-foot figure of Clara Barton, by then sixty-one years old. It had been her fight, now was her triumph, and was to be for a score more years her unending, never slacking challenge of leadership.

But on that March day she wrote, "So it was done. . . . I had waited so long and got so weak and broken I could not even feel glad." And she added that she used a wet towel to "wipe off the sadness and tears."

On July 26, President Arthur formally proclaimed the adherence of the United States to the Treaty of Geneva. The story won only routine and slight treatment in the press. It even seems to have been an anticlimax for Clara Barton, who by then had gone to her house at Dansville, New York. She had purchased this house in 1876, and occupied it intermittently until 1884. It was her legal residence during these years.

III

What sort of woman had won this triumph? The following description was written by Dr. William E. Barton, Clara's cousin and biographer:

> Ladylike, sympathetic, energetic, and marvellously forceful . . . still patient, still persistent, rising at 4 or 5 o'clock in the morning and working until late at night, living with such simplicity of life that no soldier ever lived upon a smaller ration or slept upon a narrower or simpler bed than that upon which she slept night after night, always with a light at the head of her bed where she might, as thoughts came to her in the night, write down those thoughts.

The "sadness and tears" expressed the normal emotional reaction of a highly charged and almost indomitable character. But they also typified to a degree that even Miss Barton could not see at that time the host of contradictions that were to plague the Red Cross for the rest of her life and long after she had passed from the scene. In fact, a perspective viewpoint of the Red Cross must take note of the contradictions both in views and personalities in order to permit any sort of clear picture of this unique organization.

The most mistaken concept that has hounded the Red Cross throughout its lifetime is the impression that it is an organization definitely established to do a few well-outlined chores under the direction of undeviating rules represented by a fixed organization. It is nothing of the kind.

The Red Cross—yesterday, today and probably tomorrow—suggests to the outside observer a combination of the characteristics that are found alike in a militant new church organization, a welfare movement founded on revolutionary ideals, and a thoroughbred horse. It suggests a new religious organization in the ideals which constitute its guiding principles. The parallel with the reform movement has occurred time and again in conflicts of viewpoints between equally dedicated but widely differing personalities. Like a thoroughbred horse, it has had periods when it has run excellent races but left its backers wondering why, for no accountable reason, it has fallen so low in the handicappers' books.

When Congress ratified the international treaty governing the Red Cross there actually was no clear definition anywhere in the world of what the treaty meant, or any physical organization remotely suggestive of the Red Cross as it exists in the United States today. It is equally true, and hardly at all understood, that the American Red Cross as it exists more than seventy-seven years later, shares little more with so-called Sister Societies throughout the world than it did in 1882 —a common devotion to ideals.

The American Red Cross today is completely American and more national in its activities than it is international. At the same time the differences distinguishing it from the 80-odd other national Red Cross Societies are essentially the source of its strength and a powerful lever in those fields where the American ideal exerts a sort of leadership in world thinking.

Here is the peculiar aspect in an extraordinary situation for which it would be difficult to find a parallel.

The very differences from other Red Cross Societies that mark the American Red Cross stem directly and in very slightly changed form from the original objectives set down by Miss Barton. If the diminutive leader did not have the gift of prescience, she most assuredly had the imagination to develop a long-range public relations program that is the goal which modern practitioners of that art might well copy.

The international conception of the Red Cross in 1882 was based on the introduction of a few humane rules into warfare—rules incidentally that have literally gone up in smoke in an era of saturation bombing of cities. The Barton thesis was that, to be worth anything in time of war, the Red Cross Societies should train specialists and volunteers by means of practice in handling natural disasters in time of peace. And that is what the Red Cross has done.

Nevertheless, a year after the chartering of the first American Red Cross Society, M. Moynier felt it necessary to set the record straight in order that the European Red Cross Societies should not be embarrassed by the American upstart.

Bowing deeply to the proud, aristocratic ruling powers of Europe, he wrote that of course the national Red Cross organizations should be "essentially an auxiliary of their respective armies." He gave a firm but friendly slap to the American group, writing that, "To use a flag which has a legal significance determined by the Convention of Geneva for undertakings of a different character from those for which it was intended is undoubtedly wrong."

It just so happened that it was Moynier himself who was out of step.

Already various Red Cross Societies in Eastern Europe were extending aid to victims of famines, epidemics, fires, earthquakes and other disasters. In England, where the Red Cross still is primarily a wartime organization, the true counterpart of the American Red Cross, called the St. John's Ambulance Society, had established by 1877 an extensive system of instruction on first aid to the injured. And in 1882, the American Red Cross and the German Red Cross each followed suit.

In September, 1884, at Geneva, Switzerland, at a meeting of the International Red Cross Committee, Miss Barton watched the American interpretation of the true meaning of the Red Cross triumph over the interpretations of the Western European powers. The open-hearted faction of the Red Cross tore to pieces the legalistic dictum written by Moynier only a year before.

The Red Cross became a truly humanitarian symbol—as yet glowing only faintly—but inextinguishable even at the hands of governments who saw a threat to power in any encouragement of the dignity of the individual.

In the United States any calamity large enough to be considered national—too big to be handled by local resources—was and is the concern of the Red Cross. And for that matter, international calamities—famine, plague, floods, earthquakes.

IV

In summarizing first steps as a prelude to chronicling the impressive history of the modern American National Red Cross we cannot overlook the garden in which the plant bloomed. The soil was a new attitude, intangible but growing; there also were gardeners.

The Red Cross symbolized a striking new conception of man's relationship to man that was slowly awakening in the western world and—we like to think—moving at a faster pace in the United States than elsewhere.

The Red Cross movement cannot be separated from the growing enlightenment of modern man, any more than that enlightenment can be separated from the evolution of factors that raised standards of living. It is perhaps true that most persons are good at heart, but the goodness comes through a lot more easily when the heart is in a well-fed body, and when the body represents a mind that feels reasonably contented and secure.

Miss Barton and her leadership came into the picture under the Red Cross as tangible evidence and form of the spirit which already was growing on every side. She was equally as necessary as the public spirit, because otherwise the recognition that all persons struck by disaster deserve the assistance of all others would have had no expression. But too often in detailing the histories of movements the great works themselves are perverted in their own greatness by enthusiastic efforts to prove that somehow they grew as freaks of individuality in a barren desert.

If there is one thing from which the Red Cross has suffered through the past half century, it has been overglorification. There has been too much effort, both within the organization by its friends and outside of it by its critics, to make it unique, a thing apart from ordinary things, a kind of godlike being that all alone is able to sweep down upon disaster-stricken peoples and make all things right for them. Of course, it cannot, and does not so claim.

If that seems to be an individual opinion—and it is one that many persons will say is unfair—I cite as my witnesses the leading figures in the organization who time after time have seen the greatest relief and rehabilitation jobs undertaken by the Red Cross followed by the stormiest criticism of the organization. On such a basis has been laid a blanket of unfair criticism and unfounded rumors ranging from dishonesty to favoritism to stupidity.

The Red Cross today, and the Red Cross in the 1890's, is and was no more and no less than the sum of its environment. Its leadership always has been the equal of the best leadership in other humane and public developments; its weaknesses organizationally and administratively have been about average.

Much credit goes to the Red Cross for the integrity of that leadership in moral and financial honesty, for its record is virtually perfect. But remember that neither have there been financial scandals involving sister organizations of great stature that sprang up coincident with it —the Salvation Army (British), the Ys, the Boy Scouts and Girl Guides (British), and more localized movements such as Hull House in Chicago and comparable settlement houses in other metropolitan centers.

When Miss Barton assumed leadership of the American Red Cross movement she had to fight for the technicalities involving recognition of the idea as an international symbol and force, but not for support of the work the Red Cross was designed to do, in so far as its first limited steps led it.

Americans were ready for the idea, by whatever name. They were ready for so many things, and free economically to express their hearts by contributing their resources to victims of all kinds of troubles that slowly were impressing man's consciousness as not the inevitable fate of the luckless few.

This was a period marked by major development of large hospitals in the cities for the free care of the sick who otherwise had been left to die in their misery. For the first time municipal groups were organizing on a permanent basis volunteers for care of the aged and indigent. Long looks were being taken at city slums by outraged civic leaders. The emancipation of women was becoming a burning issue.

Orphanages—however gruesome some of the century-old ones seem in retrospect—were becoming commonplace as refuges for children who earlier had lived cast-off lives and died in alleys. The United

States was just beginning a fantastic growth in church membership coincident with the development of church programs planned to make them neighborhood centers as well as places of worship for their congregations.

In this chronicle there will be many citations of "firsts" recorded by the Red Cross in community, humane and welfare activities. But none would have been possible except for acceptance, support and financing by the communities themselves.

This all represented a whole new concept of community life, the bringing together of whole communities as groups, and knitting communities into larger families. The county or the town was ceasing to be the shell within which individuals must live or die—and too often die within a cell within a county or city, unregarded and unattended.

In any great disaster—flood, earthquake, fire—which hits with dramatic impact, there are four steps to meet the needs of the stricken. The first is an immediate mustering of the resources available among the victims themselves of housing, food and medical care for those surviving the blow. This is personal emergency relief. Second, within hours this is supplemented by aids from the surrounding countryside, which usually suffice.

But two greater steps which move more slowly then must be taken. One is restoration of public services, such as roads, schools and utilities. These are by far the most expensive elements of rehabilitation and are properly the charge of governments, both state and federal. Since they involve great sums of money they overshadow all other costs and win the headlines. But they leave out one essential feature.

Public funds, aside from such relief as may be given while the ground is yet wet from receding floods, go to restore *things* for all the public. The rehabilitation of *people* is traditionally, in the United States, the job of private agencies. That was true before the Red Cross was founded. It is true today.

V

Now let us turn from the soil in which the Red Cross took root to the flowers—a few individuals who cultivated that soil and created the works that were the Red Cross flowers.

Here we see most clearly Miss Barton as chief of staff and drillmaster, as well as her own and the Red Cross's only recruiter. While seizing with one hand every chance to obtain the best possible publicity through activities, she demonstrated extraordinary capacity to bring into her circle extremely skilled and oftentimes brilliant men from the business and professional fields. And it is worth noting that this self-acknowledged homely and unprepossessing lady, already past middle age, held the continuing loyalty of her male associates over long periods of years.

The publicist and the politician, who had been such valuable allies in the special efforts to obtain recognition for the Red Cross, were supplanted immediately after its founding by the new types the Red Cross needed. Among them were doctors, lawyers and businessmen, and each, whatever his primary interest, proved to be a superb diplomat.

It might be suggested that only a natural-born diplomat could survive the pace set for her lieutenants by Miss Barton's own example. And it is well worth remarking that while many women became active in the Red Cross even in the early days, the positions of leadership all were held by men.

Take Dr. Julian Hubbell as a prime example. Dr. Hubbell first came into the Red Cross in 1881 when he served as Red Cross agent at the time of the Michigan forest fires, the first relief operation into which the new organization threw its meager resources. Hubbell was a student volunteer from the University of Michigan, where he was studying chemistry.

Miss Barton advised him, upon return to his studies, to switch to medicine. He did. In the twenty years thereafter, during which Miss Barton headed her little flying wedge of relief groups, Dr. Hubbell was always present and on the job with the Red Cross. Dr. Hubbell lived to inherit Miss Barton's Washington house.

In her last days, the giant bearded doctor watched over the aged little woman, tended her garden, made jellies in her kitchen—all the while as a world-known figure he directed development of the medical resources of the Red Cross.

Dr. Hubbell was far more than a dedicated volunteer medical man serving the Red Cross. In 1884 he accompanied Miss Barton to Geneva as her personal physician, and turned out to be the principal reporter of activities of the American delegation. Dr. Hubbell gave the name of

"The American Amendment" to the enlarged concept of the Red Cross conceived by Miss Barton. He worked alongside the official American delegate to that conference, Judge Joseph Sheldon of New Haven, Connecticut.

Judge Sheldon, who in 1890 became a vice president of the Red Cross, was already marked as one of the most brilliant delineators of the Red Cross idea. He was a militant standard-bearer for the contention that the Red Cross should operate as a continuing society to relieve and mitigate the effects of disaster in peacetime as well as war.

Judge Sheldon met and reputedly had a romantic interest in Clara Barton when both were young. Later he married one of her closest friends, Abby Barker. For fifty years the Sheldons and Miss Barton were an inseparable trio.

Judge Sheldon had not written the original charter of the Red Cross, approved by the District of Columbia in 1881. This was the work of Stephen Barton, Clara Barton's nephew, who served as her aide throughout her entire Red Cross career. However, Judge Sheldon refined and revised Stephen Barton's original manuscript in the form of a bill for submission to Congress in 1890 when it again was hoped that the Red Cross could obtain a national charter. The effort to obtain that charter was to be frustrated for another decade but Judge Sheldon's work in 1890 resulted in the classical description of the Red Cross still embodied in today's legal authorization.

As a third and fully equal partner of Hubbell and Sheldon among Miss Barton's dedicated aides, was Dr. Joseph Gardner, former college classmate and lifelong friend of President Benjamin Harrison.

Dr. Gardner also entered the Red Cross circle by marriage. When he married Enola Lee, Miss Barton's first notable expert in handling distribution of supplies at disasters, he fell into a pattern that still holds today—the devoted husband first helping his wife in Red Cross work and afterward awakening to the fact that he has adopted a second career.

Dr. Gardner and Judge Sheldon joined forces in 1893 to head off another European organization, calling itself "The Good Samaritan Union" whose backers proposed to organize a world-wide society to provide relief in cases of natural disaster unconnected with war. Such a program would have cut the ground from under all of the plans to make the American Red Cross a vital, continuing organization instead of simply an adjunct to armies in time of war.

Here was a perfect example of the teamwork—and political acumen —by which the founding group of the American Red Cross swung into action on the diplomatic level:

On August 22, 1893, Miss Barton publicly rejected the idea of the Good Samaritan Union as an organization separate from Red Cross, emphasizing twelve years of prior activity by the American society in this field. Within twenty-four hours Dr. Gardner wrote to M. Moynier urging immediate adoption of "The American Amendment," and Miss Barton followed up Gardner's formal appeal with a personal letter to Moynier. Judge Sheldon composed within a few days the official protest of the American Red Cross Society, citing all possible arguments of law and priority in the relief field as judicial reasons for squelching the competing movement. That was the end of the Good Samaritans.

As one other example of the type of volunteers Miss Barton mustered to her cause we see constantly recurring a tall, shrewd and reticent figure—George Pullman, wealthy, vigorous and distinguished nephew of the founder of the Pullman Company, who handled the business organization behind Red Cross relief operations that already were assuming very large proportions in relation to the money values of the eighteen-eighties and -nineties.

George Pullman was a different sort of friend from Hubbell, Sheldon and Gardner. Less a personal disciple of Clara Barton, he was at the same time more illustrative of the foundations she had laid in what seemed such a long time ago. There always lingered a bit of the shadow of President Lincoln's close friendship in Miss Barton's prestige and among her resources.

President Lincoln's regard for her was inherited by Tad Lincoln, his son. Tad had become a successful partner in the Pullman Company. There his closest friend was George Pullman and he brought his two friends together or, more precisely, placed George Pullman under Clara Barton's spell.

VI

Yet even with such support as this, what was Clara Barton's Red Cross Society?

It was little more than the name adopted by a handful of persons, incorporated as a group in the District of Columbia, and not even dignified by Congressional recognition.

It was true that they sometimes got lots of publicity, but always connected with disasters. Newspaper headlines were generous in praise of Red Cross work in times of extraordinary occurrences such as the Ohio River flood in 1884 and the Johnstown, Pennsylvania, dam-bursting deluge in 1889. However, between whiles the organization consisted of little more than Miss Barton's own self and three or four clerks crowded together in one room.

This meant no slackening of interest among the family of aides enumerated above, but—like their volunteer counterparts today— these notable volunteers must spend the major share of their time attending to business, practicing their professions, earning a living.

Directors of services who maintain continuity in organization and training must be permanently employed, paid staff members; there must be a liaison office to handle communications between other cooperating groups. Someone must collect money, disburse it and account for it. At the very minimum this requires organization—paid organization.

No such organization existed, except in one regard. It all perforce had to be in the person of Clara Barton, the unpaid Number 1 Volunteer who in her extreme old age would have to defend herself—and successfully—against charges that all the while she had profited from the Red Cross. More of that later.

There developed early several Red Cross Societies, in the wake of disaster relief work. The first was a tiny, devoted group in Dansville, Miss Barton's home—the first formed outside of Washington. This growth of chapters parallel with disaster work is told later. Here perspective requires some grouping of legal problems that would continue for years in the future.

This Red Cross organization was, and could be, no more than a loose association of organizations lacking a common charter. Only one, the Washington group, was covered by the International Red Cross Convention and recognized as part of the world movement.

Judge Sheldon's classic concept of a federal charter was introduced in Congress in 1890. It simply lay in a pigeonhole. Three years later the measure was recognized as dead. The concept of the Red Cross as the thing for which the Barton coterie had fought seemed to be dead for all time. In a moment of despondency Clara Barton wrote its epitaph on her copy of the bill:

"It has no changes, no criticisms and has no assurances and little hope of a future existence."

The temporary depression in hopes for a national charter did not last long. There must be a new strategy. If the Red Cross was dead as a recognized national agency it still must survive in some form. Miss Barton turned to an effort to obtain some form of legalization that would remove the taint of bastardy, through the local government of the District of Columbia. She reincorporated the Red Cross under a name to which it had not the slightest current right—The American National Red Cross.

Here was a transparent attempt to use the power of suggestion to give to the Red Cross the national status that it seemed to have no hope of getting in fact, to claim it for what it was not as a means of working on the public mind.

There were, however, other things that justified in fact, if not in all ethical practice, this grandiose assumption. These things were acts. And who could fairly quarrel with that?

By 1900, when the Congressional charter that seemed so distant in 1893 was suddenly won, there was no quarrel.

✛ ✛ ✛ ✛ ✛

5

On the Job—
When Disaster Strikes

WITH ITS FIRST little charter tucked under its belt, the miniscule Red Cross faced three alternative directions in which it might travel. It could be a paper organization crowning with prestige the sixty-year-old Clara Barton, who had at last reduced its ideals to some form of recognition in the Capitol of the United States. It could build up a long list of leading "names" graciously awaiting calls upon it for assistance. Or it could become an aggressive agent of mercy going out and meeting disasters face to face, seeking out need for the services it proposed to offer.

There never was doubt for a moment as to the course the Red Cross would take under the leadership of Clara Barton. Old she might be by the standards of her day, a part-time invalid subject to fits of depression and exhaustion that often held her in tight grasp, but she was not one to head idly an idle organization. Whatever the peculiarities of her tenacious battles, they always were on the side of activity, never organization for organization's sake.

In the fall of 1881, the first big challenge to prove whether the new Red Cross organization was designed for action or for paper planning came into being. That challenge came with the outbreak of fire in the forests of northern Michigan that wiped out countless settlements and villages and destroyed the homes of hundreds of families.

Dr. Hubbell's report to Clara prompted her to write in her first appeal on behalf of the Red Cross relief work that, "there is no food left in its track for a rabbit to eat and, indeed, no rabbit to eat it, if there were."

The description, it is true, was on the melodramatic side. But consider the time and the setting. Red Cross headquarters was the place where Clara Barton happened to hang her hat, not some imposing headquarters with national and regional offices and staff. In this instance, the "headquarters" was not even in the national capital, but at Dansville, where Clara was spending some time.

At Dansville, Clara had the nucleus of a branch chapter organization, and she had pioneered chapter operations in the larger cities of Rochester and Syracuse. These just about accounted for the Red Cross in 1881, outside of the handful of Washington friends, although one should not discount the powerful press and other individuals who stood ready to rally to any cause espoused by Clara Barton.

Small as was the organization, Clara ran up the Red Cross flag for the first time over her Dansville home, to mark it as the disaster headquarters of the Red Cross for the Michigan relief operation. And before she had finished her organization campaign she had in hand $80,000 in donations, either cash or provisions, to be dispensed through the field organization set up by Julian Hubbell. This was not a great sum compared with almost $900,000 dispensed by local committees in Port Huron and Detroit, but the Red Cross operation established two precedents that were to stick.

One was that here existed, for the first time, an organization ready and able to raise and dispense relief funds on a responsible basis, acting as liaison between the sources of contributions—however far removed from the immediate scene of disaster—and without regard to social or economic barriers.

The other was more important and far more basic in laying the groundwork for the long-range American operations of the Red Cross. The key word in the new development—and mark it carefully for the future—was *rehabilitation*.

Only sketchily defined—in fact never yet clearly so in technical and legal terms—rehabilitation is the greater part of the Red Cross work today. When disaster strikes, whether in the form of weather or man's more bestial side, there always are responses in some degree of aid donated at the moment by shocked and sympathetic onlookers. And government agencies move to restore public works such as schools, roads and the like.

However, every disaster leaves dangling on the end of the line, long after the waters have receded or the first-aid and field-kitchen groups have departed, the families that face hopelessly ruined futures if left to their own resources.

A program for these few but forgotten ones—as far as nationally mustered aid is concerned—was part of the original American Red Cross meaning given to rehabilitation. Definitions and practices under that word would be debated for decades, but the act became a fact of operations from the start.

This was part and parcel of the same philosophy that broke the American Red Cross away from the original European conception, and that made the Red Cross great in the United States from the start.

In developing this procedure, the Michigan forest fires and a relatively small flood on the Ohio River in 1882 were in effect practice sessions—practice in developing rehabilitation techniques, in making appeals for funds, and in doing the Red Cross job in a manner to win future support for its appeals. Out of these first steps grew the hard core of the first Red Cross organization, directed by Clara Barton and her loyal lieutenant, Dr. Hubbell.

Organizationwise, the Red Cross would remain virtually unchanged for the next fifteen or more years, but circumstances would seem to have been almost arbitrarily arranged to shape its character despite its organizational limitations.

When disaster struck, action would be signaled by as simple a thing as Clara Barton wiring the Associated Press and a few of the leading newspapers that the Red Cross would accept and distribute contributions. A typical message to the Associated Press that touched off a national flood of gifts was stated as simply as this: "Everything is needed; everything is welcome."

In such ways, based on constantly growing integrity, the Red Cross was to raise and distribute an estimated more than $2,000,000 worth of relief and rehabilitation supplies—about 90 per cent of the value in goods and only 10 per cent in cash—in the regime of Clara Barton.

How was this done?

The answer is best described in a few high lights, domestic and foreign, of work done in the years prior to the Spanish American

War, which itself served to set a precedent for activities by the Red Cross in wartime, under the formalized rules already established by the International Red Cross.

The roll call of peacetime work in the nineteenth century, and the gradual development of the meaning of the American Red Cross, runs through such occurrences at home as the Ohio-Mississippi flood of 1884 that made 7,000 families homeless, the Johnstown flood in 1889 and the Sea Island hurricane in 1893. For foreign action side lights, the record embraces a famine in Russia in 1892 and special relief distributed in Armenia, personally directed by Clara Barton, in 1896.

And between times we see Miss Barton, with the ever present Judge Sheldon and the ubiquitous Dr. Hubbell walking across the international stage, bemedaled and beribboned, at international conventions of the Red Cross, first at Geneva in 1884, then at Baden-Baden in 1887, and at Vienna in 1897.

II

On February 15, 1884, telegraph wires carried the news that the Ohio River in full flood had crested seventy feet at Cincinnati, and that this upsurge of angry waters was covering not only the city's streets and adjacent lowlands but building up into record proportions as it broiled down through the plains and on into the Mississippi.

Clara Barton, with Dr. Hubbell and her little crew of helpers, issued an appeal for Red Cross contributions, and started to the Ohio Valley. She reached Cincinnati coincident with military relief forces dispatched to the area by the government. Thereupon, the Red Cross set about its first major task in which it demonstrated what it could do without duplicating official relief work and what it could do that was not provided by government.

In this emergency, while the federal government distributed $500,-000 in relief supplies, the Red Cross raised and distributed supplies accounted as worth $175,000. The government provided tents, blankets, army rations and $50,000 cash. The Red Cross supplemented these with fuel and clothing, set a precedent by distributing food for beleaguered farm livestock, and wound up in the task of home rebuilding and individualized "helping people get back on their feet." No longer would a question be asked as to the place of the Red Cross in disaster work.

Miss Barton looked around Cincinnati and "the surging river like a devouring monster" swirling through the city. She wrote that "bankers and merchants stood in its relief houses and fed the hungry populace, and men and women were out in boats passing baskets of food to pale, trembling hands stretched out to reach it from the third story windows of the stately blocks and warehouses of that beautiful city."

The Red Cross group asked itself: since this was the condition in an organized city, what was transpiring through the long reaches of the low country, in the flooded villages and on the farms abutting the ordinarily placid waters? And they realized that there was only one sure way to find out.

Already supplies were coming into Cincinnati to a warehouse rented by the Red Cross and into another storage depot at Evansville, Indiana. These would go down the river. Miss Barton herself chartered at Evansville a small steamer, the *Josh V. Throop*, loaded it to capacity with coal, clothing and other provisions, and headed downstream.

With the Red Cross flag flying from its jackstaff, the *Josh V. Throop* made its way to Cairo, Illinois, and back to Evansville, while the weather turned back from the warmth that had caused the flood to freezing cold. Wherever there was isolated need, the Red Cross supplied what help it could, and with the help it gave impetus to cooperative relief.

Here was another important precedent, this cooperation. On this relief venture Miss Barton added to her staff volunteer members from other organizations and oftentimes turned over to local groups supplies from the warehouses in Cincinnati and Evansville. There was no question of pride as to the dispensing hand. And time was taken, too, to organize in the midst of the flotsam impromptu new Red Cross auxiliaries.

Without such organization any Red Cross aid would have been surely localized to a few cities; by its means, it spanned thousands of miles. In fact, after the initial work, as the flood waters raged down the Mississippi, broaching dikes and shifting the ordinarily turgid river's channel by many miles, Miss Barton repeated the water convoy program by chartering in St. Louis the steamer *Mattie Belle*. She loaded this ship, from the mountain of contributed supplies, with clothing, medicine and food for humans, and also with hay, oats and corn for livestock, and journeyed all the way to New Orleans and back again.

And when the waters had gone back to normal, the dead had been buried, and the immediate needs of the victims fulfilled, the Red Cross workers—again chartering the *Josh V. Throop*—set out to help wherever possible to mend the lives of families and individuals among the otherwise forsaken poor in the rural reaches of the river country.

This first flood-relief venture took the Red Cross into Clara Barton's dream of community cooperation—of "people helping people" in contrast to an organization impersonally doling out aid—the pattern for future chapter operations.

As an example: six boys and girls in Waterford, Pennsylvania, gave a public entertainment for the benefit of the flood sufferers. They raised $51.25, which they turned over to the Erie *Dispatch*. This newspaper dubbed them the "Little Six" and sent along the money, which Miss Barton promised to give to a specially worthy recipient. At a spot on the Illinois side of the Ohio River known as Cave-in-Rock she found the proper place for this money. There, in a corncrib, lived a Mrs. Plew, with her six children. Her husband and home had been lost in the flood. Clara waded through deep muck to visit Mrs. Plew, and reported that she found "misfortune, sorrow, want, loneliness, dread of future, but fortitude, courage, integrity and honest thrift." She presented the "Little Six" gift with enough extra to make the contribution an even $100. When Clara next steamed by Cave-in-Rock, she saw a new house for the Plews going up, and on the bank a board with the inscription, "Little Six Red Cross Landing."

The work went on until June, before Miss Barton, having dispensed all the contributions over a path of 1,500 miles, hauled down the Red Cross flags and left the river country in its budding clothes of spring.

Neither she nor her co-workers probably realized what had been accomplished in demonstrating the national spirit without which the Red Cross could not have flowered. Something of it was expressed by an editorial in the Chicago *Inter Ocean,* in March, 1884:

> There is no doubt that the day is not far distant—if it has not already come—when the American people will recognize the Red Cross as one of the wisest and best systems of philanthropic work

in modern times. Its work does not stop with the alleviation of bodily suffering and the clothing of the destitute—blessed as that work is when wisely done so as not to break down the manly spirit of self help. The Red Cross has become a grand educator, embodying the best principles of social science, and that true spirit of charity which counts it a privilege to serve one's fellow man in time of trouble. The supplying of material wants—of food, raiment and shelter, is only a small part of its ministry.

It was small wonder that Clara Barton's friends felt that she had capped her career with this work, and perhaps thought it wise to hasten tributes to her if she were to hear them in her lifetime. She had traveled 8,000 miles in this great venture, personally supervised the allocation of all relief supplies passing through Red Cross channels and with her own hand written acknowledgments of all contributions. Now she was tired and ill, but her old friend, Secretary of State Frederick T. Frelinghuysen knew the medicine that would do Clara Barton the most good —activity, not rest.

Before Clara Barton returned to Washington, a message had already arrived inviting the new American Red Cross Society to send a delegate to Geneva to the first quadrennial International Red Cross Conference to be held after ratification of the Geneva Treaty by the American government. Clara Barton put on her formal attire to call on the Secretary of State and ask him to name a delegate.

Secretary Frelinghuysen said there was none other to be appointed than herself, but Clara Barton protested that she was both tired and ill.

"That's because you have had too much fresh water, Miss Barton," the Secretary of State told her. "I recommend salt, and shall appoint you."

Of the prescription of salt water, more a little later. At this point it can be reported that Clara Barton made a full recovery on the spot.

After the flood episode of 1884, the Red Cross—while without organization, national status or even a set of books—was definitely in business, or in whatever it chose to make its business, the record would indicate. In 1885 Miss Barton went to Texas to visit regions hit by a severe drought, but decided that local resources were sufficient to handle the situation. In 1886 she visited Jacksonville, Florida, where the Red Cross cooperated with the Howard Association in combating a scourge of yellow fever and actively recruiting nurses for this work. But this was not the same pattern of high and glorified activity. A scandal aroused by reports of the behavior of some of the nurses, whether justified or not, clouded for the first time a major work in which the Red Cross injected itself.

When word of this epidemic reached Washington, Miss Barton assigned relief organization to F. R. Southmayd, secretary of the Red Cross at New Orleans and a former colonel in the Confederate Army who had lost an arm at Shiloh. Colonel Southmayd recruited about thirty nurses—some white and some Negro—who by previous experience had indicated immunity to the disease.

Most of the nurses were sent into Jacksonville, despite resentment expressed by the local medical group. It is not clear whether objections were raised because of the color question or otherwise. The official complaint was that the nurses were "intemperate," which in Victorian English could cover a lot of ground. And it is true that in this early period of nursing the profession embraced many women seeking adventure as well as the trained, dignified and dedicated young women who were the forerunners of today's nurses.

At Jacksonville the Red Cross learned two lessons it still remembers: (1) never attempt to give relief anywhere it is not welcomed; and (2) use the greatest possible care in selecting personnel.

On the other side of the coin, the Jacksonville epidemic provided a baptism in Red Cross service for a young woman, fresh from nurse's training in the North, who would later win a place among unforgettable humanitarians in professional Red Cross service. Along with the alleged intemperates and the others at Jacksonville was Jane Delano.

Rehabilitation of the Red Cross prestige needed to await, however, only another major opportunity, and this came in the form of the Johnstown flood. In 1889 swollen waters burst a dam above the little city of 30,000 persons and within minutes the community was all but wiped out.

The flood struck on June 1. Eventual statistics would show that 2,142 persons were drowned in its onslaught, but for the survivors the picking up of the pieces of their lives was as much a tragedy as the deaths.

Five days after the waters swept over the town, Miss Barton arrived on the scene with Dr. Hubbell and a small staff. The Red Cross appeal for relief funds and materials already had been nationally broadcast. The Red Cross mission remained for five months, distributing relief in kind estimated at a value of $200,000 and $39,000 in cash, including for the first time salaries for clerical workers hired to assist with the business of the Red Cross on a relief mission.

To keep the Red Cross work in perspective, it should be noted that in the same period the Johnstown Flood Relief Commission disbursed $1,600,000, but there was no conflict. There was, however, a strange echo that was to arise in later years to haunt Miss Barton and her reputation.

As part of the Red Cross work, barracks were built to house temporarily displaced families. When homes were rebuilt, the Red Cross planned to dismantle the barracks and sell the lumber. Protests by local merchants against such "unfair competition" required disposal of the lumber elsewhere.

The final decision, made by Clara Barton, saw the lumber shipped to Washington where it was used in the construction in suburban Glen Echo of a headquarters for the Red Cross, including a personal home for herself.

It would be eight years before the elderly woman would close her town house in Washington and occupy Glen Echo as her exclusive residence, but henceforth the grave question would be raised repeatedly as to whether the organization could be used as a private preserve for Miss Barton's comfort and convenience. Oddly enough, there was no hint of such a question from the contributors to the Red Cross. The issue was to be raised internally, and to become part of such a feud that even today its reverberations are heard and felt.

But the little whirlwinds that were to mount into a tempest of controversy seemed all but submerged in more dramatic events.

As one more example on the home side, there was a hurricane that freakishly swept across Sea Island off the coast of South Carolina in 1893—a region thickly populated by 30,000 persons, of whom thousands perished and the survivors lost houses, livestock and tools. Almost all were Negroes.

Here was a new problem in relief work, and dramatic indication of what the Red Cross was beginning to mean. Miss Barton personally felt that the task was too great to be handled by her organization. But no other group of organizations came forward to lend a hand. Presi-

dent Grover S. Cleveland and Governor Benjamin P. Tillman of South
Carolina joined in a personal appeal to the Red Cross to do the job.

The Red Cross was on the job at Sea Island for ten months—
months of hard work, of virtually training ignorant and frightened
persons how to mend their shattered lives, of appeals to the outer
world for such simple things as any sort of castoff clothes, and even
for hoes with which to cultivate gardens.

The job was dramatic in retrospect but it was not one that aroused
great public sympathy. At one point Miss Barton wrote: "I cannot
talk, cannot sleep." But she pulled up her reserves of sheer personal
force and wrote again, "We shall stand in this great work by ourselves,
with no help, no funds back of us, and no one to create them. It is
a perilous situation. If we fail, we are lost."

But the Red Cross did not fail, and its humane reputation was enhanced. When Joel Chandler Harris visited the scene to write about
it for *Scribner's Magazine,* he recorded: "There are no exhibitions of
self-importance. There is no display, no tortuous cross-examination
of applicants—no needless delay. The perfection of its machinery is
shown by the apparent absence of machinery."

III

In the year that Clara Barton became seventy-one years of age, the
Red Cross had thrust upon it an international operation quite distinct
from the role anticipated in the Geneva Convention. Not war but
famine raised the curtain on this phase of its work, and the impetus
came—of all places—from the so-called isolated and nationalistic section of the United States, the agricultural Middle West.

The voice of America demanded that the Red Cross act as agent
in a humane gesture toward alleviating in some degree the effects of
a famine of historic proportions that swept over Russia.

Foster Rhea Dulles, the noted historian, writing the history of the
Red Cross in carefully documented form, ascribed this outburst of
sentiment to the feeling that Russia—then as now a political enigma
but not considered a threat to the Western world—had been a true
friend of the Union in the Civil War. Russia had sent its Fleet on a
visit to New York at a crucial point when it was feared that Great
Britain and France would recognize the Confederacy, and perhaps

helped to stop such action with the threat of world conflict if European powers meddled in the American dispute.

In any event, when the farmers of Iowa, Wisconsin and adjoining states read of the plight of Russian peasants trading their possessions for bits of food, and burning the thatched roofs of their cottages for fuel, their hearts were aroused.

When Miss Barton agreed to accept the call on the Red Cross, Iowa growers dispatched an initial shipment of 225 carloads of corn to New York, in care of the Red Cross. This was only the first of many massive contributions of food.

The Red Cross chartered a ship for the first consignment. Dr. Hubbell personally took it to Riga and thereafter traveled to the famine-stricken districts in Russia to supervise the distribution of this and subsequent donations. Large as was the gift in the aggregate, it was small in comparison to the need. But it represented again the unique status of American feeling for those in need; the same sentiment on which Miss Barton had built the Red Cross idea.

The Czar of Russia particularly noted the meaning of the gift when he personally decorated Dr. Hubbell as representative of the American Red Cross. No longer was the little society in Washington, or its satellites growing in other cities, simply a provincial movement of do-gooders.

And having wet its feet in the international field, it was logical that the Red Cross could not thereafter retire, even though the next call had more political complications than either the Red Cross or the American government desired. That came in 1896.

The scene was Armenia, and the occasion was a renewed flareup of the historical Moslem-Christian warfare in which periodically, later as well as then, the Turks perpetrated appalling atrocities on the Armenian minority. This outbreak was particularly brutal, and aroused deep resentment and pity exemplified through such American organizations as the American Board of Foreign Missions and the Armenian Relief Committee.

These organizations were helpless to work in Turkey, where government policy aimed at extirpation of the Armenians held no note of sympathy for outsiders helping the victims. But Turkey was an adherent to the Red Cross Convention. Hence the Red Cross was asked to be the agency for Armenian relief. Reluctantly Miss Barton accepted the call, and in January sailed for Constantinople in a role more quasi-diplomatic than otherwise. Accompanying her were Dr. Hubbell and a staff of four.

In Constantinople, Clara Barton called first on Tewfik Pasha, Minister of Foreign Affairs, who with a courtesy that surprised her asked her plans. The seventy-four-year-old unofficial ambassador, prim in her bonnet but as regal in her deportment as her royal friends in Europe, told him frankly:

"We have brought only ourselves. No correspondent has accompanied us, and we shall have none, and shall not go home to write a book on Turkey. We are not here for that. Nothing shall be done in any concealed manner."

She added, "I shall never counsel nor permit a sly or underhand action with your government, and you will pardon me, Pasha, if I say that I shall expect the same treatment in return—such as I give I shall expect to receive."

So she gave, and so she received, but the task was almost overwhelming. Fiasco threatened the venture at every turn. One expedition set off under the direction of Dr. Hubbell. Another worked under Dr. Ira Harris. At headquarters in Constantinople, where Clara Barton remained, George Pullman attempted to handle the accounts for disbursement of some $115,000 in contributions.

At the height of the operation medical teams were fighting typhus and the other diseases of poverty and malnutrition over a range of country that required six weeks for delivery of a message, and handling communications in a babel of languages including Turkish, Armenian, Greek, Arabic, Italian and Kurdish. And while medical relief progressed, the Red Cross was importing at first, and then having made on the spot, tools for the planting of grain crops.

Obviously much good was done, but the venture was not a happy one. From America and from England came questions as to whether the Red Cross under Miss Barton had not become the dupe of the Turkish government, and other questions as to the wisdom of the manner in which funds were handled. There were no definite charges, just questions that rankled, and that caused Clara Barton to strike back in correspondence to many trusted friends—to M. Moynier in Geneva, to her nephew Steve holding the fort at home, and to Frances Willard, who was working with Steve. One letter to Steve said, "I feel we are doing so much for humanity that no one else could do, and that there is so much gratitude on all sides, that it is almost a comfort to know we have suffered something for it."

Thus the grand old lady of relief brushed off the flies of criticism, and as a treat to herself, with the mission completed, sailed up the Danube to Budapest and traveled to Germany to visit her old friend, the Grand Duchess of Baden.

+ + + + +

6

Publicity, Propaganda and Politics

FOR THE FOUNDLING Red Cross the years between 1882 and the Spanish-American War involved much more than forays into disaster relief, basic and important as these were to its growth. The years were marked by as strong a propaganda effort as could be mustered, and for this period of time this activity was the comet flight of Clara Barton, trailed by her galaxy of followers. The trail led back and forth between the United States and Europe, from the drawing rooms and meeting halls of America's leading cities to the courts of Europe.

When Secretary Frelinghuysen prescribed "salt water" for the Red Cross leader in 1884, he launched her on a phase of her career that undeniably aggrandized the Red Cross but also did equally as much for the Clara Barton legend.

Clara Barton went to Geneva, to attend the Third International Conference of the Red Cross with an appropriate train. Her fellow delegates were Judge Joseph Sheldon and Adolphus S. Solomons, vice president of the American National Red Cross. As personal aide she had Antoinette Margot, officially serving as interpreter.

Geneva was a triumph for Clara Barton. She was the only woman delegate to the meeting, and certainly the outstanding point of interest.

In fact, the Geneva meeting almost seems to have been planned to honor her American work, with Judge Sheldon himself denoted as the keynote speaker. Who then could forecast more than twenty-five active years still ahead of the sixty-three-year-old Miss Barton—a woman so fatigued by recurrent illness and many labors?

Judge Sheldon said:

I hesitate here in her presence, and without time to suggest details, to speak fitly of her work already done . . . nobly and successfully, where many eminent statesmen and men of influence and ability utterly failed. And if the history of our relations to that treaty [the Treaty of Geneva, 1864] and its ratification, and the relief work under it shall ever be adequately told, it will present all the elements of a career worthy of high admiration by all interested in humane work.

I cannot now state what will be plainly seen, that she has done her work with the skill of a statesman, and the "final perseverance of the saints."

Be it noted that Judge Sheldon spoke within a few weeks after the subject of his oration had concluded four months of day-and-night relief labors, mostly aboard river boats, succoring flood victims in a path she traveled back and forth between Cincinnati and New Orleans.

His speech in which he paid this tribute was followed by a vote of acclamation for the tiny woman who was credited with having brought the United States singlehanded into the International Red Cross.

The picture of Clara at Geneva was glowingly reported to America by Antoinette Margot, who sent news dispatches to the *Tribune* and *Graphic* in New York. Miss Margot wrote that the other delegates watched Miss Barton for any signal of agreement or disagreement with proposals put forward at the conference, particularly during the rather tense debate over the so-called American Amendment officially approving the peacetime role of the Red Cross along the pattern already set in the United States.

As a personage, Miss Barton also played her role well. Even her clothes—the apparel of the formerly mouselike schoolteacher and Patent Office clerk—were a matter of remark, as well as of some concern to her. In fact, Annie Childs, who had become a sort of adviser to Clara in matters of dress, had taken considerable pains to see that the American Red Cross leader should hold her own in competition with the famous and fashionable personages who would be at Geneva.

It is recorded that Clara Barton had for outdoor wear a long, close-fitting coat and a bonnet with ribbon ties and a fur piece. She took along a silver basque for evening wear and a black satin dress with jet trimming for evening wear. She possessed "a tight-fitting dress of silk" for street and church wear, a garnet skirt, a polonaise and an "old green dress" that had been freshened with new velvet.

With the formal clothes, she had now begun to wear medals and decorations, of which she seemed to be inordinately proud. Each addition to these—whether from societies in the United States or from foreign governments—was a new thrill to her. She accepted these as she accepted friendships of celebrities, as a normal and necessary attribute of the career she had laid out for herself.

Those who thought they were paying tributes to Clara Barton at the end of a notable career, when they honored her at Geneva in 1884, could not have been more wrong in their estimate of the stamina of the frail little woman, then 63 years of age. She returned to the United States, closed for all time her house at Dansville, and moved into a house in Washington larger than the one on I Street had been. By now, her house was a beehive with comings and goings of aides, visitors and officials. Her interests were as wide as those of any political leader, her influence often greater.

As head of the Red Cross, Clara Barton had the official position and prestige that she so obviously desired. With this prestige firmly in her grasp, she used it to the hilt to bring attention to the Red Cross.

At one moment in 1885 she was calling upon former General Grant, by now on his deathbed. At another time President Cleveland was requesting her to look into a politically and socially troublesome situation in Texas. This threatened trouble for the Red Cross and for the Administration alike, inasmuch as the Red Cross responsibilities still were to be defined by law.

In any event, Texas was suffering from a prolonged drought. From one quarter, led by a country preacher, the Reverend John Brown, came demands for Red Cross relief for sufferers pictured as numbering 100,000 families. From other quarters—the land-owning families— came reports that such descriptions were exaggerations that served only to hurt the name of the Lone-Star State.

Clara Barton and Dr. Hubbell acceded to President Cleveland's request to look into the situation. The Red Cross leaders crisscrossed northwestern Texas, at best a barren stretch of endless plains, by horse and buggy, studying conditions.

With Yankee forthrightness, Miss Barton reported on the spot that conditions affecting many persons were pitiful, but that this was a situation that Texas should handle with its own resources. And it is a strong indication of the prestige already won by the Red Cross that the recommendation was accepted. Furthermore, in the role of leadership she had assumed, Miss Barton set about showing Texans how to do it.

Clara went to see an old Civil War friend, Colonel A. H. Belo, owner of the *Morning News,* in Dallas. He opened a public subscription list, starting it with a gift of $5,000 and announcing that Miss Barton personally was contributing to the fund. While this fund grew, the Texas legislature appropriated $100,000 for relief of the drought-stricken farmers.

Clara Barton remained in Texas until wagons of relief supplies, feed and seed were rolling through the stricken area—in fact, until rains came and broke the drought.

Then she hurried back to Washington, to attend the first encampment in the capital of the Grand Army of the Republic. Honored there as a noted veteran of the Civil War, she busied herself with seeing that the Red Cross flag was much in evidence and that the now familiar Red Cross brassard was sewed on the sleeves of all surgeons, nurses and others attached to the medical staff of the G.A.R.

II

All this time the façade of publicity was designed for a purpose far greater than the sporadic raising of relief funds or the personal glorification of Clara Barton. She despaired at times of ever seeing the Red Cross grow into anything like the image of it that was in her mind.

She had continually thought of the organization as she had described it in prospect in letters to Dr. Appia in 1877—a national one with headquarters in Washington connecting area and state groupings of local chapters. In other words, a truly coordinated National Red

Cross such as it is today, differing perhaps in many details as the Red Cross has evolved through the years, but the same in concept.

What the Red Cross actually was at the start of the Clara Barton regime consisted of nothing more than the Washington society chartered by the District of Columbia government, plus the incalculably valuable names of prominent persons who gave their support to Miss Barton. Among these were Senator Omer D. Conger of Michigan; Richard J. Hinton, the nationally known newspaper correspondent; Judge William Lawrence; General and Mrs. N. V. Boynton; Judge Sheldon; Mr. Solomons, one of those rarities in Washington, a local and highly successful businessman; and such younger followers as her nephew, Steve Barton, and young Dr. Hubbell.

One technicality must be cleared away to make clear the limited status of the Red Cross that Miss Barton headed when she went to Geneva to the Third International Conference in 1884, and later to the Fourth International Conference at Karlsruhe in Baden in 1887. The United States government had signed, and the Senate had ratified, the Geneva Treaty, but no provision had been made for chartering a National Red Cross under that treaty. Hence the American organization had no national standing. And the effort to obtain a charter from Congress was to prove about as difficult a task as had been the obtaining of ratification for the treaty.

This accounted for the constant propaganda and political effort, the pulling of wires in Washington, and the publicity on the international stage that occupied Clara Barton and her associates almost full-time between the disaster operations that in themselves were the best fuel for the publicity fires. This in turn accounts very largely for the seemingly insatiable publicity efforts, and the kowtowing to leading names on the world stage that increasingly marked Clara Barton's advancing years. She gathered publicity where she could, and in return for it gave adulation that at times threatened to warp her own judgment of the world in which she lived.

The British upper classes paid her no heed, so she never returned to England for a second visit after the first in 1872. The French people likewise did not strike her as hospitable in the manner of supporting her American work.

On the other hand, the German—particularly the Prussian—royalty lionized her through the Emperor's daughter, the Grand Duchess

Louise—undoubtedly using Clara Barton as a tool to win favor with the German emigrants in America and as part of the propaganda to offset the bad taste left in many mouths by the brutally pursued conquest of France in 1870 and the annexation of Alsace and Lorraine. But to Clara Barton the Germans were the cream of Europe and, it would seem, the only ones worth knowing.

Yet in her likes and dislikes she was devotedly sincere. If snobbery or ambition prompted her to cultivate Louise in her struggling days with the Red Cross, the fact remains that when Clara Barton was failing in 1912, only six weeks before her death, the aged lady penned a note to one of Europe's almost forgotten royal characters, the equally aged Louise, with the salutation, "Dearest, dearest Grand Duchess."

Whatever the other reasons might have been behind Clara Barton's courting of the spotlight, the Red Cross fared well in world publicity when it still had stiff work to do to obtain official recognition in Washington.

In Karlsruhe, in 1887, where Clara Barton headed again a delegation of three, this time accompanied by Dr. Hubbell and the prominent woman physician, Dr. Lucy M. Hall, she was Louise's personal guest. That was remarked around the world, together with the fact that while Miss Barton and Dr. Hall held credentials that permitted them to sit as delegates in the convention, the concourse of German royalty, eminent members of the international legal and medical fraternities, and heads of military establishments were restricted to viewing the proceedings from the galleries.

At one reception in Karlsruhe, Clara Barton discussed as an expert from her Civil War experience, casualties with those eminent creators of battle casualities, Prince Bismarck, Germany's "Iron Chancellor," and Count von Moltke, Field Marshal of Emperor William's conquering armies.

Emperor William himself, still active despite his own advanced age, sought her out for a visit during a reception in his daughter's palace, and noted with pleasure that among her many medals she wore one bestowed by himself, doubtless at Louise's suggestion, when special medals were struck to celebrate his seventy-fifth birthday.

On this occasion Clara Barton made probably the silliest gesture of her life in kowtowing to "name" figures, but in the setting it did no harm and possibly a little good for the continued popularity of the Red Cross in Europe. As Ishbel Ross reconstructed the story, the Emperor noted that alongside his and other medals, Miss Barton wore one given to her by the *Verein Deutscher Waffengenossen* of Milwaukee, Wisconsin, a group composed of emigrant German survivors of the Franco-Prussian War, who had elected her a member of their society in recognition of her own humane services in that war.

"And they make good citizens?" the Kaiser asked her.

"The best that could be desired," Clara Barton replied, adding, "industrious, honest and prosperous, and, sire, they are still yours in heart, still true to the Fatherland and its Emperor."

William is quoted as having replied, "I am glad to hear this; they were good soldiers and, thank God, true men everywhere." And he went on to make his compliments to America.

In fairness it must be stated that, away from the pomp of court life, Clara Barton was her old self when she showed Dr. Hall the sights of Strasbourg and recalled "the poor wretches, all covered with ragged and festering wounds," for whom and among whom she had worked so hard after the siege of that city in 1870.

All of this made quite a story for Dr. Hall to report in an article she wrote for the *Vassar Miscellany*.

On the other hand, Clara Barton showed ingenious touches of self-consciousness in this period of publicity, fanfare and propaganda. When invited to speak before the Sorosis Club in New York, she was genuinely concerned about the clothes she should wear in order to make the proper appearance. So she wrote to Mrs. M. Louise Thomas, who had invited her. Clara knew that this was a signal honor.

In the invitation Mrs. Thomas had pointed out that this was the only time each year when outsiders—gentlemen and "gentlewomen" —were invited to a club affair. She named P. T. Barnum, Robert Collyer and Will Carleton among those who would attend, together with many editors, judges and literary men and women.

Mrs. Thomas duly wrote to Clara that she herself, as chairman of this meeting, would wear a black velvet gown with a train and her Sorosis badge, and would carry a fan and flowers. Good diplomat that she was, Mrs. Thomas suggested that Clara wear a lace on her head, otherwise whatever costume she desired, but to be sure to include "your well-earned decorations, all of which I want you to wear."

III

Clara Barton became seventy-five years of age on Christmas Day, 1896. This anniversary came only a few months after her strenuous relief foray into Turkey. It found her exhausted and again going through a despondent mood that extremely worried Dr. Hubbell, George Pullman and Dr. Lucy Hall, who had now become Mrs. R. G. Brown.

In retrospect this might have been the best historical moment in which Clara Barton could have stepped down and let the Red Cross develop as an organization rather than as the entourage of her personality. Just as much of its strength had come from the indomitable leadership of Clara Barton, so had the one-woman rule developed many weaknesses.

There were strong and large societies in New York, Philadelphia and Boston, and scores of other smaller ones reaching from the Atlantic to the Rocky Mountains. The trail of organizations roughly marked the routes over which the Barton trail had wandered in disaster relief. But it is notable that there are few records of leaders in name or action in those early societies.

One hears only of Clara Barton and her followers—rushing here and there to alleviate the effects of disaster, traveling half around the world, dominating world conventions. But where were the others? Submerged under a cloak of anonymity that would explode within a few years into a violent controversy, which first would threaten to tear down the whole idea, but out of which would come the enduring structure.

But weak as Clara Barton might seem to be in the winter of 1896–97, she was far from out.

In the fall of 1897 she again headed her delegation, to the Sixth International Conference of the Red Cross, convened in Vienna. She had not gone to the fifth conference, held in Rome in 1892. Dr. Hubbell had reported for her. No more feebleness marked Clara now. In Paris she paused to see Sarah Bernhardt, to shop and to visit the Eiffel Tower and the Jardin des Plantes. And each day she found the energy to spend hours preparing reports on the work done by the American Red Cross in the five years since the last conference had been called. Those reports now had come to be accepted as laboratory experiments pounded out in actual experience in disaster work—experiments that already were affecting profoundly the world-wide conception of the Red Cross in peacetime.

Between the making of reports, there was more of the lionizing of Clara Barton that contributed probably most of all to the American Red Cross stature. Hers was the most prominent seat at the general sessions. Her views were the most sought-after when debate showed divisions of opinion. It was she who attracted most attention at the court reception given for the delegates, and it was she who was chosen to walk with the Mayor of Vienna at the head of the procession of Red Cross delegates into the Jubilee Hall of the Rathaus where the city paid its hostly dues. There was even a special train provided to take Clara Barton to Kahlenberg to view the poetic stretches of the Danube and the Vienna Woods.

It was things like this, too, that caused the stature of the American Red Cross to grow at home in proportion to the celebrity achieved by its founder. There were such tributes as importunities from Frances Willard for Clara to back actively the temperance program to protect students at Yale from the "saloon influence." There were countless invitations to lecture, which Clara declined because of the press of her other work.

She returned from Vienna to settle in her last home, the house at Glen Echo built with the lumber salvaged from Johnstown, Pennsylvania.

This house, which combined the functions of Red Cross headquarters and personal home for Clara Barton, provided a suitable setting for the retirement years of one of the most colorful careers carved out by any woman in the nineteenth century.

Its gardens, dairy and trees were the particular responsibility of Dr. Hubbell, who throughout his lifetime had a great affinity for the soil. Almost pretentious in size for its time, it was a busy house, with numerous apartments for the entertainment of guests. Clara's flag collection was displayed in its corridors; the rooms overflowed with treasured furnishings which had come mostly as gifts to her from admirers, such as a gold settee from the Grand Duchess Louise.

In surroundings of her choice, Clara Barton could settle here— working to the degree she desired, and pampered by her household— completely protected from the rigors of super-activity and the storms of controversy, whenever she chose to delegate her leadership elsewhere.

But to her such a thought was absurd.

Within a few months after returning from Vienna, the battle-toughened septuagenarian was off to another war, this time in Cuba, after first winning a preliminary skirmish to keep other would-be leaders from intruding upon her dominance. Never would she permit another to displace her in the first wartime operation by the American Red Cross in the Western Hemisphere since its authorization in 1881 under the Geneva Convention.

+   +   +   +   +

7

First Test by War

IN THE SPRING OF 1897, more than a year before the outbreak of the Spanish-American War, Cuba became a focal point of interest to many North Americans interested in extending a humane hand of friendship to a plundered populace. The thing that sparked this interest was the plight of the so-called *reconcentrados* in Cuba, the natives who, as a result of resisting Spanish tyranny, had been herded into concentration camps.

The plight of these Cubans had won concern on the part of the Red Cross before Miss Barton sallied off to the Vienna conference that year. But under her leadership the American Red Cross societies had moved cautiously because of the complications involved in relationships between the United States, Spain and the insurgent forces in Cuba. Oddly enough, it was the activity of another group composed of women calling their organization the National Relief Fund for Cuba, that precipitated Red Cross interest in taking direct steps.

This group, derisively dubbed by Clara Barton "the Court Ladies," so aroused her ire that she called personally on President McKinley in July to discuss the situation. Despite an asthmatic attack that made it difficult for her to lay the problem before him, he sided with the Red Cross and suggested that Miss Barton confer with the Army and Navy. This she did, without confiding to the President that she already had held detailed negotiations with President Moynier of the International Red Cross as to possible courses of action.

Within a few days, when Clara called again on President McKinley, he told her that she had been chosen as "the most efficient source of aid" to collect and dispense funds for the benefit of the *reconcentrados*.

Miss Barton moved fast, now that the politics of the affair were settled. President McKinley personally issued an appeal for funds to support the Red Cross work and the Central Cuban Relief Committee was formed in New York to receive money. Miss Barton declined an invitation to serve as chairman of this committee but nominated her nephew Steve, who took the post; with Charles A. Schieren, representing the New York Chamber of Commerce; and Louis Klopsch, of the *Christian Herald,* as fellow members.

On February 4, President McKinley wrote a letter which read in part as follows:

> Miss Barton's well known ability, her long devotion to the noble work of extending relief to the needy and suffering in different lands, as well as her high character as a woman, commend her to the highest consideration and good will of all people.
>
> I bespeak for Miss Barton, wherever her mission may take her, such assistance and encouragment as she may need in prosecuting the work to which she has devotedly given so much time and service.

Two days later, accompanied by Dr. Hubbell and J. K. Elwell, formerly a merchant in Santiago, Cuba, and a fluent speaker of Spanish, Miss Barton sailed at the age of seventy-five to her last great battlefield adventure.

Before it was over she would have carried the Red Cross banner through three phases of Cuban operations—*reconcentrado* relief, the Spanish-American War, and orphan and hospital relief work in Cuba in the spring and summer of 1898.

In that year and a half, never once interrupted by illness or fatigue despite her advanced age, Miss Barton would reach another summit of her career, and come perilously close to wrecking the very organization she so sincerely desired for the Red Cross. As for the Red Cross, this would be its last long step toward accreditation as a national organization instead of a loosely knit group of local and state societies; and one so strong that rumblings of discontent over the one-woman nature of its leadership would almost, but not quite, topple the old lady from her pinnacle.

For two months, broken by one dramatic interlude, Clara Barton, Dr. Hubbell and a party of some twenty helpers worked among the sickening sights and smells of the concentration camps, dispensing what comfort they could to hundreds of thousands of Cuban political prisoners. A showplace villa was placed at Miss Barton's disposal, but busy days found her traveling from one camp to another, organizing what comforts and relief were possible with the bounty of stores sent from New York—from Havana to Cienfuegos, to Matanzas, Artemisa and a score of other camps she traveled.

The dramatic interlude was one more example of history's coincidental creation of Homeric backgrounds for Clara Barton. Immediately after she had arrived at Havana she was invited to lunch aboard the battleship *Maine*. Two days later, while she was working into the night on correspondence, the doors of her room facing the sea flew open, a deafening blast shook the furniture, and all inferno seemed to have torn loose in the night.

The *Maine* had just been blown up. Miss Barton left her current work, sent a telegram to New York stating simply, "I am with the wounded," and for several days thereafter did whatever was possible to augment the assistance given by the Navy authorities ashore to their own—what Miss Barton, never an admirer of official medical organizations, now termed "excellent Navy care." Then she hurried off on the rounds of her original mission.

Senator Redfield Proctor went to Cuba to observe what the Red Cross was doing. When Miss Barton showed him some examples of the concentration camps, he saw the almost hopeless task that had been assumed.

Senator Proctor returned to deliver a speech in the Senate that— added to the inflamed feeling caused by the sinking of the *Maine*— certainly advanced the possibility of a declaration of war on Spain. He charged that 200,000 of Cuba's population of some 1,600,000 already had died in these camps. His praise of the Red Cross work, as handled by Miss Barton, was unstinted.

"I especially looked into her business methods," he reported, "fearing that there might be want of system, waste and extravagance, but found she could teach me on these points. In short I saw nothing to criticize, everything to commend. The American people may be assured that the bounty will reach the sufferers with the least possible cost and in the best manner in every respect."

This endorsement was to mean much to the Red Cross in the weeks and months ahead, when the still immature organization faced all the usual demands of war, small in scale but a challenge to organization.

II

With all of its lack of organization, inexperience and the limitations imposed by its monolithic leadership, the Red Cross hammered out much of its character in the Spanish-American War. Furthermore, this was the crucible that refined much of the theory evolved by the older international organization into practical experience for greater tests of the future, because with the exception of the brief Franco-Prussian War in 1870 there had been no major conflict in the world since the Geneva Convention was framed.

Thus the American organization, already marked as the great pioneer in peacetime relief work, had the opportunity to turn high-sounding articles written on pieces of paper into sweaty and trying activities on the home front and the battlefield alike, however miniature in scale the war might be.

In a brief span of months, in 1898, the American National Red Cross—not yet national at all, be it remembered—achieved several notable results:

1. It won acceptance for, and put into practice, the idea of recruiting female nurses for duty with troops in wartime.

2. It demonstrated its power to weld persons with humane instincts into a compact organization for the raising of funds and provision of nonmilitary supplies. For instance, the shipment of 800 tons of ice from Maine to Cuba was a godsend beyond price.

3. It developed the unique Red Cross field worker assigned to duty with military units, to work with *but not under* military command.

4. Most of all, it won acceptance of the need for the job it could do.

The Red Cross actually had no program to put into operation in the Spanish-American War. There was no time to develop one after hostilities commenced. What was done was evolved under emergency conditions, always handicapped by the absence from Washington or New

York of Miss Barton, who should have been directing staff work there. But somehow the program got done, and generally it was a credit to the Red Cross.

At President McKinley's suggestion, the New York Chamber of Commerce sponsored a committee to collect money and supplies for Red Cross use in Cuba. This was called the Central Cuban Relief Committee. It quickly won the support of the whole country, and served as a rallying point for the scattered Red Cross Societies throughout the country. It mustered the support of ninety-two auxiliary committees covering the United States east of the Rocky Mountains. Later the California Red Cross State Association, numbering forty branches, received authority from the national society to act in the Philippines and other sections of the Pacific theater of war.

On April 22, 1898, the Navy declared a state of siege of Cuba. On that very date the New York committee had completed loading a chartered steamer, the *State of Texas,* with supplies intended for relief of the Cuban civilian population. The *State of Texas* was dispatched to Key West, a naval base, on April 23 to await developments. Then the United States declared on April 25 that a state of war existed with Spain. Miss Barton, who had hurried north in early April for coordinating conferences, returned south and joined the *State of Texas* at Key West upon its arrival there. She left to an emergency committee in Washington and to Steve Barton the task of working out a plan for Red Cross operations with the forces.

In this situation the Red Cross floundered through the war. The American National Red Cross in Washington was the only agency recognized by the government under the Geneva Convention which became invoked automatically with declaration of war, but the so-called "national" organization was simply a group of individuals in one city.

However, war helped to define Red Cross responsibility. Displacement of Cuban rebel work marked the end of the Central Cuban Relief Committee. Now the same leadership set up in New York the American National Red Cross Relief Committee. It actually mustered the other societies for war work with the Army but acted almost independently of the National Red Cross. Finally, there was nothing in law or precedent to divide lines of operation between the Red Cross and the Army Medical Corps. Recruitment of nurses for duty with the

Army was taken over by an organization called Committee on Maintenance of Trained Nurses, Auxiliary No. 3 of the New York Red Cross
committee.

The politics of the situation were even more complicated. On May
24, 1898, the State Department officially proclaimed the National Red
Cross as "the proper and sole representative in the United States" of
the International Red Cross Committee to carry out functions "for the
relief of wounded in war"—the first official recognition, in fact, by
this government of the legal status of the Red Cross under the Geneva
Treaty.

But there still remained the Army Medical Corps, headed by Surgeon General George M. Sternberg, whose views on volunteer civilians
serving with the Army, particularly female nurse volunteers, were precisely in accord with those of his Civil War predecessors. Now there
was no strong-willed Clara Barton to carry the contest to a solution or
compromise. She was glued to her self-designated post on the *State of
Texas* and there she would remain until late June when this ship was
permitted to sail for Cuba.

But bit by bit, largely because the need and the time for its potential services at last had met, the Red Cross overcame obstacles, among
which the greatest were perhaps within itself.

III

Out of the welter of uncoordinated and oftentimes unrelated activities
were hammered in essence the Red Cross Services to the Armed Forces
as they have grown and been proved in major tests since 1898. As
examples of these services:

The Red Cross Relief Committee and its affiliates, composed often
of men and women with keen memories of troop hardship in the Civil
War, set out to raise money and procure those things that always get
lost in red tape.

Hospital and camp equipment, abdominal bands and underwear for
wounded or ill men, canned goods, pajamas and nightshirts, delicacies
and the priceless ice—these were among thousands of items purchased
or gathered as contributions in kind. Remembering that the year was
1898, the size of the contributions is impressive: more than $100,000
raised in California, $50,000 from Cleveland, as examples. The

A.N.R.C. relief committee in New York dispatched provisions valued at $360,000.

These were not stacked up to await need on the battlefields. The hardship phase of the Spanish-American War was as acute, or more so, in camps on American soil as in Cuba. And the first Red Cross field representatives acted as agents to search out such needs and supply them.

At a training camp at Chickamauga, 500 cases of typhoid fever developed in one day, whereupon Steve Barton, acting as chairman of the National Red Cross Executive Committee, authorized any necessary work "to alleviate the suffering without stint." Another field agent reported from Jacksonville that many hospital patients had neither sheets nor nightshirts. The Red Cross went into action, supplementing gifts of these things with fresh milk, ice and other supplies and, when Army medical supplies ran low, supplying sterilizing apparatus, hypodermic needles and syringes.

In the meantime, from New York to San Francisco Red Cross women were creating the substance if not the formal organizations of the subsequent Gray Ladies, Recreation Services, and Canteen Corps, among others; by entertaining embarking troops and establishing rest and recreation tents, with game rooms and reading and writing facilities, for men in transit and in hospital and recuperation camps. They penned letters dictated by soldiers too feeble to write. They organized games and in a few instances took on the responsibility of providing emergency relief for families whose men had gone away to war.

The old and sketchy records of Spanish-American War Red Cross activities necessarily deal mostly with the broad picture and the generalities of fund-raising, supplies collected, and in particular with the figure of Clara Barton. But there comes through this picture here and there evidence of the vital factor that marked the adolescent stage of the American Red Cross—the springing up of chapters as the arteries and veins of the body that made it truly "national" and "American," as distinct from these words denoting the Washington hierarchy.

While the records of 1898 mention ninety-two Red Cross auxiliaries cooperating with the successive New York committees and the California Red Cross State Association with its forty branches, these mean so many individual cooperating community groups that are today known as separate chapters. In these cities men and women raised amounts of money phenomenal for the day, particularly as there were no national fund drives with organized broadside publicity. In addition, many women sewed.

The collection of supplies often meant making thousands of units in Boston, Philadelphia, Cleveland or Denver and *assembling* them in New York. Or it meant the ingenuity, noted by Miss Barton, of "some lovely committee of home ladies," who collected the funds and loaded a ship with 800 tons of ice to send to Santiago.

In the South, Red Cross work in primitive and often fever-laden camps—all the little touches to make the sick comfortable and the well less depressed—was done by *local women*. In San Francisco, then a relatively small city, hot lunches and coffee were served by Red Cross volunteers to 17,000 men awaiting debarkation. Oakland, California, anticipated military procedure by many years when an ingenious and unnamed volunteer sparked the idea of providing each soldier embarking from San Francisco with an identification badge—so often the only means of identifying the dead or wounded.

Finally the Red Cross won a fight, quite independently of Miss Barton, to provide some of the nurses so badly needed by the Army Medical Corps and yet so strenuously opposed by the Surgeon General. His fears were not entirely based on whim; there was a strong feeling among the medical fraternity that such nurses as might be drawn to military service would be impelled by motives other than sheer service, and that, in addition, the introduction of women to essentially all-male installations would impose new burdens of housing and care beyond the offsetting value of the work they would perform.

The ice was broken, not by the Red Cross, but by a committee of the Daughters of the American Revolution, headed by Dr. Anita N. McGee, who was to become an Acting Assistant Surgeon General charged with organization of the Army Nurse Corps. Dr. McGee undertook to procure volunteer nurses; but only for work in general hospitals; not overseas or in training camps or in the field. She became a relentless enemy of Clara Barton, still attacking her after the latter had died.

The Red Cross, through its Committee on Maintenance of Trained Nurses, took its claim of right and duty under the Geneva Treaty right to President McKinley. He arranged a meeting with General Sternberg, who in turn agreed to accept nurses recruited by the Red Cross.

The Red Cross committee had as its chairman one of the strongest-willed of American women, Mrs. Whitelaw Reid. She was typical of the emerging type of feminine leader in America already challenging Clara Barton's self-defined monopoly of Red Cross leadership. Fortunately, at that time nursing had reached an advanced stage of development in the United States. It was a recognized profession, to which admission was gained only by educated young women after long training in residence in accredited hospitals or schools.

Soon thereafter the first nurses, now recruited by the Red Cross and serving under the Army, made such a good record in general hospitals that they were granted some of the opportunities that General Sternberg had first opposed so strongly. A few got to Cuba, a few to the Philippines, and many to camps and field hospitals.

Before the Spanish-American War ended, the Red Cross had recruited about seven hundred nurses, one-third of the total employed by the Army. Half of the Red Cross contingent was maintained at the expense of the Red Cross.

The final decision on this experiment was written by a Congressional Committee after the war:

"Our recent experience may justly be held to have shown that female nurses, properly trained and properly selected, can be duly cared for and are of the greatest value."

IV

Having stated that the whole Red Cross operation in the Spanish-American War suffered from Clara Barton's preoccupation with getting to Cuba, it is only fair to add that her presence in the battle zone also wrote a large chapter of Red Cross history.

In May of 1898 we find her, in company with Dr. Hubbell, nine nurses and a small staff on board the *State of Texas:*

The ship, not really accredited as anything, is neither a war vessel nor a white-painted hospital ship. As a chartered Red Cross vessel it will have no status until the State Department acts at the end of that month to notify the War and Navy Departments of the Red Cross's official status.

Loaded with 1,400 tons of supplies for Cuban patriots, now badly needed by our own forces, the *State of Texas* at one time acts as a mercy ship by treating medically the crews of Spanish merchant ships that have been captured and interned. It is simply a curiosity, occasionally visited by newspaper correspondents to see the celebrity who is managing it, and again visited on May 23 by General William R. Shafter to learn what he may expect in the way of aid from it for his Cuban expeditionary force.

What Clara Barton belatedly came to recognize, and what was clearly seen by George Kennan, the former newspaper correspondent now Vice President of the National Red Cross, was that the massive and active relief committee in New York had thrown her paper organization into the shade. Even the name of Clara Barton, in absentia, was no match for the vigorous activity on the home front of Levi P. Morton, New York chairman, and such other figures as Mrs. Reid, Bishop Henry C. Potter, William T. Wardwell and Dr. George F. Schrady.

None of these tried to undercut the national organization; in fact, they had outfitted the *State of Texas* and had pledged full support to the national organization. But as a group they were far bigger, more active and doing more things.

On June 20, at long last, Rear Admiral William T. Sampson, naval commander and the victor at Santiago, issued orders permitting the *State of Texas* to proceed to Guantanamo Bay, where the Marines had landed.

Aboard the *State of Texas* when this historic order was delivered were Miss Barton, twenty Red Cross medical and nonmedical workers and a crew of thirty-five men. All were civilians. On the hull of the ship and on its smokestack was painted the Red Cross symbol. Its barnacle-covered hull made such slow progress that its assigned port of Siboney was not reached until the night of June 26.

At Guantanamo the medical staff joined the Reserve Divisional Hospital at Siboney, while Clara Barton and her nonprofessional staff —and her supplies— were welcomed for the relief work they could do.

It was not a pretty sight they saw on land. Already the Rough Riders had been hit, losing among their dead Hamilton Fish, son of the former Secretary of State. Many of the American wounded still lay in their bloodstained clothes in native huts. As always, supplies were desperately short. Patients lay on bare floors even in the so-called hospitals. There was little or no protection from dirt, flies or lice—the barest sanitary facilities, if any.

At Siboney, Clara Barton found the Army welcoming her supplies but a little appalled at the thought of her female nurses serving ashore. The weather was adverse, but unloading began—medical supplies, meal, flour, coffee, tea and canned goods. Hour by hour, the little woman who could not possibly have such energy at the age of seventy-five, directed work aboard ship, until finally word came from General Shafter that she should proceed to the front.

Here was the repeat performance of the Clara Barton triumph in the Civil War. Penciled with General Shafter's own hand was an order authorizing Clara Barton to seize any necessary transport and get along with blankets, tents, food and medical necessities. She did just that.

Through a pounding surf separating the *State of Texas* by half a mile from the beach, Clara went ashore with her staff—Dr. and Mrs. Gardner, Major James A. McDowell, a Civil War veteran, and others.

The first contingent of Red Cross supplies was loaded by Dr. Hubbell onto two six-mule Army wagons and headed toward the 1st Division Hospital of the Fifth Army Corps. Clara and her group hailed a hay wagon and followed it, to find what George Kennan described as follows: "If there was anything more terrible in our Civil War, I am glad I was not there to see it."

The forward "hospital" was situated in a valley surrounded by dense jungle east of Santiago. It was made up of three large tents, six smaller ones and a scattering of individual "shelter halves" of Army tents (half tents carried by soldiers in their packs). In and around the tents were wounded men. Eight hundred were there when Clara Barton arrived. Without blankets or covering for more than a fraction of them, the broken bodies were lying on soaked earth and wet grass. Many whose clothes had been cut off so that their wounds could be treated were naked, as there was neither clothing nor cloth with which to cover them.

New arrivals were brought in almost continually, to this gory back alley marking the realistic portion, so quickly forgotten, of the now famous and gallant battles of El Caney and San Juan Hill. They were "Rough Riders" at the front, but here only the same pitiful and helpless creatures that Clara Barton had come to know so well in Virginia a generation earlier.

If the scene was repeated as though there had not been more than thirty intervening years, so the sight brought out the fundamental spirit of Clara Barton, whose aging body refused also to admit that those years had passed by it. Her therapy was based on food as a primary requisite. Others could handle the medical work.

With McDowell, Clara looked at the cooking facilities and condemned the amateurish outdoor structure that she saw. With her own hands, assisted by McDowell's, she built an outdoor oven and fought to get a proper fire going. It was difficult, because the rain was falling and the wood was green, but the old campaigners made their fire and started kettles of water to boiling.

A few hours later Clara wrote, "I had not thought to ever make gruel again over a camp fire," but make it she did, and before the evening was over these men in the swamp had a hot meal, supplemented with milk, chocolate, rice and tea. Also, she evolved that night what she called "Red Cross cider" made from stewed apples and prunes, mixed with lime juice and cooled in a stream.

As the night wore on, a night in which seventeen men died and walking wounded continued to come down from the heights, Dr. Hubbell went back for more supplies and Clara Barton tore up unbleached muslin into strips to cover the naked men. In passing she recorded her opinion that the battle was being poorly fought, sending gallant charges of men against entrenched troops without preparatory artillery barrages.

Clara Barton remained at this post for two days, working closely with Major Marshall William Wood, Chief Surgeon of the 1st Division, watching operations carried on by day and night, on rough plank tables set in the open. The rain stopped briefly and it was the season of bright moonlight, which made possible more night work but also had its risks. Two Red Cross workers—one from the official Red Cross group—were killed by sharpshooters in moving supplies from the beach to the field hospital. Three times Clara made this trip herself as supplies were fetched until all the men were covered—and what the Red Cross could provide was in ample supply, if anything is ever ample in wartime.

And one morning Clara had a visitor, as she herself described it:

We were very glad to meet the gallant leader of the Rough Riders. After a few moments conversation he said, "I have some sick men with the regiment who refuse to leave it. They need such delicacies as you have here, which I am ready to pay for out of my own pocket. Can I buy them from the Red Cross?"

"Not for a million dollars," said Dr. Gardner.

"But my men need these things," he said, his tone and face expressing anxiety. "I think a great deal of my men. I am proud of them."

"And we know they are proud of you, Colonel. But we can't sell Red Cross supplies."

"Then, how can I get them? I must have proper food for my sick men," he said.

"Just ask for them, Colonel."

"Oh," he said, his face lighting up with a bright smile, "then I do ask for them."

On the spot a sack was filled with malted milk, oatmeal, canned fruits, rice, tea, chocolate, meat and vegetables, and Clara added in her account:

Before we had recovered from our surprise, the incident was closed by the future President of the U.S. slinging the big sack over his shoulders, striding off, and out of sight through the jungle.

V

The Red Cross work in Cuba was as brief and dramatic as the fighting. On July 4 the Spanish Fleet was destroyed by Admiral Dewey in the Battle of Santiago Bay. A few days later San Juan and El Caney were captured, although at a cost of 1,475 killed and wounded, many of the latter of whom streamed through the hospital where Clara Barton, her civilian helpers and a Red Cross medical staff labored. Then on August 13 yellow fever broke out in Siboney, striking at the Red Cross medical staff among other victims.

Since the *State of Texas* could no longer unload medical supplies at Siboney—in fact, the Army soon ordered the town burned to check

the spread of fever—Miss Barton and her party embarked for Santiago, where she reported to General Shafter, asking permission to
enter Santiago and resume the work of relieving suffering Cuban
civilians.

Here was another incident of the dramatic ups and downs encountered throughout its history by the Red Cross.

Permission first was refused for the *State of Texas* to enter Santiago
at all, since it had come from Siboney and therefore was suspect as a
carrier of the dreaded yellow fever. For four days it lay in the road-
stead, while the military and naval authorities were preoccupied with
organizing the victory procession with which the city would be taken
over formally from the defeated Spaniards.

Then, without notice, a launch appeared alongside the *State of
Texas* with official orders that the dirty, black-hulled little steamer
with its Red Cross insignia should be the first ship to steam into the
harbor, ahead of all the armed might of the victors. Someone, somewhere, never identified, apparently had an auspicious sense of public
relations.

As the *State of Texas* proceeded on its historic little voyage into
Santiago, Miss Barton—ever more eloquent as her age advanced—
jotted down the following:

> Could it be possible that the commander who had captured a
> city declined to be the first to enter—that he would hold back his
> flagship and himself and send forward and first a cargo of food on
> a plain ship, under the direction of a woman? Did our commands,
> military or naval, hold men great enough of soul for such action?
> It must be true—for the spires of Santiago rise before us.

With the war ended, the Clara Barton mission returned to its originally planned role of assisting Cuban civilians, remaining until September of 1898. Again in 1899, Miss Barton personally led another
relief expedition to Cuba, but now the bloom was off the vine for
such personal forays by the leader of the Red Cross. The scope and
importance of the Red Cross demanded another reappraisal. Here its
history pivots from the field of personal inspiration to that of organization.

+   +   +   +   +

8

By Authority of Congressional Charter

IN 1900 THE CONGRESS of the United States granted to the National Red Cross a charter designating it as the official agency for the rendering of certain services to the armed forces. But the charter was anti-climax. That which was granted already had been offered and accepted in practice. And the charter affirmed a legal status that had existed in fact for so long that already grave revolutions in concept and leadership were threatening either to tear the Red Cross to shreds or to hammer it into the truly national status that it had long claimed but never held.

The Spanish-American War had, in many respects, proved to the Red Cross what it could be; at the same time it had shown that the Red Cross as conceived, created and led by a single individual, however gifted, could never assume the posture required by a modern nation.

As in every revolutionary social change written into law, the Act of Congress incorporating the American National Red Cross set forth a series of standards that gave small indication of the forces behind the legislation. The law of incorporation, dated June 6, 1900, authorized and directed the Red Cross to furnish volunteers to aid the sick and wounded of the armies in time of war; to serve as a means of communication between the armed forces and the people as well as with other Red Cross societies; to provide relief in times of peace for sufferers from national calamities; and to devise measures for preventing suffering from such events. Also, to furnish the federal government with an annual report of receipts and expenditures.

The articles of incorporation, preserved in every subsequent revision of the Red Cross's massive rights and duties on the American scene, provided precisely the recognition for which Clara Barton and her intimate followers had fought for almost twenty years. Yet they were written at a period when a dissident group of powerful names brought to bear every pressure possible to strip the aging leader of her authority.

While Red Cross operations were continuing in the midst of the Spanish-American War, there were restless stirrings in New York for businesslike management, particularly in the accounting for funds. At one point, when Steve Barton became disturbed by the pressure, Clara Barton wired her nephew, "If insisted on, refuse cooperation with Committee."

In retrospect it seems that the doughty old lady was economical to the point of frugality in dispensing Red Cross assistance. But her mistake was an imperious conviction that since she was the Red Cross leader the contributors should take her leadership as it was without question. She was not alone, in an era when Cornelius Vanderbilt, building up his railroad empire, said, "The public be damned."

But Clara Barton's "public"—her most important contributors—were not the sort to accept such an attitude; they represented the business and the new businesslike attitude of a country that gave much to, and demanded much from, its publicly supported organizations.

Support for the Red Cross by the New York leaders never wavered, but neither did their determination to make the Red Cross a truly public society. Notable in this contest was a public statement, signed by Bishop Henry C. Potter, Spencer Trask, Cleveland H. Dodge, Robert C. Ogden and Mrs. Whitelaw Reid:

> The undersigned persons, who, in times of previous activities and during the War with Spain, have been associated with the American National Red Cross, desire to state that in their judgment the financial arrangements of this organization need reorganization in order to meet the confidence of the American public.

Beneath the surface, and far beneath the level of such dignified public statements, there was growing another schism that was to leave echoes haunting the Red Cross into the very period of its maturity following World War I.

Some have called it a power struggle. Others have termed it the normal progression of an organization grown out of the bands of its swaddling clothes. Whatever the cause or its true nature, there was shaping a battle royal, in which the Barton opposition was to rally around another woman of intense personal determination, and furthermore a wealthy and ambitious figure—Miss Mabel Boardman.

Miss Boardman was the daughter of William Jarvis Boardman, a lawyer and businessman. Her mother, also wealthy in her own right, was the daughter of Joseph Earl Sheffield, founder of the Sheffield School of Yale University. This new leader had been born in 1860 and was to live until 1946. She never married. In making the Red Cross her prime interest in life she was destined to dominate it or cast her shadow across it for a period far longer than the founding leader, Clara Barton. But with the vital difference that others shared her leadership.

Seldom in organization history has the bitterness of an almost unaccountable hatred so shadowed an otherwise noble progress. Even at this writing there is difficulty in placing the Barton-Boardman antagonism in proper perspective, shorn of the personal animosities of the respective supporters and critics of the two women. And at this writing it still is a notable fact that no memorial yet has been erected to Clara Barton in the national headquarters of the Red Cross, no reminders of a personal nature save an engraving of her likeness hanging on the wall of the main floor corridor, and an oil painting on the second level.

And it must be noted here that Miss Boardman, when she won control of the Red Cross from Miss Barton, restrained her own ambitions to the point of refraining from ever seeking either the presidency or chairmanship of the Red Cross, either of which she might have had for the asking. Officially she was simply a member of the Central Committee.

A woman of majestic dignity, she suggested the late Queen Mary—so much so that when the Duke of Windsor, as Prince of Wales, met her in the 1920s he exclaimed, "My God, there's Mother."

II

Despite the conflicts raging around her, the earliest years of the twentieth century continued on the surface at least to be a triumph for Clara Barton, both in the field and throughout the world. At the age of seventy-eight, she took charge of a major disaster in the field, returned to Washington to beat down the first onrush of criticism and opposition, and emerged in such high fettle that in 1902 she would shatter seemingly overwhelming opposition ranged against her.

Let us look at these occurrences in order, for they are part and parcel of the Red Cross, the glory of its beginnings and the foundation of what was to come.

On September 8, 1900, a tidal wave and hurricane swept over the port city of Galveston, Texas. When it subsided, between 5,000 and 6,000 of its 38,000 inhabitants were dead—so many that bodies were cremated in batches for the lack of means to give proper burial. Rich farmlands were inundated and every building suffered some damage. Thousands of survivors fled to Houston, abandoning everything that they owned.

Within the shortest possible time after the news wires flashed details of the catastrophe across the country, Clara Barton and a staff arrived on the scene, and she issued her now familiar call for relief —contributions of money or things. The New York *World* led the campaign for contributions in the east, and the Wells Fargo Express Company conveyed supplies contributed to the Red Cross without charge.

Soon money and supplies estimated at a value of $120,000 were sent in response to Clara's call, but the echoes of the inner struggle of the Red Cross floated like a cloud over this operation.

For one thing, the contribution of the Red Cross, large as it was, figured as relatively minor in the total of contributions to Galveston's needy. For another, a nasty controversy broke out on the spot.

This latter stemmed from a report issued in Galveston by Mrs. Ellen Spencer Mussey, the Red Cross counsel, that Clara Barton was too old and ill to direct the work properly. Clara's response was to transfer her work from a room in a hotel to more spectacular outdoor activities and to send Mrs. Mussey back to Washington. Thereafter Miss Barton worked literally day and night on the spot for two months.

And in late October she went to Houston to work for the rehabilitation of the Galveston refugees who had fled to that haven.

This work completed, she returned to Washington, there to face again a barrage of criticism because there was no specific procedure for making an accounting of disposition of gifts to the National Red Cross.

In Washington once more, however, the storms generated in New York seemed far away.

In the White House was President McKinley, one of Clara Barton's staunchest friends. He had presented to her, in fact, the pen with which he had signed the bill incorporating the Red Cross.

That bill had provided for the establishment of a Board of Control of the Red Cross. The bickering seemed to be one concerned with details, and details could not dent the leadership of the Founder and her old guard. And another year passed uneventfully, except for the inner-circle political maneuvering. Then, in September of 1901, an assassin killed McKinley.

For the third time, the assassination of a President removed a supporter and powerful friend from Clara Barton's circle. What had been only personal skirmishes within the Red Cross became, with the passing of President McKinley, vital threats to the old guard.

Already, in January of 1901, the anti-Barton forces had put a series of resolutions through the Board of Control, consisting of sugar-coated criticism of Miss Barton. These resolutions bestowed high praise upon Miss Barton's service and long devotion to the Red Cross, but also directed, among other things, that thereafter "all moneys for the American National Red Cross shall be paid to the Treasurer directly and shall be disbursed by him directly."

The Barton group responded to this implied criticism at the annual meeting in December of 1901 by pushing through reorganization abolishing the Board of Control and substituting for it a Board of Directors.

Now Miss Boardman's leadership—that of a confident and independent woman in the prime of life—came into dominant view. And the goals of her leadership at their highest level embodied the conception of an entirely new type of Red Cross—one controlled and led by the born or self-made leaders of American society, with emphasis on wealth and social prestige. Only such leadership, Miss Boardman contended, could attract to membership the wealthy individuals to whom the Red Cross must look for support if it was to become the national organization she envisaged.

By 1902 the dissension had become so great that Clara Barton's supporters were planning maneuvers to confer upon the president, Miss Barton, enlarged powers for life, apparently believing that she would live forever.

The opponents of the elderly lady, while recognizing her strength as one of the best-known living American women and a great popular symbol, became equally convinced that their plans for the Red Cross of the future could sprout only in soil from which every vestige of Barton leadership had been torn. Since Miss Barton apparently never was going to die or resign, she must be dismissed.

Now it was a clear-cut contest between the Boardman forces and the Barton forces. Ranged behind Miss Boardman were money and social position, plus now the President of the United States, for it was President Theodore Roosevelt who sat in the White House, and his sister, Mrs. Anna Roosevelt Cowles, was one of Miss Boardman's strong allies.

The Boardman forces worked to enlarge the Board of Directors. The Barton group concentrated on the gathering of proxies from chapter members, to obtain the required two-thirds vote necessary to change the bylaws and elect Miss Barton president for life.

Apparently to the surprise even of Miss Barton, her administration won all along the line. The Board of Directors declined to enlarge its membership, and thereupon her proxy-gathering friends pushed through the life presidency.

To Miss Barton, writing in her diary on Christmas Day, 1901, her own eightieth natal day, she confided, "The Red Cross is in the hands of its friends." But opposition such as she faced hardly paused to catch its breath before hurling an attack far more destructive than the intramural voting at the new life president.

On January 2, 1903, the same impetuous individual who, as a colonel in Cuba had praised Clara Barton's Red Cross work, delivered as President the most devastating blow he could level at her leadership, shattering the cordial relationship that had existed for more than twenty years between the White House and the Red Cross.

III

Opening her mail on January 2, Miss Barton found a curt note from George B. Courtelyou, secretary to the President, informing her that the President and his Cabinet declined to serve as a Board of Consultation for the Red Cross, an honorary body incorporated in Red Cross practice since the first small organization was chartered in the District of Columbia in 1881.

The note cited reports from "ladies and gentlemen of high standing" protesting against the manner in which the new bylaws had been adopted, as well as a recent resignation of the treasurer of the Red Cross in protest against the manner of accounting for funds. Its crowning blow was notice that "the President directs me to have it publicly announced that the President and the Cabinet cannot so serve."

Miss Barton replied to this letter after days of heart-searching thought, but her reply was never published. And in the meantime her opponents seemed intent upon hounding her out of the organization. In fact, students of the Red Cross are still confused as to the multifarious course of events at that time, a matter of relatively small importance except for the ultimate results. It appears, however, that Miss Barton was confronted variously with offers by the opposition to retire her with a pension if she would resign or, on the other hand, to subject her to a Congressional investigation if she remained in office. In the meantime the old lady was not sitting still, and the Executive Committee, under her control, suspended Miss Boardman and her principal lieutenants right after the threatened step by the latter to present a memorial to Congress had been taken.

Throughout the year 1903, in which no major disaster or other event occurred to focus particular attention on the Red Cross, the intramural contest raged. But fever rose to such a pitch that the minority group headed by Miss Boardman refused to attend the annual meeting in December, 1903.

Clara Barton's controlling faction accepted the conclusion that there was no alternative except to subject their leadership, and Miss Barton's own conduct, to a public investigation. But the resolution passed at that time stipulated that the study should be made by the general counsel for the Red Cross rather than by a Congressional Committee.

Since Richard Olney, former Secretary of State under President Cleveland, was the general counsel, this procedure was accepted by the minority. He in turn named a committee of three members, of which the chairman was Senator Redfield Proctor, who had studied Clara Barton's work in Cuba. The other fellow committee members were General Fred C. Ainsworth and William Alden Smith.

Judge Sheldon advised Clara that he felt too old and feeble to carry the burden of representing her, so she was represented by L. A. Stebbins and Thomas S. Hopkins, while Leigh Robinson represented the minority group.

The battle actually seemed to stimulate Clara Barton, who was described by one reporter who interviewed her as "serene and confident." And she did not lack for well-wishers. The American Woman Suffrage Association made a point of inviting her to its Washington convention in February, 1903, where she stood beside her old friends, Susan B. Anthony and Carrie Chapman Catt. Soon thereafter the entire group of Spanish-American War veterans, meeting in convention in Washington, went out to Glen Echo to pay their homage.

When the investigating committee met, there were piles of evidence introduced by each side, but mostly it was inconclusive and so prejudiced as to hardly warrant the word. It became more and more evident that here was a washing of dirty linen in a contest that had little more meaning than a cat-and-dog fight between the "ins" and the "outs" of an organization both sides wished to control.

The remonstrants pressed many charges, including one that Miss Barton might have diverted $12,000 worth of Russian relief contributions to the purchase of a farm. But this farm had never been her personal property and it long since had reverted to its former ownership, when a project to turn it into a supplier of food for relief operations failed to materialize.

The end of the investigation came abruptly, when Senator Proctor declined to continue hearings and declared the whole affair "the most outrageous proceeding that has ever come under my investigation."

Of course, this was in many respects the worst thing he could have done. Miss Barton's side claimed this as complete vindication. The remonstrants said the inconclusive nature of this termination was meaningless.

But the clarification of Red Cross atmosphere, which history was pressing to have accomplished, was worked out. On May 14, 1904, Clara Barton resigned from her lifetime presidency. Fortunately the prestige of Proctor and Olney was so great, and Miss Barton's exit so graceful once her name had been cleared, that the way was left open for rebuilding of the Red Cross into the organization that the country's growth demanded.

On June 16, 1904, a temporary authority was established under the presidency of Rear Admiral William K. Van Reypen, former Surgeon General of the Navy.

As far as the public was concerned, the bitterness was ended and a nationally respected old lady retired to a well-earned rest. The Chicago *Inter-Ocean,* then a newspaper of national importance, wrote: "Clara Barton cannot resign her place in the world as the one real, true representative of the Red Cross in this country."

Within less than six months, early in January, 1905, the Red Cross was reincorporated by a new charter passed by Congress (written by John W. Foster) and immediately signed by President Roosevelt. This created in substance the Red Cross as we know it today; it evolved a form of organization that could not kill the bickering, as no law can, but which made the Red Cross both essentially scandal-proof and a truly national organization.

From the standpoint of organization, the "new" Red Cross answered almost every demand of the leadership that at last had succeeded Clara Barton. The governing body was to consist of a Central Committee of eighteen members, of whom six would be elected by the incorporators, six would be chosen by state and territorial societies, and six would be appointed by the President of the United States. The last six would consist of the chairman of the Central Committee and five Cabinet members, representing the Departments of State, War, Navy, Treasury and Justice. Furthermore, the new law provided that the War Department should annually audit the accounts of the Red Cross.

Thus the Red Cross became at long last a quasi-official organization, with its rights and privileges conferred by law, its unique international status reaffirmed, its affairs set in order, and at the same time a public organization wholly supported by private contributions. William Howard Taft, a close friend of Miss Boardman, became the first president of the new corporation, and Surgeon General Van Reypen the first chairman of the Central Committee. Clara Barton's pre-eminence, now that she was stripped of power, was assured by her being named as the first of sixty-five "incorporators," but the reorganization effectively wiped out the old guard, including the aging Judge Sheldon, bewhiskered and loyal Dr. Hubbell, and the nephew Steve, who had grown into middle age in the personal service of his aunt.

Clara Barton severed completely her connection with the Red Cross, retiring to her home at Glen Echo. But she remained active until a few months before her death on April 12, 1912, at the age of ninety. In her eight remaining years she organized the National First Aid Association of America, from which she sallied forth to attend many public meetings, and an increasingly introspective development caused her to study intensively the fad of spiritualism.

9

Groping
and Reshaping

DESPITE ALL THE fanfare over the "new" Red Cross, under its 1905 charter the organization came perilously close to being a "pretty face with naught behind it." It appears in retrospect to have been in 1905 all names and no money, all authorization and no activity. And as for leadership in fact, it had torn itself apart to overturn a "one-woman leadership" only to settle down into the same state before the ink was dry on the signatures on the new document.

Of names there was no lack. The sixty-five incorporators were a roll call of leaders in finance and industry. The Central Committee included dominant members of the President's Cabinet. Finally there was an Executive Committee, consisting of a fraction of the Central Committee.

The president of the Red Cross was William Howard Taft, and the chairman was Major General George W. Davis, retired, a Civil War veteran.

And hovering over all—the "boss" even of Taft and the only regular attendant at meetings of the Executive Committee—was Mabel Boardman, suggesting, ordering, devising plans.

Yet in the first year of its operation under the new charter the Red Cross resources were so meager that it spent only $2,902. Much of this came from a fund of $10,000 representing the resources turned over to the new organization by Clara Barton. There was a slight income from legacies and contributions, but the enrolled membership of the National Red Cross stood at only 3,337 persons.

Under the Barton regime, when the Red Cross existed virtually as a name only between disasters, such an organization had sufficed. But it was intolerable to the new regime, which had set as its goal the creation of a truly national organization with divisions and chapters covering the country, ready to meet the demands upon itself that the Red Cross had set forth in framing its pattern of exclusivity.

Something was needed to bridge the gap. The "something" became an obsession with the idea that the Red Cross should make itself the pet object of support by the wealthy, the socially prominent and the ambitious. And that was how it went for more than a decade.

This was the strength that Mabel Boardman brought to it, and this was the weakness that became so ingrained in the Red Cross structure that in the 1950s, at the broadest period of operations it had yet achieved in peacetime, the Red Cross needed the weightiest of publicity campaigns to muster the contributions necessary to finance the calls upon it.

Many times in recent years the Red Cross has echoed a statement written into one of the earliest issues of the *Red Cross Bulletin:* "Publicity, in point of fact, is the great present need. Relatively few people know what the Red Cross is."

Fate must have realized this need, because in 1906 the San Francisco earthquake and fire gave the almost dormant organization a publicity opportunity of the best sort, the kind in which need and services could be demonstrated, without which even Miss Boardman's energy and name-gathering might have failed to hold it together.

II

On April 18, 1906, hell itself seemed to explode in San Francisco. At this time, the Red Cross had no staff worth mentioning, no organization except a few scattered societies still torn apart by the feuding a year earlier, only a few thousand dollars in the till and not a single person trained in disaster relief. But it had a friend in the White House, now that Miss Boardman was its spark plug and Mrs. Cowles was her friend. And the friend, President Theodore Roosevelt, was impulsively quick to act in all matters.

Without consulting even the Central Committee, President Roosevelt issued a public proclamation declaring the Red Cross to be the best-fitted organization to take over relief work in the stricken city!

This was the responsibility publicly placed on an organization which hardly existed—to be responsible for sheltering more than 35,000 temporarily homeless people, to feed at the period of greatest stress some 200,000 persons, to exert leadership in restoring the lives of one of the largest cities of the country.

While Congress was hastily appropriating $2,500,000 to assist the stricken city, and business leaders in San Francisco were setting up their own notable Committee of Fifty to cope with the crisis—and while countless other highly organized groups in other cities and states were swelling the generous outpouring of assistance—Roosevelt took another step that for sheer gall is almost without exception.

He telegraphed Dr. Edward T. Devine, General Secretary of the Charity Organization Society of New York, already enroute to San Francisco, to represent the Red Cross there—in effect naming the embarrassed Dr. Devine as director general for a shadow organization taking precedence over local as well as other cooperative relief work. Dr. Devine accepted the assignment, stopped in Chicago to pick up Ernest Bicknell, a noted social-work director, and went on to San Francisco to prove himself both a prime diplomat and an able relief administrator.

Within a few weeks, the Red Cross found its new stature, sharing responsibility and working harmoniously with the San Francisco Committee of Fifty.

Once more the heart of America poured out gifts, and the amplitude of contributions undoubtedly lessened what otherwise would have been high tensions resulting from competition between hard-pressed relief groups.

The Red Cross and the Committee of Fifty set up a corporation named the San Francisco Relief and Red Cross Funds. The corporation eventually received and accounted for $8,537,871 in cash subscriptions alone. Of this total about one-third was given through the Red Cross—more money in fact than the Red Cross had collected for all of its relief work in all peacetime disasters prior to that time.

Dr. Devine concluded his work with the organization phase of this operation. When he returned to New York, he delegated direction of the Red Cross work to Ernest Bicknell, who unknowingly began what was to be a quarter century of Red Cross service.

Between the two men the Red Cross achieved a stature it had not had before, and in fact its work laid a protective covering over the feuds and petty quarrels, the ambitions and the jealousies that had threatened to smother its development.

Much more was accomplished too. Here was an opportunity on the grand scale, considering the size of the country and its resources, for exemplification of cooperation with other organizations. In this case the working arrangement became one in which the United States Army handled emergency distribution of food and temporary shelter, both with government resources and the contributions to the Red Cross.

The Red Cross took over the longer-range task of rehabilitation. Here was further development of the primary idea behind the plan of Clara Barton, and further enrichment of what has since become the Red Cross's historic and primary, if not exclusive, disaster role.

Almost as soon as the Army's tent shelters and bread lines were in operation, the Red Cross moved into the work of rehabilitation—floundering in the great mass of requests, unequipped by experience and dependent entirely on the size of contributions which as yet could not be measured.

The city was divided into districts, each assigned to a volunteer committee. Mindful of past criticism, the Red Cross established an accounting system before all else. Devices were improvised for screening and investigating requests; because unfortunately in all disaster rehabilitation operations, then as now, the chiselers and the cheats commingle generously with the honest persons. To this task came a host of social workers from agencies in San Francisco and other cities.

The caution was almost too great. Delays and complaints threatened again to give the Red Cross a black eye. Then came another improvisation: the establishment of a Bureau of Special Relief with authority to act quickly in cases of obvious and great need. Each of these steps was a landmark in building Red Cross experience.

Since San Francisco is a damp city, and a chilly one, the first major job was to get residents out of tents and into weather-tight shelters. The answer to this problem was one of the first mass developments of portable houses. Families who agreed to build such small houses in parks or other assigned open spaces were granted construction bonuses of one-third the cost, up to a limit of $500, with the understanding that when the ruins were cleared the houses could be removed to normal residential sites.

Next a system was set up of granting up to $500 to families as tide-over assistance until jobs and livelihoods could be restored. Some loans were made, but in these cases the Red Cross had its first and last sorry experience with disaster relief loans.

The bad feeling arising from attempts to collect eventually resulted in cancellation of those still outstanding. Loans were never tried again in disaster relief.

It is not unreasonable to assume that the old lady then living in retirement in Glen Echo chuckled understandingly at seeing this result from the violation of her own principle against lending money to persons in distress.

In fact, the loan problem was not the only black eye that the Red Cross had to nurse. There came eventually the old complaint about improper accounting of funds—not charges of dishonesty but of carelessness. And there was another furor raised by millers when plans were announced to sell the surplus of the flour they had contributed. The millers complained, with justification, that the dumping of their contributions on the market would break prices and ruin them as a result of their own generosity. Finally an agreement was worked out for sale of the flour for export only.

But on the whole, capitalizing on its new experiences, a wiser Red Cross emerged from the San Francisco disaster work. The *Overland Monthly* gave it a treasured tribute: "When the people of San Francisco regard the aftermath of the earthquake and fire in the growing perspective of time, the work of the Red Cross Society will be appreciated more and more. The half can never be told of their devotion to their duty and their high ideals."

It may be fairly said that the Red Cross contributed mightily to the relief work in San Francisco, and it can be added with equal honesty that the experience and reputation gained by the new Red Cross in that work saved it from a questionable fate. After San Francisco the Red Cross was in business for keeps.

III

It soon became apparent to the dedicated group in Red Cross organization, however—and they were dedicated, whatever their individual motives—that even a San Francisco catastrophe could not alone make the Red Cross a vital element in the public mind.

Miss Boardman and her Central Committee were cheered somewhat in 1906 when Red Cross membership (the total number of persons who contributed to it) rose to 9,262; but they fell back into glum depression when in 1907 the membership dropped to less than 6,000.

Red Cross officials agreed that the public must understand the Red Cross and support it. One published statement frankly conceded, "No plan is worth considering which does not attract public attention, which is not natively interesting to the people." And by people it meant multiple persons—everyone, everywhere.

It was all very well to know that J. P. Morgan would write a handsome check every time an appeal was made for assistance in some headline disaster. But without continuing organization, a cadre of trained paid personnel, active volunteers with some degree of training in every locality, and a reserve fund to finance immediate first steps in any emergency, each new call on the Red Cross would be simply a repetition of past headaches and mistakes.

The Red Cross was actually sitting on the horns of a dilemma of its own creation. Over a quarter century it had fought to become the recognized agency to handle on behalf of all the people the relief needs of the stricken. It had achieved that role in law, but no law or charter could make it so in fact without organization backed by mass support.

And that support furthermore must be primarily in the form of money, which in responsible hands could be apportioned in rehabilitation work where it would do the most good. Then, as in more recent years, the Red Cross found too often that contributions to sufferers represented the working off of surpluses that could not be sold in any event, and even when made with the best intention had no relationship to the realities of need.

For instance, in the San Francisco experience, the millers who protested so vigorously about selling excess flour had dumped into San Francisco enough of the white stuff to fulfill the city's normal needs for fourteen years. Furthermore, the harassed relief workers found themselves holding a twenty-five-year supply of condensed milk and enough clam juice to meet normal requirements for a future extending from twenty-five to forty years.

Now the Red Cross faced the dilemma of self-aggrandizement as a necessary means of doing the job it was expected to do. And it began to take its case to the public.

On the one hand it prepared documents almost legalistic in scope for the major societies whose support it must have. On the other, it hired a press agent.

A case in point illustrating the former was a memorial written in 1908 to the Trustees of the Russell Sage Foundation. This said in part:

> Such requirements [chapter responsibilities] place upon the Society [Red Cross] the duty of instructing its members and the public at large in the methods best fitted to mitigate suffering after great calamities, for only by such study and instruction can a proper system be continued and carried on. The preparation for relief measures, if successful, must be made beforehand. No community is liable to suffer twice in a generation from a great calamity, so that experience gathered by local relief committees is not available for future use unless a general relief society such as the Red Cross is enabled by means of an experienced representative to collect and study the data provided by each successful [handling of a] calamity and furthermore, to impart the results of such study to the local Red Cross branches with instructions as to successful relief methods.

The press agent, E. R. Johnstone, was short-lived. This high-pressure expert was appointed at a salary of $6,000 a year and expenses, underwritten by some of Miss Boardman's moneyed friends, early in 1908. His work was to be part of a program to build up the Red Cross to a membership of 1,000,000 contributors and volunteer workers.

A jump from less than 6,000 members to 1,000,000 sounds overly ambitious. But there was a galling sting behind this goal. It was the fact that the United States, then at the peak of its "biggest-and-bestest" boasting was anything but that, as far as the Red Cross in comparison with sister societies abroad was concerned. Many other countries had societies with memberships which would make even a million-member United States National Red Cross seem puny. In 1908 Japan had an enrolled Red Cross membership of nearly 2,000,000. In most European countries the Red Cross had become so well established and so important that it was operating large undertakings including hospitals, shelters, hospices and ambulance brigades.

However, neither the high-sounding papers nor the press agent provided the answer. The year 1908 closed with an American Red Cross enrollment of less than 12,000 names, and the promoter had long since been fired.

The Red Cross had moved, however, into an appreciation of the need for something broader than the exclusive group courted and led by Miss Boardman, and it must be stated to her credit that she led the move for change.

In 1908 the first professional welfare worker of national reputation joined the Red Cross as paid director of activities. The new man, and the shaper of the Red Cross in its professional activities for a quarter century to come, was Ernest Bicknell, who had served and perhaps saved the Red Cross at San Francisco.

Now, with Miss Boardman's loyal legion and Bicknell's professional talents as organizer and money-raiser, the Red Cross had its feet planted solidly on the ground. It would move slowly, but always ahead.

+ + + + +

10

Progress
and Programs

THERE CERTAINLY WAS no financial inducement for Ernest Bicknell to cast his lot with the Red Cross in 1908. His own words show the grim humor with which he surveyed the job he was embracing:

> For an organization of such meager resources, the ponderous machinery provided for in the new charter and the formidable objects set forth impressively in that charter, may have seemed to some critics rather incongruous. With Mr. Taft at the head and Mr. de Forest as vice-president; with a Central Committee of eighteen members of whom six were appointed by the President of the United States to represent the Government; with a Board of Incorporators of sixty-five eminent citizens representing the country at large; with an annual audit by the War Department and a report to the Congress—gaze on all this front and then look into Room 341, State, War and Navy Building, and see Miss Boardman and three paid employees, a handful of decrepit furniture and a total annual income of $20,000.

So there was the challenge, only two years after the San Francisco disaster was presumed to have settled once and for all the stature and prestige of the Red Cross—in fact, its unique status as the sole recognized legal agency of the public to organize and supervise relief and rehabilitation of victims of national disasters.

Now Miss Boardman and Bicknell, with the support of the "ponderous machinery" of committees set about establishing a system of financial accounting that would be above reproach before seeking out substantial contributions. This plan provided for the separation of endowment funds, special relief funds, and contingent and general funds.

The endowment fund was to be, and is, an untouchable capital fund from which only the interest may be used, like a family trust. Controlled by a special board of trustees, the income from the endowment fund was to be used to cover overhead expenses. Special relief funds were to consist of the contributions received in response to appeals for great disasters, with all receipts and expenditures separately accounted for, on the basis of each particular job. The general and contingent fund was to comprise, in addition to interest on the endowment, annual membership dues, incidental receipts and a tax of 5 per cent on gross receipts from relief contributions, to cover the extra and special overhead costs involved in operating special relief assignments.

The only problem in this scheme was that ingenuity still was required to raise money so carefully earmarked for these funds. Membership dues, in fact, only climbed to $19,377 by 1915.

But in 1908 the Red Cross first hit the jackpot by introducing a project long since forgotten as an original Red Cross program, but still a fantastically successful money-raiser for the cause it was designed to assist. This was the project to sell Christmas seals to finance anti-tuberculosis work. The idea was a discovery rather than an invention, and credit was freely given for that fact.

Miss Emily Bissell was at that time secretary of the Delaware Red Cross Chapter. She read in a random article about the sale of tuberculosis stamps in Denmark and passed the idea along to National Headquarters. It evolved into a plan for Red Cross volunteers to sell such seals in sheets of 100 at a dollar a sheet (inflation has never changed the original price). The Red Cross was to bear all expenses in return for a percentage of the take—first set at one-third and later reduced to 10 per cent.

Gross receipts from the stamps hit $165,899 in 1908 on the first try. By 1916 sales topped $1,000,000.

In 1918 the Red Cross decided to turn the whole project, and all financial rights in it, over to the National Tuberculosis Association within the next year. But in the decade that the Red Cross developed, promoted and sold the seals, it was officially estimated that sales aggregated $5,652,500, from which the Red Cross took a total of $496,800 and made a profit of $285,000.

This project alone would have justified Mr. Bicknell's work with the Red Cross, but it was only one of many ingenious developments. In the meantime, moving a little more slowly but relentlessly, Miss Boardman was hammering away at the endowment project. It got under way in 1910, with a public announcement by President Taft.

The endowment goal was $2,000,000. Typical of the thinking led by Miss Boardman—that the Red Cross appeal should be made primarily to people of wealth—was the fact that one-fourth of the quota was assigned to New York, where the biggest money was to be found. Henry P. Davidson accepted the chairmanship of the endowment campaign in New York and J. P. Morgan led off the subscription list with a gift of $100,000 conditional on others making up the remainder of the half million. By December, President Taft was able to announce the successful conclusion of the New York campaign.

But the half million dollars raised in this manner in New York was in a way a handicap that might never have been overcome by the Red Cross but for the later occurrence of wars that gave the public a feeling of self-participation in the organization's work.

Hardly anyone of moderate means contributed to the endowment fund; in fact, there was no public appeal made at all. Only sixteen persons, the records show, gave less than $2,000 and seven persons gave an aggregate of $300,000.

The failure of the campaign to give the general public a feeling of participation in the work of the Red Cross was amply demonstrated when the effort to raise the endownment fund was carried to other parts of the country. Special campaigns were staged in sixty-two other cities. In only eight were the assigned quotas, based on population and community wealth, successful. The only individual outside of New York who contributed $10,000 or more was William J. Boardman, father of Miss Boardman. Two years after the endowment-fund effort had been started only half of the goal of $2,000,000 had been reached.

This meant that not only was the general public little interested in the Red Cross as a continuing national movement, but the very planning which had started the endowment campaign in New York had apparently alienated the support of the thousands of wealthy and leading figures in other cities.

There was one happy note of contrast to this apparent apathy toward making the Red Cross a secure and self-supporting endowed institution. When disasters occurred, whatever the type or cause, there was an immediate and generous outpouring of contributions. Nothing anywhere comparable to the San Francisco disaster was to occur in the next decade, but in the years prior to 1917 the public which had contributed through the Red Cross almost $3,000,000 to the San Francisco victims also gave another $8,000,000 in response to appeals on behalf of the victims of other major calamities.

II

While bending administrative energies toward money-raising, the Red Cross was branching out in another undramatic but methodical path to identify itself with the sources whose support it must have—the communities of America. This was in line with Bicknell's determination to do things that would attract the sympathy, the support and the self-identification of persons whose desire for public service was large out of all proportion to their bank balances.

At first an effort was made to align the Red Cross with other established agencies in the welfare and social-service fields. But this plan did not work very well. There was plenty of cooperation but some complained that there was no Red Cross identification.

Yet much that made the Red Cross great in the field, and that set a pattern for chapter development in later years, came from the cooperative work with other agencies whose personnel were enrolled as "institutional members." For instance, James F. Jackson, head of the Cleveland (Ohio) Associated Charities, and a Red Cross disaster volunteer.

A skilled and methodical man, Jackson put together a personal disaster kit—rough clothes, disaster-relief needs, stationery, registration cards and a Red Cross flag—and he asked the newspapers to

notify him if anything in the way of a disaster in the surrounding
territory should occur.

With his usual warm humor, Bicknell wrote down an episode in
tribute to this pioneer Red Cross disaster-relief worker:

> To his immense satisfaction, the looked-for disaster happened.
> A cloudburst in the panhandle of West Virginia drowned eight
> persons and destroyed a large amount of property. For Jackson,
> everything worked exactly as planned. He was called by tele-
> phone from his bed. He dashed off with all equipment, caught a
> train, reached the scene of disaster almost before the prostrated
> community had fully comprehended the extent of its calamity
> and calmly opened headquarters with the Red Cross flag flying
> over the door. He organized the relief and carried it through with
> the help of a local committee. I visited the scene later and found
> the community unanimous in warm gratitude to that "big Red
> Cross man" who had come so promptly, almost mysteriously to
> their aid.

But such sporadic activities were not enough, whether by cooperating volunteers or by members of Red Cross chapters. Each effort
in this direction proved that if the Red Cross was to grow it must
grow by the route of showing how badly it was needed, every day in
the year. And to be ready for disasters and war it must have within
itself the nucleus of trained personnel and skills so urgently required
to direct and spearhead emergency operations.

What was more natural than to turn to the nursing field, in which
the Red Cross already was chartered to recruit in time of war and
emergency?

In 1909 Miss Boardman broached a suggestion to ally the Red
Cross with the Federation of Nurses in recruiting nurses under the
general direction of the War Relief Board. This opened the field
whereby in succeeding years professional nurses were to become not
only the symbol of the Red Cross most generally pictured on posters
and in campaigns, but the first general group of professionals who
served on call in the Red Cross as unpaid volunteers.

Here again, circumstances brought into the Red Cross a woman
with talents making her one in a million—a figure as commanding in
her own right as Clara Barton or Mabel Boardman, although one

without the personal ambition or organizing drive of the other two, except in her own special field.

This woman, number three in the long history of Red Cross leaders, who entered the Red Cross rolls in 1909, was Jane Delano. She was to leave those rolls only in 1919, when she died on duty in France, but not from wounds, soon after the close of World War I.

Born in 1862, Jane Delano was one of the pioneers of the modern type of nurse, and in addition a handsome woman, almost beautiful, with a warm personality that glows out from the portraits painted during her lifetime. When she joined the Red Cross as chairman of the National Committee on Red Cross Nursing Service, Miss Delano was the recently appointed superintendent of the Army Nurse Corps, which had come into being in 1901. She already had been director of the nursing school at Bellevue Hospital, New York, outstanding among its kind. But more important from an organizational sense was experience with the Red Cross reaching far back into its pioneer days under Clara Barton.

In 1886, when Jane Delano was only twenty-four years old and a fledgling nurse, she had been one of a handful of nurses to volunteer for special work with victims of the yellow fever outbreak in Florida, and her interest in the nursing phases of Red Cross activities had been continuous for virtually all of her adult life.

It was the luck of the Red Cross to obtain such a figure to guide development of its first professional volunteer corps because, disguise such feelings as we may, there always has been and always will be a hesitancy on the part of skilled professional personnel to place themselves as volunteers at the sole disposal of amateurs.

As it turned out, the success of the program hinged on two prime factors: First was the professional direction. Second was the requirement that only nurses with the highest professional standing would be accepted. Thus from the start the Red Cross nurse became a member of an elite corps.

But Miss Delano recognized that the Red Cross could do far more with its nurses than simply hold their skills in abeyance for possible wartime call. Had there not been a peacetime program of solid and rewarding service opportunities the Red Cross would not have been able to enroll 8,000 nurses who were ready when World War I broke over the United States.

How were the nurses used? In the first instance, the professionals assisted in establishing a basic Red Cross function—training for women in home hygiene, family health care and as nurses' aides. In disasters the nurses went as volunteers on field work, and by 1915 Red Cross nurses were serving as volunteers with hospital units sent to France, Belgium, Germany and Serbia, among other European countries.

Coincident with the start of the Red Cross nurse program was established the Red Cross First Aid Department, a former pet of Clara Barton's, but dropped by the new regime as impractical and beyond the financial resources of the Red Cross. Impetus for it actually came from the field, where the state and local chapters, after surviving the bruises of the reorganization quarrels, began to show signs of ambitious activity.

New York was one chapter that simply had refused to abandon first-aid work and training and had built up "trained relief columns" that were winning a national reputation. This single chapter "covered" President Taft's inauguration in Washington in 1909 with a corps of trained workers manning twenty-four stations along the route of the procession.

This ground swell from outside finally prodded the national organization in Washington to approach President Taft in 1909 with a request to designate an Army medical officer as national director of the First Aid Department. Major Charles Lynch, whom he named, has lost out in the listing among notable pioneers in the Red Cross, but in many ways his pioneering was comparable to that of Jane Delano.

Already experienced as a volunteer Red Cross lecturer on first aid, he accepted the assignment and plunged into a whole new field of industrial training in first aid. The anachronism of red tape required, it seems, that the Red Cross give first-aid training only as part of its war-preparedness program, so Major Lynch worked under the supervision of the War Relief Board. But he and his staff soon were deep in the midst of devising and promoting training programs for a wide range of industrial groups including miners, lumbermen and telephone and telegraph employees.

The Pullman Company provided a special touring training car. A program was developed to promote railway safety. The cooperation of the Y.M.C.A., closely affiliated with railroad workmen, was obtained, and countless manuals and training guides were published. The first-aid handbook was thus taken to the host of immigrant workmen in their own languages, particularly Polish, Italian and Slavic.

While membership remained low, and money for administrative operations was still hard to obtain, the Red Cross—or shall we say Miss Boardman and Bicknell—kept selling the Red Cross through service.

In 1912, whether voluntarily or by prompting one cannot say, President Taft requested development of still another program that has since been tightly locked into Red Cross primary activities—water safety. The populace of the United States was taking to the water in great numbers for the first time—swimming in it, boating on it, and fishing. And individuals were drowning themselves with appalling frequency. As a result, when President Taft made his request the public was ready for the program.

Thus it came about that the Red Cross, while continuing to function with increasing efficiency in great disasters, found itself an organization that was reaching the people, its work seen and felt by millions; fully accepted as a cooperating society by industry, by organized labor and by such other popular organizations as the Ys, the Boy Scouts and Girl Scouts.

A few statistics tell a graphic story of some of the accomplishments in this new phase of work, generally described as preventive work, reached in the year 1916, just before a great war cast its challenge to the organization. In that year alone:

Certificates for completion of first-aid training were issued to 10,000 men and women.

Sales of first-aid textbooks and training kits approximated $50,000.

One thousand members were enrolled in 151 life-saving and water safety corps.

Special cars traveled 21,000 miles carrying staffs that gave safety lectures and demonstrations to 66,000 railroad employees.

This was a far cry from the original design of the Red Cross at Geneva, to create a "neutral" corps to assist the wounded in time of war. It marked at the same time a long step toward development of the dream of Clara Barton, which she fought through Geneva in 1884 as the American Amendment.

III

The disaster work of the Red Cross in these years itself became a testimonial to the value of the intrusion by the organization into more prosaic training fields. Experienced hands, in the chapters as well as with Bicknell in Washington, were learning how to use their new machinery, and to look with imagination on the true meaning of relief and rehabilitation. And Miss Boardman was expounding a running flow of common sense.

The Red Cross saw that its mission was to help victims over the first hard steps toward rehabilitation. It never could become an agency using contributed funds as insurance policies to replace all losses. It could supply the machinery to train and organize relief work, but it always must work with other like-minded organizations, never try to dominate or displace them. There always have been and always will be violations of such hard-learned rules, but the pattern was set.

In San Francisco some of these lessons had been proved, but at the price to the Red Cross of assuming a secondary role. By 1913, when the Ohio River again went on a historic flood rampage, the Red Cross found it had won its spurs.

In March of that year, the Ohio gave a repeat performance of the 1884 flood which had drawn Clara Barton to the scene. But in twenty-nine years there had been a multiplication of population and of values of property to be lost. On the night of March 25, at the end of five days of torrential rainfall, the ordinarily placid river became so flooded by its tributaries that its waters wiped out scores of communities, buried all its banks under water and obliterated $200,000,000 worth of property. It left an estimated 300,000 persons dependent on emergency relief supplies, 3,000 families homeless and 70,000 other families without shelter until their dwellings could be restored.

Governor Cox simply handed the problem to the Red Cross, first by establishing the Ohio Flood Relief Commission—composed almost exclusively of members of the State Board of the Red Cross—and then by designating the National Red Cross as administrator of the relief program.

Such was the change in social and economic conditions that the same Red Cross which had expended $175,000 in relief following the Ohio River flood in 1884 now faced a $3,000,000 job.

The money tells such a small fraction of the story. Through its National Committee on Nursing Service the Red Cross was able to mobilize 238 needed nurses and 66 experienced social workers—all working regularly with other organizations but available as Red Cross volunteers. Relief headquarters were established in forty-three communities. And the job was done. After the immediate relief work there was the long, hard problem of fair and humane assistance in rehabilitation.

The total of nurses mobilized in this flood of the Ohio turn from a statistic into an example of how the chapters, normally dozing in quiet reserve at that period until summoned to relief work, responded to calls upon them. The nurses had been enrolled by chapters, and were an important part of the rolls of volunteers who made their living otherwise, but dropped all routine to respond to Red Cross calls.

Seventy-seven of these went to duties assigned by the Cincinnati committee within forty-eight hours after the flood struck. Within another two days the force of trained specialists was augmented by details from Chicago, St. Louis, Detroit, Cleveland and other cities, some far from the flooded areas.

This corps of volunteers from the chapters staffed emergency relief stations and dispensaries and augmented hard-pressed hospital staffs. And when the waters subsided, leaving a film of slime and decayed filth everywhere, the nurses methodically went through the mess, into refugee quarters and occupied residential quarters, instructing and showing what to do to avoid possible epidemics.

A contemporary report from Dayton at the time reads:

> A city street, river mud and debris piled high on either side; houses off their foundation or entirely washed away; a very different looking "Red Cross lady," serenely picking her way around wrecked furniture, sodden mattresses, ruins of porches and sheds; wearing rubber boots, skirt kilted high, wet nearly to the waist, sending sick people to the hospitals, inspecting plumbing, back yards and cellars; superintending all sorts of work from feeding the baby to the digging of trenches. . . .

In such cases the American Red Cross's national headquarters coordinated the work that was done, but the working force of the Red Cross came out of America's crossroads.

In the midst of the latter problem, Bicknell wrote a report that almost constitutes the permanent Red Cross testament as to what it can do and cannot do, something always to be remembered by both the friend and the critic of the Red Cross:

A month has passed since the flood occurred. Cities and towns are rapidly cleaning and repairing their streets, removing their debris and setting their public utilities in order. Emergency relief activities have been gigantic and have accomplished wonders. The excitement and rush have passed. The inspiration and enthusiasm in helpfulness aroused by the danger and suffering of many thousands of fellow men are subsiding.

And now comes the true test of our efficiency. Our work is only fairly begun. It must go forward without the inspiration of early days. Family by family we must calmly and sympathetically consider the right thing to be done for each. We are dealing with individual problems, complex, various, infinite. We cannot restore losses. Our relief fund is not an insurance fund. The amount of a family's losses is not an index to the relief which may be afforded it. The only guide for us is the extent of each family's need and its inability to re-establish itself. We must do what is necessary to help the hardest hit family to its feet and start it forward in self-support. Only that. Our fund will not permit more.

Now, in addition to the so-called natural disasters, the Red Cross was receiving calls for another form of assistance in the cases of industrial disasters, important here only because they set two precedents.

One notable case was the explosion in a mine in the little town of Cherry, Illinois, which caught 500 miners below ground, and resulted in the entombment of half of them. Here was the first instance of the Red Cross accepting responsibility for relief in such a disaster.

From many sources as well as Red Cross contributions came contributions of more than $400,000 to assist the survivors, mostly of foreign origin and many speaking no English. Instead of handing out proportionate capital sums of relief money, the Red Cross put into operation its first deferred-pension plan, with monthly payments to widows and orphans. The sequel was reported as follows: "This scheme worked out successfully, and because so many of the widows remarried after the mine was reopened and new workers moved to

Cherry, the monthly allotments of the remaining widows were later increased."

The test worked out so successfully, in fact, that it was the model for similar operations when in 1911 a fire in New York, the historic Triangle Waist Company holocaust that caused revision of fire laws, claimed 145 lives and caused serious injury to 70 others among the workers in the loft building.

In sum, the Red Cross, rather than struggling for recognition, became in a decade after 1905 the disaster-relief agency which, instead of having to offer its services, was expected to answer those calls by a public that had nowhere else to turn for similar assistance.

✛ ✛ ✛ ✛ ✛

11

War and Its Challenges

F ROM 1905 TO 1914 the American Red Cross kept its part of the bargain to assist sufferers of disasters in foreign countries to the extent of raising and distributing about $3,000,000. Of this sum, $1,000,000 went to one vast effort, relief of sufferers from an epochal earthquake that struck Messina, Italy. Another million was spent in China, and there were few parts of the world that did not receive something.

But all of this practice in international operations was dwarfed—in fact, the stature of the Red Cross itself in the prewar years appeared puny—by contrast with the opportunities and the expansion that started slowly in 1914 and exploded in 1917. The Red Cross would never again be as it had been in the quiet years.

The new era in Red Cross development was graphically symbolized on September 12, 1914, when a gleaming white ship, christened for its voyage *The Red Cross,* steamed out of the Narrows separating New York Harbor from the Atlantic Ocean and headed for Europe.

The ship aroused almost as much rhapsody in prose from the pen of Miss Boardman as earlier Red Cross exploits had called forth from Clara Barton. The former, usually more identified with the prosaic writing of businesslike statements, jotted down:

Cheered by the crowds on the passing boats and saluted by the flags of all nations from the many steamers lying at their docks, she went. As the white ship passed the great statue in the harbor, Liberty for the moment seemed to grasp in her uplifted hand the flag of the Red Cross flying from the foremast, and to hold it forth as a token of America's sympathy for suffering Europe.

The chartered ship was unique and, despite some adverse criticism, as a symbol, a successful venture at the moment. Aboard it as passengers, with their supplies as freight, were 170 surgeons and nurses recruited by the Red Cross, divided into units of three surgeons and twelve nurses each. One team or more was being dispatched to each country involved in the European war that had broken out in the previous summer.

Here was a new type of Red Cross venture, the cultivating of a new field of humane activity, almost spontaneously conceived and under way before there had been more than a hint of public reaction. Miss Boardman personally and alone is credited with the idea, acting as precipitously as Clara Barton once had been accused of acting in any earlier day by the Boardman group itself.

When news of the European war flashed to America, Mabel Boardman was vacationing at Murray Bay, Canada, the fashionable resort where one of her neighbors was former President Taft, who held the title of chairman of the organization's Central Committee. She hurried to Washington and personally directed the sending of cables to sister Red Cross Societies in England, France, Germany, Austria-Hungary, Russia, Belgium, Serbia and Holland, offering American assistance.

On August 3, 1914, appeals for a special relief drive were sent out from National Headquarters simultaneously with the proposal for the relief ship. Something of a record was set with dispatch of the ship one month and nine days later.

On the whole the project was popular, although there was some editorial criticism and serious question as to how badly it was needed at the time. But any doubts raised by the project were dispelled by the public itself. Before the ship had unloaded its teams and supplies in Europe, contributions covering its cost of $350,000 already were in hand, and before the end of 1914 more than $1,000,000 had been collected in response to this appeal alone.

Later additions to the complement of the *Red Cross*—it was popularly known as the "Mercy Ship"—brought to sixteen the total of American Red Cross teams assisting the nations then at war, trying in so far as possible to provide neutral relief.

In keeping with the chart curves of response to all such activities, contributions that so quickly reached a million dollars soon tapered off. Up to 1917 only one more million was added to the first, but in the meantime, the American Red Cross had written a new chapter in its history and learned much from the experience.

The Red Cross teams actually saw the European war from as many differing angles, according to their assignments, as the reports about the elephant written by a group of blind men from variously examining it with their hands.

In England two teams settled down to their work in a traditionally luxurious house in South Devon. The French government contributed to its volunteers a former casino. Germany and Austria supplied the typically efficient hospital units that were required. But in Russia the Red Cross workers first had to cool their heels through a long wait, until they were located in a renovated building of the Polytechnic Institute at Kiev.

Closest to tragedy, and involved in actual battle, eventually were the three teams assigned to Belgrade, in what then was Serbia and now is Yugoslavia. Working in unsanitary conditions of the worst sort, the teams had to fight a typhus epidemic, which they conquered, and eventually treat battle casualties direct from a front a stone's throw away when a battle was waged in Belgrade.

The story of this service, involving much self-sacrifice on the part of the 350 surgeons and nurses who eventually worked in it, could be dropped right here with a bow to its glory. Actually, however, it was a rather sorry experience until time healed some of its bruises and the film of propaganda could be cleared away from the facts.

In October, 1915, all the teams were withdrawn from Europe. In fact, before 1914 was ended, plans were being made to do this as fast as could be gracefully done. The slackening off in contributions made the project financially insupportable. Britain's blockade of Germany was not relaxed even for the shipment of supplies to the Central Powers, on the ground that there was no means of differentiating between Red Cross supplies for generally humane purposes and those that might be of military value to Britain's enemy. And there was a less defined but broadening question about the element of intrusion in the affairs of other countries involved in this gesture. It was technically and legally within Red Cross charter rights, but still a long way from either the Clara Barton Civil War precedent or the pattern of disaster relief.

In a moment of frankness a decade later, Ernest Bicknell wrote:

> I, for one, harbor a suspicion that these countries which accepted these units found that the accompanying responsibilities largely outweighed the benefits; while, on the other hand, I have reason to believe that the American surgeons and nurses in many instances felt that the conditions under which they worked were cramping and irritating.

With the "Mercy Ship" venture ended, the Red Cross switched to a policy of assistance to, and cooperation with, other organizations conducting relief operations for all war victims, and prior to April, 1917, extended aid to 130 of these. In this the Red Cross took a back seat.

It became clear that, lacking direct involvement by the United States in any war, there was no more than lukewarm support for any Red Cross overseas war-relief program. Earthquakes, famines, plagues —these were fields accepted by the public as proper Red Cross responsibilities, but apparently not indiscriminate relief of populaces whose governments had ordered them to shoot at each other. Right or wrong, the psychology existed:

But should the United States become involved?

No one could guess the result, to be so graphically demonstrated in 1917.

And future perspective indicates the jotting down here of a few simple facts about the Red Cross in 1917. It had at that time less than $200,000 in working funds, it consisted of 267 chapters and a total paid staff of 167 men and women specialists. But around these bones of organization existed the nucleus of the future greatness of the Red Cross—the professionally trained volunteers and the willing hands of untrained volunteers who, when needed, would respond by the million.

Herein lay the as yet unknown strength of the Red Cross, when the public was convinced that it was needed to do a job. And the new Red Cross that was to emerge would bring into being the third genera-

tion of leaders, the new America of business and professional men—
with heavy emphasis on men rather than women—and men, too, who
from the moment they took control would sweep out the influence and
in most cases the actual personalities of the old hierarchy.

Their rise marked the decline and fall of the dominance personi-
fied by Mabel Boardman, the leisurely gentleman-politicians represented by William Howard Taft, and the social position that had sat
securely on Mrs. Whitelaw Reid's throne.

Only twelve years separated 1905 from 1917, but there was a full
generation of change for the snug group that had taken over the Red
Cross from the pioneers and so recently built an imposing edifice in
Washington—financed, of course, by their own group—as the emblem
of their dominance.

II

Within twenty-four hours after severance of diplomatic relations with
Germany by the United States, on February 3, 1917, the third phase
of the American Red Cross began to take shape, as Eliot Wadsworth,
acting chairman of the Central Committee, under Mr. Taft's titular
chairmanship, telegraphed the 267 Red Cross chapters to be prepared
immediately for all eventualities.

This preparation began now in earnest, with enrollment of volunteers—8,000 loyal nurses already were on the rolls—preparations for
intensified work in the field of readying hospital supplies and shaping
basic resources into units for duty.

The chapters, be it remarked, had not all waited for this call. Far-
seeing men and women, whose names were not even known to the
tight little hierarchy that held the reins in Washington, had assumed
responsibilities in their communities far beyond routine. As one example, there existed, as organized units, the personnel and supplies for
twenty-six base hospitals to go wherever the Army needed them and
could supply quarters. Here was an echo of the experience gained by
the experimental "Mercy Ship" operations that paid dividends.

But even these preparations were paltry compared with the demands that some foresighted Red Cross leaders could see in the offing.
Money and personnel far beyond any prior effort would be needed,
and these must be obtained in competition with all the other forces of
mobilization.

Wadsworth took the picture directly to President Wilson, with a plan for action that marked him as the Red Cross leader of the hour. He saw the need for big leadership, big plans and big money. And President Wilson agreed. Furthermore, Wadsworth was a man big enough to subordinate his own personality in a program to bring these together.

On April 21 the first meeting was held by the new leadership, the type of men that Wadsworth and President Wilson needed for the Red Cross, and they heard the keynote talk of the meeting delivered by a man as big as themselves, Secretary of War Newton D. Baker.

"There is simply no measure of our opportunity," Baker told the audience he faced. "It is limitless and everything we can do will fall short of what could be done if our means were larger."

Such words, and their source, made sense to the group, which included Henry P. Davison, now a fifty-year-old partner in the house of J. P. Morgan and Co., Cleveland H. Dodge, John D. Ryan, George W. Hill, and Jesse H. Jones.

The conversation at that meeting dealt with sums of money and a Red Cross organization potential that would have been laughed to death had the conferees been simply a collection of professional do-gooders. But these men were serious, and they were practical. Furthermore, they would be the principal contributors. The first item on the agenda was a fund-raising campaign, with talk of figures as high as $25,000,000 to $50,000,000. Wadsworth pushed the goal for the first drive up to $100,000,000. (This was oversubscribed early in June!)

But it all had to be tidy and businesslike. Big activity would demand big management, and meticulous planning. In one letter Cleveland Dodge put down on paper what this meant, when he wrote to Colonel E. M. House, the right-hand man of President Wilson:

> The great trouble is that the business men of the country today have not much confidence in the Red Cross due largely to the fact that until comparatively recently the organization of the Red Cross was not effective. The organization in the last year has been thoroughly reorganized, and is first rate as far as it goes, but it is utterly inadequate to cope with any enlargement of work.

So in effect business took over, but with such regard for the delicacies of the job that the chapters—now heart and soul of the Red Cross in national mobilization—liked what they saw, and approved.

There was established a War Council, including the leading figures already named. Mr. Taft was doubtful about the legality of such a move under the Red Cross charter, and his views as chairman of the Central Committee were respected, because after all he had become almost the patriarch of the rechartered Red Cross. The problem was solved by making the War Council a temporary substitute for the Executive Committee, technically acting under and as a subcommittee of the Central Committee.

However, committees never have got things done on any venture. Ultimate authority must rest in an individual. The individual was at hand in the person of Henry P. Davison.

Mr. Davison, living in an age prior to the broad development of public relations and publicizing of individuals in business, was known only to a relatively small circle of persons. But the circle included those who now counted most. Quiet in speech but eloquent in expression, he had become a major figure in the house of J. P. Morgan and Company. He knew relatively little about the workings of the Red Cross, but he had a high vision of it. He pictured the Red Cross as an agency to assist nations and peoples, not individuals, and he offered all that he had to that service.

Davison became, on Cleveland Dodge's recommendation, chairman of the War Council, pledging to give his full time to the volunteer assignment for the duration of the war. He accepted the job in these words:

> The Red Cross has given me a new conception of America and the American spirit. It is with the zeal of a convert that I invite the American people to come in with me under President Wilson and make it the nationwide organization that is demanded by these times. . . . Our job in the American Red Cross is to bind up the wounds of a bleeding world. . . . Think Red Cross! Talk Red Cross! Be Red Cross!

Against what background could Davison so speak? For his language was eloquent yet carefully phrased. He spoke from the pinnacle of financial success as a banker, yet did not talk down to the public. His background was that of the new American—as plain as the crusading Clara Barton's but through his own efforts as elegant as Mabel Boardman's. He could speak to both their houses.

Born in Troy, Pennsylvania, in 1867, fired with the desire to be a banker, Davison became a runner for a Bridgeport, Connecticut, bank at the age of nineteen. Five years later he got a job with the new Astor Place National Bank in New York, and soon then moved to the Liberty National Bank. In 1899, at the age of thirty-two, he became president of the Liberty, and the youngest bank president in the United States. In 1909 he was invited into the Morgan circle and won international note among the elite of the banking business.

It was Davison who then had to guide the War Council through the shoals of policy determination, now that the United States had taken sides in a conflict covering most of the western world. Without a policy there could be no coherence. Serious questions—never before encountered—required serious determination.

How far could the Red Cross proceed as an *American* auxiliary to the war effort without compromising its position as an international neutral force to relieve suffering? Even the word "treason" crept into heated debate in the conference room of the still new and incompletely furnished headquarters so recently occupied in Washington.

The answer came in August, 1917, with adoption of a policy statement by the War Council which stood the test not only of World War I but of the subsequent wartime operations of the Red Cross. It is notable both for its realism and for the brevity and simplicity of its language:

> When war was declared between the United States and Germany, the neutrality of the American Red Cross ended automatically. The American Red Cross can cooperate only between the lines of the armies of the United States and its allies. But the Red Cross knows no such thing as the nationality of a wounded man. Any wounded enemy turned over to the care of the American Red Cross will receive as kindly treatment as any friend. The Red Cross will not only extend every aid and comfort to the army and its allies, but it will assist in every possible way the sick, wounded and afflicted among the civilian populations among our

allied countries. This is in conformity with the practice of the
Red Cross in every country.

And so it was.

III

Here the Red Cross story in World War I—the almost unbelievable
story of its development in response to the need—leaves temporarily
the Washington scene to find its proper places, in the communities of
the United States, with some indication of what individuals were doing. After all, the Red Cross is not so much an organization as it is
the individual infinitely multiplied—individuals forming both a core
of paid and trained technicians and the millions of volunteers whom
they guide, counsel and train.

Before that departure, however, there is one note of qualification:

This is the story of the Red Cross, and to this one subject it is
confined. But perspective requires the note and constant recollection
that the Red Cross was not alone by any means in service to the armed
forces in World War I or since. Under its charter the Red Cross held
unique responsibilities for serving the wounded but it was no monopoly, and did not seek to be one, in giving assistance and comfort
to the ablebodied serviceman.

There were eight other volunteer societies who enriched their traditions in World War I. They were the Y.M.C.A., the Y.W.C.A., the
Knights of Columbus, the Jewish Welfare Board, the Salvation Army,
the Society of Friends (Quakers), the American Library Association
and the War Camp Service.

After a preliminary hassle over fields of activity, the War Department set up a Commission on Camp Training Activities that eventually worked out parallel roles to be played by all these organizations
in providing recreational, educational and religious activities for servicemen. The feuds and criticisms of the time are long since past, and
have no place here.

So we shall return to the Red Cross story.

+　　　+　　　+　　　+　　　+

12

Chapters Come into Their Own

PRIOR TO 1917, it seems fair to state as a generality, the picture of Red Cross chapters was one of wisps and whims that developed without rhyme or reason. Clara Barton long before had made clear her feeling that on the whole the local chapters should be considered as fund-raising media when called upon, but otherwise should lie low and not presume to intrude in the affairs of the national organization.

Mabel Boardman had advocated a limited and definitive chapter program, with continuing activities and training work for volunteers. But except for sporadic acceptance of such things as the Christmas seals program, the chapters remained much as they had been before—fund-raising devices primarily and recruiting agencies for volunteers to a modest degree.

These attitudes, both from the National Headquarters standpoint and from the localities where the Red Cross often had its highest acceptance, present an untidy picture of development that utterly abolishes any attempt at presenting a continuity of chapter growth. There is not even a clear statement as to the origin of the term "chapter" for local branches.

In the early days there were societies and auxiliaries, according to how they chose to term themselves. These grew first in the wake of disaster operations—just as Clara Barton organized Dansville, Rochester and Syracuse in 1881.

New York, Philadelphia and Boston came into the picture early, but as independent units. There was no love lost between these large city groups and Washington. At one international convention in the nineteenth century, Philadelphia sent its own delegate, a man quickly sent packing by Clara Barton but not before he had confused several issues. The Washington Chapter, on the other hand, substantially controlled the national operations from 1904 until 1917.

At the time of the Spanish-American War there were state associations in New York, New Jersey, Connecticut, Pennsylvania, Indiana, Illinois, Missouri, Tennessee, Kentucky, Arkansas, Mississippi, Minnesota, Texas and California, but none was really a part of the Barton organization. In fact, New York insisted, as has been noted, on setting up its own committee for the Spanish-American War, and Minnesota sent its own delegation to the troops.

Despite all the talk in 1905 of encouraging state branches, there were no ground rules and no real procedures. Primary emphasis was on the enrollment by National Headquarters in each state of a primary committee of prominent and wealthy persons, seeded with leading political figures including the governor wherever possible.

Later Bicknell suggested development of state branches, and the formation of local chapters within the branches. But however one slices the records and background, it all remained a paper plan of a paper organization. The trouble was, there was so little to do between disaster appeals.

In 1910, Bicknell said he thought that "chapters are chiefly and must always be chiefly dormant." By 1912 he wrote—about coincident with the start of the water safety program—that "to be successful the Red Cross must be a part of the life and interest of the community."

And there at last he put his finger on a great discovery.

This was exactly what many of the outstanding auxiliaries and societies had long since begun to do, but more in their own name than in that of the headquarters group in Washington. The most common continuing activity by the Red Cross societies revolved around the "sewing circles" of the period, in which members did sewing for the needy in the name of the Red Cross.

The Brooklyn, New York, Society, which was far more active in the early years of the twentieth century than those in the other New

York City boroughs, founded a nurses' training school. Philadelphia was pioneering many types of social service through cooperative work with other established organizations.

All of these together were the nuclei of the Red Cross to which was addressed the first war appeal on February 2, 1917, when, by all the totaling of such units in the cats-and-dogs organization, Eliot Wadsworth could find 267 Red Cross "chapters."

A 1914 report shows the cleavage that existed right up to this time. In that year the Red Cross had three broad administrative areas in the United States. The Central Area covered practically all of the country from the Alleghenies to the Rocky Mountains. Yet in all that territory there were Red Cross chapters only in Chicago; Burlington, Iowa; Topeka, Kansas; Detroit and Grand Haven, Michigan; Milwaukee and Madison, Wisconsin; San Antonio, Dallas, and El Paso, Texas. And only three—Dallas, El Paso and Madison—were on sufficiently good speaking terms with Washington to hold charters from National Headquarters.

The trouble was—the Red Cross as a whole had little to offer and less to do.

II

Then came the explosion, signaled by the trumpet call to action in 1917. There was such a response that for months records could not keep up with the facts.

As the statistics piled up they seemed improbable, if not impossible, prompting one anonymous reporter to set down the conclusion that "their enthuiasm was matched only by their ignorance of what they were to do."

Bridgeport, Connecticut, which already had a staunch local organization, took in 18,000 new contributing members within two weeks; New Orleans and Atlanta reported 7,000 new members each before the end of February; Chicago burgeoned immediately into an organization with 30 chapter branches and 635 auxiliaries dedicated to specific tasks. The examples could be continued indefinitely.

By August of 1917, the number of local chapters had grown to 2,279, and in November to 3,287. A peak was to be hit in 1918 with a chapter total never reached since, 3,864, when it could be reported that there was not a square mile of territory in the United States that was not enrolled in some Red Cross Chapter. And it was harmonious, cohesive and on the whole efficient—with cooperation between Washington and chapters eventually running smoothly through the agencies of the thirteen regional branches of National Headquarters.

Within a few months the Red Cross chapters knew what they were to do and were going about doing it. And the Red Cross was at last a part of American life, national and community alike.

Adult enrollment reached 20,390,173 in the year ending June 30, 1918, with more than 8,000,000 children brought into the Junior Red Cross when it was formed in 1917.

The members of the chapters not only gave money: they worked. More than 8,000,000 women were organized on a regular service basis to cut bandages, roll surgical dressings, knit sweaters and make hospital garments. The traditional American sewing circle became an efficient production line, working on materials purchased out of funds contributed to the Red Cross. In most cases the contributors and the workers were the same persons. Any prior dynasties of money or social cliques were submerged, for the moment at least.

Take Chicago as one recorded example of what this organization meant: In this one city Red Cross contributions in the eighteen war months reached a total of $13,000,000. For many months the volunteer workers sent to the soldiers and sailors under arms supplies valued at $8,000 a day.

III

Through the chapters there now fanned out the personnel that operated, unsurely at first and then with more vigor and understanding of their jobs, the many new services that characterized the work of the Red Cross on the home front in 1917 and 1918.

In perspective it is a little easier forty years later, but not always simple, to separate the "glory" descriptions from the actual practical applications. The individuals always seem to become obscured by the atmosphere in such mass upheavals, and the Red Cross most assuredly shared the same confusions, mistakes and wonderful individual experiences that characterized the mass mobilization suddenly thrust upon the United States by a totally unprepared leadership in 1917.

It took almost a year, until the beginning of 1918, for the Red Cross chapters to begin to function smoothly as an auxiliary of the military—as a "shock absorber" between the men in uniform and the civilian population—but it also is true that it took the military that long to settle down to the task of training and equipping an army of 3,000,000 men.

In that period, the Red Cross developed somewhere in the middle ground between the sentimental posters screaming the legend of "the Greatest Mother in the World" and as a working organization. It became an organization of many thousands of hard-working anonymous male and female volunteers whose uniforms gave them the privilege of doing some glamorous work but more often vexing and sweaty jobs reimbursed only with a great sense of satisfaction.

On one side the picture is one of statistics. On the other it is a montage of human beings hard at work.

The accounting procedures of the Red Cross, so long under fire, actually swung to almost an absurd extreme. It is meticulously recorded that in World War I, the chapters turned out 23,000,000 articles for soldiers and sailors, 14,000,000 items of hospital supplies, 6,000,000 refugee garments and 300,000,000 surgical dressings. Some 15,000,000 pounds of wool went into articles knitted by Red Cross volunteers and there are due records of millions of meals served, cups of coffee handed out, *et cetera ad infinitum.*

One final hard statistic shows that the Red Cross chapters purchased $61,000,000 worth of raw materials in World War I, and turned it into finished products with an estimated value of $94,000,000. That was big business, a classic memento to volunteer hands working by the million and incidentally relieving commercial production facilities that could be turned to other war needs.

No such records can give an impression, however, of the individuals and their work.

The Red Cross production picture in World War I finally became one of mass efficiency unparalleled since, because in meeting the needs of World War II such efforts had been outmoded by industrial development. In the helter-skelter of 1917–18 the Red Cross work by the women so often teased for being a gigantic sewing circle was priceless. That war caught the United States unprepared militarily or industrially even to feed and clothe a mass army. When women knit sweaters they knitted necessities—not luxuries to displace some item of standard issue but a garment that otherwise in the main the wearer would not have got at all.

When surgical dressings and hospital supplies were wastefully trimmed and rolled by hand, they supplied a need for which machines to make these in such quantities simply did not exist.

By the early part of 1918 such proficiency and efficiency in delivering these items had been demonstrated by the millions of unpaid women working in the Red Cross chapters that the military authorities considered the Red Cross a major source of supply. Requisitions were sent to National Headquarters, just as orders went to munitions-makers; quotas of work according to chapter organization were allocated, and deliveries were made, as in the case of military commercial contracts. And on the whole the system worked well.

Of course, the usual bad reactions occurred. Here and there someone sold a sweater, and occasionally an article with the Red Cross label found its way through the black market into commercial channels. But this was not the Red Cross; this was the inescapably normal fringe thievery that always has, and always will, characterize the black markets of wartime.

And there were military regulations, too, that gave rise to other rumors of Red Cross sales, just as these cropped up again in World War II. Under certain conditions the Army required that the Red Cross make nominal charges for meals served in canteens to military personnel, or for coffee, in the United States and abroad. It is the nature of the human mind to have remembered down through the years the fact that charges were made, but to disregard, either out of ignorance or malice, the reason for the charges.

Coincidentally, while millions of women became a volunteer production force for the troops, their co-workers (or often the same women multiplying their shifts of service) were making the Red Cross, now characterized by a new authorized uniform, the symbol of a tireless female auxiliary to the fighting forces.

IV

To the soldier in World War I—or in later wars for that matter—there was no differentiation between the chapters and the National

Red Cross, or even any understanding of the almost military organization and discipline to which Red Cross staff workers and volunteers gladly submitted.

The soldier saw a Red Cross worker serving coffee and doughnuts in a canteen during the interminable waits imposed upon troop trains, or a Red Cross worker in a hospital penning a letter for a bedridden man, or another passing out cigarettes at a port of embarkation and doing her best to leave him with a smiling impression of good wishes. Too often he contrasted these individually small services with the overglorification of the Red Cross in the posters and advertisements of fund drives presenting (not always through the fault of the Red Cross) such workers as super angels.

But to the Red Cross, national and chapter alike, the war brought a challenge of organization and service development that turned it in effect into a civilian army. This was an army administered, organized and trained by a skeleton paid staff and filled in its ranks by the volunteers.

The paid staff grew in the national organization to approximately 10,000 members and the chapters individually employed about one-fourth that number. But among the national paid workers were the field directors, camp service directors, clerical help and the omnipresent auditors. For each paid worker there were hundreds of volunteer men and women. Each gave at least a few hours a week. Some devoted substantially full time to the tasks that were kept in order and supplied with materials by the paid staff.

In this war on the home front grew up three special services—in addition to nurse recruitment and other subsidiary activities—that had no precedent in Red Cross work in the United States or in any other country. They became known as Canteen Service, Camp Service and Home Service.

The Canteen Service was perhaps the greatest accidental big business in which the Red Cross ever found itself involved. It became both a headache and an opportunity and, let it be noted in passing, simply one activity that would have required far more persons than the entire paid staff of the Red Cross had it not been for the work of the trained volunteers.

It all started along the standard line, of some little thoughtful touch for the soldier in camp or en route to war—coffee and doughnuts, a cigarette and a smile. Similar things were being done by many other organizations, notably the Salvation Army and the Y girls. Then suddenly, in the confusion of 1917, the work burgeoned.

The tables of organization might expand or contract, the statistics grow mountain high; but the real character of the Red Cross was being shaped by the individual in the specific place where there was a job to do. From the records . . .

Aboard a train in Arizona, a soldier on transfer orders was found suffering from smallpox. The Red Cross took him off, along with a Pullman porter exposed to the man's illness, hospitalized them and saw them back to health.

Another soldier became seriously ill while detached from his unit. Red Cross workers saw him hospitalized. He died, and a local chapter sent his body home, paid expenses, and arranged, when they found he was a man without family, to send a delegation to attend his funeral.

Location of fiances became a routine task, and marriages were arranged and held in those cases where the willingness antedated a "war romance," in some cases while a troop train with the man aboard stopped to refuel at a junction.

Someone noted that men were being held for hours on troop trains without any feeding preparations made by a hard-pressed military. Permission was given to the Red Cross to pass out to them sandwiches and coffee, chocolate bars or whatever was available. Finally, the "permission" to do this was accepted by the Red Cross and the military as a duty under the old charter of the Red Cross.

In a third step the Army realized that this chore was becoming an essential military service and it requested the Red Cross formally to prepare to go all the way.

In summary, at the end of the war the Red Cross was operating 700 fixed canteens, or restaurant-snack bars in the United States. It was providing light meals aboard countless trains, and giving emergency relief ranging up to medical care for troops in transit. In the formal background of organization were operated 85 canteen depots, provided out of Red Cross funds and managed by other Red Cross workers, from which the Army itself often requisitioned supplies.

In 430 of the canteens there also were reading rooms and miscellaneous extras such as first-aid stations, lavatories, showers and free telephone booths.

All of which took an enormous amount of work—cleaning and cooking and dishwashing and carrying out the garbage. Who did this? Some 55,000 women who found time away from their homes and children, or their own regular wartime jobs, to be Red Cross volunteers.

By the end of 1918 the Canteen Corps found that demobilization was not for it, for a long time to come. The same troop trains that had moved soldiers to war now were moving them home, and among those moved home were 500,000 sick or wounded, the casualties of war. In fact, the postwar end of this job became so heavy that the Red Cross and the military authorities had to revise their own procedures in order to enable the Red Cross workers to give the best they had to these relics of the fighting.

It was the military, too, who inadvertently contributed to the most damning black eye the Red Cross has ever suffered, through the Canteen Corps; and one which still plagues it despite explanations so simple that one would think any informed person would understand, if they wished.

The canteens that served meals aroused the bitter enmity and cupidity of commercial restaurants in their vicinities, even at a period when any business worth patronizing was strained to meet its opportunities. Always sensitive to criticism by voters, the Army ordered the Red Cross to make nominal charges for meals in these rare cases. The Red Cross did so, as it was forced to do overseas in off-post canteens again in World War II.

As a result, even thirty years later, thousands of persons who have not the least idea what the Red Cross really is or does will blithely damn it because "it charged the soldier for what we gave them." Of course, such a charge also makes a convenient excuse not to contribute to the work of any public philanthropy, regardless of its nature.

V

While the Canteen Service was unique in its birth and operation, the Red Cross chapters, working as the extended arms of the national organization, successfully turned the turmoil of World War I into a development plot for delivering all the other promises of wartime service set forth in its charter.

Work abroad, of course, was for the professionals, and will be treated briefly later. At home in 1917–18, the organization discovered and responded to a thousand implications never dreamed of by the pioneers.

What was to be done to carry out the Red Cross promise when training camps mounted to a total well over three hundred, with all the personal problems of young men suffering the loneliness of mass herd life in them; with family problems mounting into the thousands daily because of separated households; and with all the other problems from epidemics to breakdown of clothing issues? What would this mean to the one organization that had fought for, and won, the exclusive privilege of acting as mercy agent for the military in time of war?

Aside from the argument of petty detail and recrimination—and the acknowledged inefficiencies that inevitably accompany the filling of such demands by inexperienced persons—or even including them all in the picture—the record is magnificent.

A staff of 1,000 Red Cross workers was recruited to serve the camps. The new job of "Field Director" was created, a man assigned to a unit who stayed with it throughout the war. With him, in larger organizations, would be also a "Camp Director" serving the able-bodied and a "Hospital Director" serving the sick and injured and, later, the wounded. And backing this group were the volunteers from local chapters.

The Red Cross field director was more than ever required to be —as had been stated in a report on pioneer work by field workers in Puerto Rico in the Spanish-American War—"a good grocer, dry goodsman, apothecary, financier, doctor and linguist." None of which he could have been, without superb assistance.

The principal components of the field director's own private army were the Canteen Service and Home Service, aided by other newly formed organizations including Motor Service and Health Service.

The daily grist of the field director and the Home Service—the chapter organizations back "where the men came from"—were illness, marital difficulties, investigation of applications for compassionate leave and reports thereon, whether valid or otherwise. The jobs were not always well done, but they were done, and the record always must note that, had there not been a Red Cross to try, how long and how difficult would have been the task of developing a substitute?

The hard fact is that mass mobilization always lays upon authority the necessity for planning operations on a mass scale. Then details slip. A kit of medicines for a vital small hospital unit goes astray; the junior officer in charge cannot go to the nearest source of supply and lay out the cash to buy such necessities, but in World War I the Red Cross man could and did. When the influenza epidemic broke out in 1918, as one example, it caught short the hospital at Camp Dodge, Iowa. The Red Cross field director bought up stocks of needed medicines from local jobbers. And the Red Cross was equally essential in plugging other gaps, from toothpaste to toilet paper and clothing, when bureaucracy got snarled in red tape.

Henry Davison gave a graphic description of what all this meant in his book, *The American Red Cross in the Great War:*

There were no bankers' hours in Camp Service. The camp turned out at 6 when the Red Cross man was on his job mapping the day's work, examining and preparing to fill orders from the camp commandant or the chief surgeon, going through a mail that was full of Home Service problems, a hundred individual cases, official communications, and "axes to grind." There might be requests for help in securing discharges, for the Red Cross— with its facilities for investigation and its standing with the War Department—could present the story of a man who had a just claim for release as well as for the man who had no claim and had yet to learn the hopelessness of asking to be released.

There were always a lot of private messes that were coming up for settlement, domestic complications legitimate or otherwise. The draft brought to light more bigamy than the law could punish. It brought many a soldier face to face in many a camp with two wives and often with more. There were reunions in Red Cross headquarters of several families with only one head. It would take a Solomon and Haroun-al-Raschid rolled into one to adjust in these cases the questions of insurance and allotment.

The Red Cross Field Director was not a judge, but he was asked more than once to sentence a foolish soldier to matrimony.

And as World War I rolled into 1918 and overseas movements of American troops, the American Red Cross "rolled with the punch" into another new ground-breaking of experiences that have become traditions.

13

✛ ✛ ✛ ✛ ✛

Europe—1917–1918

IN WORLD WAR I the American Red Cross accepted and handled in a historically notable manner the task of demonstrating to a heretofore skeptical Europe the depth and breadth of humane feeling of which the United States was capable. No such proof, nor many of the accompanying activities, were required of a non-governmental organization in the conflict of the 1940s. In many respects government had taken over this task. But in 1917–18 the story was far different.

What was lacking in experience was made up in energy, as was so often the case in military operations themselves. And the qualification must be set down that in breaking new ground every day the Red Cross, like the military and other civilian organizations authorized to operate abroad, had its own share of misjudgment, bumbling and ineptitude. But the results were what counted.

Those results were such that the Red Cross emerged from the ordeal with apparently more honors, and fewer scars of criticism, than any other official or non-governmental organization engaged in vast enterprises.

Yet everything that was done in Europe in 1917–18 on behalf of the Red Cross was done by amateurs. No amount of domestic experience in the fourteen or fifteen years of the existence of a Red Cross organization supplied precedents for even the daily routine of operations. This was no venture in which a few people collected a pittance of contributions, loaded a ship and sent it off to an island war.

This was real, it was big and it was international. It began with "morale" operations in France, embraced nursing and care of the sick and wounded of the American Expeditionary Forces and their allies, and it tapered off into civilian postwar relief operations extending the length and breadth of Europe and leaking over into the Middle East and the steppes of Russian Siberia.

Before the job was done the Red Cross national organization had expended overseas about $120,000,000, or 70 per cent of all of its World War I budget. It had sent its own expeditionary forces into a score of foreign countries. Besides that—in some fields that had ceased to require its services by the time of World War II—the Red Cross was performing actual military support services that in effect meant the devising of means to do quickly what the military found difficult or impossible.

This was the era of actual staffing and manning of hospitals by Red Cross personnel, of moving just behind the lines in the late and bloody struggles of the conflict, of taking care of countless streams of shocked and hopeless native refugees (as in Italy after the disaster of Caporetto), and of introducing to haggard and battle-worn troops of Allied forces the niceties of canteens and comforts already rehearsed in the work in America's training camps.

General Pershing was to write later of the work of the Red Cross, "The value of the service is beyond computation."

And in Italy, Premier Orlando told the Italian Parliament: "Our soul is stirred again with appreciation and admiration for the magnificent dash with which the American Red Cross has brought us powerful aid in our recent misfortune."

To complete the record prior to giving some indication of the human story, General Merritte W. Ireland, Chief Surgeon of the AEF, reported that the Red Cross "rendered an essential service to our men the value of which can never be fully known."

What a long way the Red Cross had come from the pioneering work by Clara Barton in the Civil War, the little foray into Cuba, or the sporadic headlines of disaster relief and rehabilitation work!

II

America's formal entry into World War I found some token Red Cross work already under way, including a large number of volunteer ambulance units operating with the French Army. By May of 1917 six base hospital units were landed in Britain. On June 18, 1917, a Commission to France, headed by Major Grayson M. P. Murphy—working in a civilian and not a military capacity—reached Paris.

General Pershing met with this commission when he arrived with the nucleus of a staff to plan for the AEF. He tersely told Major Murphy, "If you really want to do something for me, for God's sake buck up the French. They have been fighting for three years and are getting ready for their fourth winter, and if they are not taken care of, nobody can tell what will happen to us."

It was all very well for the mass of Americans to think that this would be a quick and easy war, now that the eagle was screaming, mostly through the exaggerations of war slogans and bond drives. But "Black Jack" Pershing knew the inevitable delays that lay ahead and the real worries over the letdown that would come to our European Allies as these facts dawned on them—the total unpreparedness of America for the total war to which it now was pledged.

The War Council of the Red Cross, already freed of any financial worry by the initial outpouring of contributions resulting from the first appeals for funds, acted far more quickly than could government. First went a check for $1,500,000 to the French Red Cross, already practically bankrupt because the impoverishment of war had dried up its resources, and now stripping its own activities to essential and minimum hospital services for the wounded poilus.

Next and even more important from a morale standpoint was the actual dispatching of American Red Cross workers, in uniform, to perform services where they not only were needed but could be seen by the French. This the War Council under Davison fully appreciated, announcing in June: "Our Army cannot get to France in force immediately, but the Red Cross is there, and it is the purpose of the Red Cross to see to it that both the French Army and the French people understand that the heart of the American people is behind them, and the impulses of that heart are expressed now in real mercy and assistance." Two years later, Marshal Petain wrote the conclusion of that policy statement, when he said of the work of the Red Cross in France, "Nothing has contributed more to the morale of my soldiers."

How was this accomplished as the first of the multiple steps that were to write the first big chapter in the wartime history of the American Red Cross, a chapter unexampled anywhere else, at any time?

It began on September 17, 1917, when the American Red Cross—already represented in the form of supplies flooding into French Red Cross canteens—opened its own canteen. The canteen was a converted barracks at Châlons-sur-Marne, near a railroad station through which were shuttled large units of the French Army on their way to and from the nearby front.

Here were dormitories equipped to accommodate many hundreds of men, a barber shop, recreation and lounging rooms, and ample bathing facilities. Completing the equipment was a large restaurant where, under military orders, meals were served at a charge of 75 centimes each, or about 15 cents. The charge was actually below cost, and in the event a poilu had empty pockets he had only to apply to the stationmaster for vouchers that gave him the meals for nothing.

The prototype at Châlons-sur-Marne soon had its counterparts at many other entraining stations and in the railway stations of Paris itself. Smaller and less elaborate canteens soon appeared close behind the lines, opened wherever French military officials suggested they be located. As a final touch fifteen rolling canteens were operating right up to the lines before 1917 came to an end.

As for capacity, even the rolling canteens were no token things, as each served between 2,000 and 4,000 hot meals every twenty-four hours. And in the canteens were hundreds of American women residing in France. From the journal of one of them the Red Cross archives contain this quotation:

> Can you imagine feeding an average of 3,000 men a day, a shifting population, infantry, cavalry, artillery, marines, chasseurs, Alpins, engineers, Turcos, Egyptians, Senegalese and, to-day, about 500 Annamese! I have just come back from the canteen. Such an afternoon. A great train of seriously wounded, which is tiring as one has to climb in all the carriages. The men adore cocoa. We get into the sanitary trains and begin with the men who are well enough to sit up and handle tin cups. . . .

And while the "morale" work in the form of hot food, hot drinks and hot baths was progressing among the fighting forces of the exhausted French, the Red Cross was branching out into cooperative work for the civilian population—displaced families, *rapatriées* from

German-occupied territory who consisted of aged, infirm, sick and orphaned young.

Here the primary job was handled by the French Red Cross, but in its bleak financial status the supplies, and much of the handling of these often foreign types of equipment, had to become a direct responsibility of the Americans. In the end, the American Red Cross took on responsibility for all refugees in Paris, and subsequently for their rehabilitation—rebuilding houses and even supplying seed for their crops—when victory liberated their lands.

The requirements for supplies and the taxation of ingenuity seemed endless. As at Evian, a gateway for *rapatriées* where in 1917 alone 50,000 of the sick, infirm and helpless refugees were released by the Germans, with no place awaiting them in already overcrowded France below the battle lines, the answer had to be orphanages and homes, built on the spot, together with hospitals and convalescent establishments.

When the civilian relief job was ended, the accountants rendered their report—expenditures of $9,000,000 on relief for refugees, $3,800,000 for relief of destitute families of French soldiers, $3,000,000 in assistance to children and $2,400,000 on a program to combat tuberculosis. The total came to $18,200,000 or more than the Red Cross spent directly on all of its activities on behalf of American soldiers in the Expeditionary Forces.

But aside from its pragmatic effect on bolstering French morale, and the uncounted values chalked up for humanity, the French program developed experience and skill within the Red Cross. Here was practical training for the work to be done when the shifting of American troops to France swelled into full flood by the spring of 1918. Old hands were there, fully experienced in the services that American troops would need, a field staff already in being to cooperate with field directors of the Red Cross who landed with the military units to which they had been assigned.

While advance military units built supply depots, training camps and all the manifold requirements of troops overseas, the Red Cross took on the task of keeping up its facilities to meet the progress of military work.

In January Major Murphy resigned as Red Cross commissioner in France, to be succeeded first by James H. Perkins and then by Harvey

D. Gibson, but the changes in command were important only in the line of authority, not in the progress of development which plunged ahead.

III

Now the Red Cross was called upon to add to its comfort and morale work the primary destiny it had set for itself in the original charter—aid and comfort for the wounded in time of war. And as emphasis shifted with the involvement of American troops in battle this became its most important function.

In World War I the Red Cross actually provided personnel and hospital units, and ran them in support of the Army's own medical program. This requires a word of explanation, since most persons even within the Red Cross ranks remember only World War II and the Korean War, in both of which this original Red Cross service had been superseded by a fully developed military Medical Corps.

In 1917–18 the Army, itself a new and vast experiment as far as this country was concerned, theoretically had a modern Medical Corps, but one that never had served forces totaling as many as 150,-000 men, and had operated only in peacetime.

The Red Cross, as experimental in its work as the Army but with the advantage of a narrower objective and fewer demands upon it, started its program with the nurses' recruitment campaign. The 8,000 professional nurses on its roster were a very large core around which to build. Eventually it enrolled 24,000 nurses, of whom 18,000 were assigned to the Army, 1,000 to the Navy and 300 to the United States Public Health Service. The rest were left in civilian work.

Upon entering military service the nurses personally became a part of the military establishment, but in the unique setup of World War I their equipment and their housing at base hospitals were supplied and maintained by the Red Cross. The uniforms worn by the nurses—at this point was developed the famous blue outdoor uniform with the blue and scarlet cape—were Red Cross uniforms. Nurses also volunteered for service overseas with the Red Cross itself, as in work with refugees, and eventually there were in France alone 600 of these nurses, in addition to 250 nurses' aides, who endured the rigors of wartime service without the pay, protection and occasional extra comfort involved in commissioned military service.

Care of the wounded and ill in this war was a prototype of the modern method, with emergency stations at the front, field hospitals immediately behind the lines, evacuation hospitals at the nearest available rail or highway junctions, and base hospitals and convalescent homes in the rear.

In general, the Army handled the work in the forward areas and the Red Cross took over the rear hospitals. But when the front moved fast, these distinctions often disappeared.

In actual fact, the Red Cross continued to operate many hospitals right through this war, because of the inability of the Army to take them over as had been planned. On paper it looks confusing, but in general this voluntary cooperation was of the kind that flowers best when almost insuperable need is faced. Thus it came about that in France there were Army Base Hospitals and Red Cross Military Hospitals handling the same types of patients, the latter entirely staffed by the Red Cross but working under military control; as well as regular Red Cross Hospitals. The last group served other Allied wounded primarily but also received the overflow of Americans from the first two types of hospitals. In the Red Cross Hospitals all doctors, nurses and staff were supplied by the Red Cross.

When the Armistice came in November, 1918, the Red Cross had established 21 hospitals in France, 12 convalescent homes, 9 infirmaries and 10 dispensaries, as well as a Navy hospital, one for Czecho-Slovak soldiers and one for auxiliary Army personnel, or civilians on quasi-military duty. In the meantime the number of Red Cross convalescent hospitals for Americans in England had grown to 13.

While these figures are the total for Red Cross facilities as such, General Ireland noted at the close of the war that the Red Cross actually had supplied 39 of the 45 base hospitals used by the military in France and England—each one geared to support 1,000 beds and served by 50 doctors and 100 nurses, plus being stocked with all technical equipment including hospital garments for the patients.

Coincident to the hospital work, the Red Cross found itself in massive hotel, restaurant and theater operations as the number of troops overseas grew, for this was the essence of the Canteen Service. Lessons learned in operating the initial canteens for the French forces stood the administrators in good stead, and eventually the number of canteens operated exclusively for American soldiers reached a total of

130. It was estimated after the war that these had served a grand total of 6,000,000 meals, in addition to operation of other recreational services.

As a footnote to Red Cross overseas service in World War I, let it be remarked that the Red Cross, outside of hospital work, was not alone. Its responsibilities and privileges were shared with other groups, notably the Y.M.C.A. and to a lesser degree by the other organizations named earlier. The result was confusion, occasional competition and sometimes downright dissension. But on the whole the Red Cross came out on top because it provided the best for the most and, unlike some of the other organizations, held strictly aloof from religious or evangelical work.

IV

The hospital and canteen work of the Red Cross with the AEF was so massive that it all but obscures in retrospect a thousand other avenues of service by which war was made endurable for combatants or for civilians in extraordinary corners or situations in Europe.

Italy and Russia furnish two outstanding episodes: the first of heroic service under conditions of grave danger; and the other of the odd political complications that befell the Red Cross in Russia, where attempts simply to mind its own business led to an extraordinary situation.

One of Ernest Hemingway's most gripping novels is *Farewell to Arms*. He gathered the material for it the hard way and, in so far as great novels can do so, he contributed to immortalizing one page of the Red Cross saga.

In the winter of 1917–18 the Italian Army—in that war fighting on the Allied side—broke at Caporetto before an overwhelming attack by German and Austrian troops. Here was a massive repetition of the story of Solferino, but modified this time by the Red Cross acting as Dunant might have dreamed.

In Italy, representing the American Red Cross was a volunteer ambulance brigade, made up of 135 ambulances and 25 auxiliary motor vehicles, manned by 104 American volunteer drivers. This brigade of ambulances, working night and day, accomplished the unbelievable feat of transporting 66,000 wounded or sick Italian soldiers

from the crumbling lines to base hospitals in the first six months of
1918. Every driver was decorated for heroism by the Italian government. One of the drivers, a youth named Ernest Hemingway, was
severely wounded and specially decorated for outstanding heroism.

Late in the war, when American troops arrived, they were accompanied by the services already so highly developed in France. It
is recorded that one unit fighting in the Alps at an altitude of 11,000
feet was served hot coffee by a canteen transported by mules and dog
teams up to the front lines facing the Austrians.

In Russia, the complexities of the Communist revolution created a
new twist for the Red Cross in its role as a quasi-official arm of the
government in international dealings. For a brief time a Red Cross
commissioner was the only American of recognized official status
talking face to face in Petrograd with Lenin and Trotsky.

In August of 1917, the American Red Cross sent into Russia the
maximum available help at the time as part of the policy of getting
something into action with each of our Allies. Colonel Raymond
Robins, acting as a civilian Red Cross official and not in his military
status, headed the unit. In his charge were a complete ambulance unit
of 125 cars, about $200,000 worth of medical supplies, and requisi-
tioning authority under which the Red Cross sent 450,000 cans of
condensed milk for distribution among the children in Petrograd.

As a gesture the mission was fine; for practical purposes in assisting
the general war effort it meant very little. Russia was already on the
way out, beaten to death, torn by revolution and treason. A provi-
sional government headed by Kerensky was trying to hold the Western
Front, but was being defeated by communism behind the lines as well
as by the Germans at the front.

The Bolshevik Revolution was over by March, 1918, and Colonel
Robins moved down to Moscow where, lacking American representa-
tion either through recognized diplomatic or military missions from
the United States, he was assigned the task of helping to mend Russia's
energy by carrying promises of more military aid. It was Trotsky who
finally broke off these negotiations, as Robins reported, when he said:

"Colonel Robins, your embassy sends you here with a big bag
marked 'American Help.' You arrive every day, and bring the bag
into my room, and you set it down by your chair, and you keep reach-

ing into it as you talk, and it is a powerful bag. But nothing comes out."

One doubts if Trotsky wanted anything to "come out." Soon thereafter the Russians sued for peace with Germany. They ceased to be an "ally" and Robins' mission ceased to have a reason for being. Some work was done thereafter with Russian prisoners of war, but in October of 1918, before the armistice on the Western Front, American military personnel, and with them the Red Cross, were withdrawn from western Russia.

In the meantime the Red Cross found itself, acting under instructions from our government, with two other confusing missions in Russia. One was in Siberia and the other at Archangel. While they assisted civilians in desperate need, both eventually were caught up in the fighting that eventuated between Bolsheviks and White Russians, as well as with American troops landed to protect American supplies, and with Czecho-Slovak forces who found themselves fighting their erstwhile Russian masters to get out of the grasp of the Bolsheviks.

As the war in eastern Europe either degenerated under revolutionary movements or came to a halt with the general Armistice in November, 1918, the Red Cross turned to problems of civilian relief all the way from Siberia southward through middle Europe and into Turkey.

This confusion in the East was graphic, but principally by contrast with the orderly manner in which such operations in western Europe blended into a pattern of rehabilitation.

With the war ended, the work of the Red Cross in Europe became a story of slogging administration of relief as one important link among many in getting Europe back on its feet, a humane story with bookkeeping overtones that is both a twice-told tale and a story of development long since obscured by repetition in more recent memory.

In summary, the Red Cross poured $90,000,000 more into European relief between 1919 and 1922, about one-tenth of the estimated total of contributions by Americans to this cause of Continental rehabilitation. But the unique feature of the Red Cross work was its disproportionate contribution of persons and skills to the administration of this task.

Out of that experience, and the reputation which it gave to the Red Cross came one overwhelming fact:

The American Red Cross—however much it might change to meet demands upon it in the future, and whatever reorganizations it must make within itself—was firmly established as a living landmark in the American scene. It would never again be small.

+   +   +   +   +

14

Aftermath of Glory

WITHIN SIX MONTHS after the Armistice of 1918, two persons looking at the Red Cross from differing aspects might have wondered, on comparing notes, if they were seeing the same organization.

In Europe, with personnel expanded even beyond its wartime level, the Red Cross was perhaps the brightest example of the humane spirit of America, of the outpouring alike of sentiment and dollars freely and voluntarily supplied for the relief of fellow men in desperate straits. In the United States, another observer might have reported with equal candor a decaying spirit of support, shrinking totals of volunteers and revenue, and a cloudburst of self-criticism and outside hostility that must have made some timid individuals wish the Red Cross idea had never been effectuated.

The question was again, but now in infinitely multiplied scale, whether an organization primarily rooted in idealism and not yet nailed down to a foundation of practicality could survive in an atmosphere other than one of troubled times.

In the foreign picture, from 1919 through 1922, the Red Cross was a prodigal servant of charity whose beneficiaries were to be counted in the millions. In Poland alone, $17,000,000 was poured into rehabilitation of a population of 18,000,000 people whose country had been devastated first by the Germans and afterward by the Bolsheviks. In Siberia, in Bulgaria, wherever among the devastated lands one looked, there was the Red Cross, either dispensing its own materials as agent for American bounty, or assisting in managing other relief funds.

In fact, the American Red Cross went beyond its own capabilities and helped to organize the International League of Red Cross Societies, to which it contributed $2,000,000 dispensed by national societies facing loads that they could not handle out of their own resources.

Not that the Red Cross was alone among agencies giving and contributing to such great works. Other American organizations were there, too, but the Red Cross was so much bigger, and so much more widespread than, for instance, the Quakers, that it got the lion's share of the glory and the major share of the work.

Davison, who sometimes was more eloquent than factual, wrote early in 1919, that "war has taught the world the tremendous possibilities of applied humanity, and the spirit of the crusades is still abroad." But his optimistic estimate was already at variance with the feeling in the United States that as soon as hostilities had ended, the thing for America to do was to get out of Europe. Many persons also made clear their belief that organizations such as the Red Cross had better revise any feeling that support for their wartime work implied any guarantee of sustenance in peacetime.

Davison is credited primarily with the idea for forming the League of Red Cross Societies, which came into being in April of 1919. In subsequent years the League survived and justified itself as (1) a means of communication between the national societies, (2) an instrument for the promotion of common aims, and (3) a coordinating agency in international relief work. Almost thirty years after its founding the League was to provide the road for a magnificent demonstration of courageous relief work in Hungary. But in its beginnings it threatened to become, by its very activity, another instrument leading to the tearing down of the Red Cross's hard-won recognition.

It was what was happening at home that counted in the perpetuation of the American Red Cross. Much was happening there, ranging from retrenchment to reorganization, all complicated by a public apathy toward everything that smacked of the recent war or foreign commitments.

It is the nature of all emergency activities that the shock of realization that the emergency is ended confronts them with a twofold problem:

On one side always are ranged the enthusiasts who insist that the opportunities for service are greater than before the emergency. On the other side stand those who contend that it is time to forget emergency activity and get about the normal business of the day. Neither attitude is ever wholly correct, whether in politics or in organization work, but the finding of a middle road of need and means always requires a period of transition, of assessment and reassessment and usually a complete "changing of the guard."

History has revealed very few examples of fiery wartime leaders capable of reorganizing their elements of genius to serve the cause of reconstruction and peace, or of fiery idealistic leaders capable of cooling their ardor to suit the long struggle of retrenchment.

The types represented by Henry Davison and Eliot Wadsworth were the spark plugs of the continued European relief effort. Immediately after the Armistice they carried the War Council into a crusading atmosphere of support for the postwar relief program. As Wadsworth proclaimed, "The great Red Cross army of mercy which the war has called into being must never be demobilized."

What size was that "army"? It was logical and modest in the midst of war, but to the eyes of a jaded peacetime United States it was huge. From an organization that in 1914 had had less than 100 employees paid something under $150,000 a year it had swollen in 1919 to a paid force of 9,000 persons and a payroll of $12,000,000 a year. There was simply no former basis of comparison for wartime budgets, which mounted into scores of millions of dollars and left a surplus of which $100,000,000 could be poured into European rehabilitation work alone.

But in 1919, while grandly spending $95,000,000 the national organization of the Red Cross awakened to the fact that all of its contribution, including the enthusiastic hang-over from pledges made while the war still raged in 1918, totaled only $58,000,000. And projects for the future reduced to an uncomfortable level a surplus that at the close of 1919 stood at about $60,000,000.

The forces of extravagant optimism and aloofness had become locked in a historic struggle. And after months of debate, there was a "new" Red Cross look, designed to win support for a big peacetime Red Cross based on big works of a kind never before attempted on a mass scale. Coincident with restoration of the form of the old organization, the faces of leadership in the American Red Cross were changed.

On February 28, 1919, the War Council dissolved itself, restoring ultimate control over Red Cross policies to the Central Committee. Henry Davison and his coterie of prominent fellow members voluntarily laid down their authority in a gesture that seems in retrospect to have been both one of modest retreat from authority and one of calculated disassociation from the peacetime "internationalism" of the Wilson Administration, as this was rapidly coming under challenge.

William Howard Taft, then in temporary political eclipse and yet to reach his next height of political achievement as Chief Justice of the United States, had resigned at long last as chairman of the Central Committee. His successor, appointed by President Woodrow Wilson, was the dynamic Dr. Livingston Farrand, college instructor in psychology and anthropology, who was to go on to become president of Cornell University.

Important as a symbol out of all proportion to authority was the fact that Taft himself, upon resigning as chairman, was unable to obtain reappointment at that time of Miss Mabel Boardman to membership on the Central Committee.

For the fourth time the Red Cross was entering a new phase, combining a fight for survival, an inner contest over philosophy and program, and a self-searching of its very structure. The single element that kept alive the machine and the ideal, it appears in retrospect, was the undeviating determination on all sides above all else to keep the Red Cross in perspective as a servant of the people, not a bureaucracy existing for the purpose of feeding itself.

II

To solve its manifold problems of transition, the Red Cross turned now to professional direction, and in doing so aroused a new storm of criticism. When Dr. Farrand was chosen as chairman, the Central Committee paid him a salary. The old tradition of unpaid chairmen standing above paid staff fell by the wayside, to the accompaniment of considerable criticism from the "old order" who still lingered in the belief that a philanthropic organization should be headed by a volunteer. That debate has never been concluded.

Dr. Farrand, who took office with the enthusiastic support of the now veteran Ernest Bicknell, was somewhat of Bicknell's stamp—a younger version, although not a professional welfare director in the sense that Bicknell was. The new chairman had earned his living first as a member of the faculty of Columbia University, and after 1914 as president of the University of Colorado. On the side, he had developed an acute interest in health and welfare work.

In a gradual transition from academic work, Dr. Farrand had been at this point—at the age of fifty-two—for nine years executive secretary of the National Association for the Study and Prevention of Tuberculosis. This was the organization that grew out of the work supported by the Red Cross Christmas seals. In the war he had been sent to France by the Rockefeller Foundation to cooperate in the work of the International Health Board.

Such a choice of chairman for the Red Cross was in many ways ideal. But current opinion within the oligarchy that controlled the Red Cross was divided over Dr. Farrand, both as a man and as the leader of the reconstruction program. Even Dr. Bicknell, his friend, expressed the view that he lacked "the weight, the brute force" to lead the organization. The more conservative element feared that he was too ambitious and regarded the fact that he was paid a salary as a trend toward too much professional leadership in what they thought should be primarily a stand-by emergency organization.

The biggest problem was the fact that the Red Cross was forced to work out its future destiny within a framework of circumstances over which it had no control. This background has been eloquently described by Foster Rhea Dulles in one brief paragraph:

> Every month saw the American people becoming increasingly absorbed in their own individual concerns—eager to get back into normal business activity and to make a living. With our former allies quarreling about the spoils of war abroad, and industry and labor battling over their rights and privileges at home, appeals for further large-scale sacrifices in behalf of any humanitarian movement carried little weight. Disillusionment had set in, and a cynical materialism was taking the place of our wartime idealism.

The opportunity for the Red Cross was essentially, therefore, that of giving leadership to the minority who believed there always was a place for the application of practical idealism, such as had flowered so often in the response to natural disasters. And as a footnote here, it is a matter of interesting record that neither in World War I nor in World War II were there disasters of such magnitude as to be called "national."

Now the Red Cross faced within its own organization the vital fact of chapter apathy. One questionnaire sent out to the chapters as to suggestions for future programs was not even dignified by a reply from three-fourths of them. One chairman replied, "Give us a rest." Suddenly the question arose as to where were the 8,000,000 women who had labored so long and hard in production work, the thousands who had labored in canteen work, and the legions of other volunteers.

In desperate anger, Dr. Farrand exclaimed that the Red Cross must not be "a drowsy giant to be aroused only by fire, sword, storm and flood—acts of God, war and pestilence." The Red Cross needed a new program, one with public appeal that would hold the membership of contributors and give volunteers rewarding work.

The answer for the time being, in so far as it could be established, lay in a new type of public health program; and Dr. Farrand moved into the field of publicity and promotion to put this into effect. Newspapers and magazines were enlisted in support of the idea even before its details were devised.

Wide publicity was given to statistics concerning American mothers dying in childbirth, mortality of infants, the deaths from contagious disease such as the still-remembered influenza that had ravaged the country, the backward state of rural hygiene.

The Red Cross thereupon pronounced its new policy:

That subject to over-all control from National Headquarters, the individual chapters would be assisted in any autonomous work to develop local health projects—with fingers of reference pointed at prevention of tuberculosis, venereal disease, mental disease—and encouragement of all types of family and home health and care.

"The Red Cross," said the official announcement opening this new door for potential chapter ingenuity and activity, "through its millions of lay members comprising every element in every community, many of them themselves the victims of the foes that cut short human life and rob it of its sweetness, can serve a community as no other agency."

Yet with all the fanfare, there was considerably more rhetoric than action. Possibly the start was made too fast, and without consideration of the times. In fact, in 1919, the chapters were busier than ever before in peacetime, although the activity was one of liquidation of wartime responsibilities rather than of new jobs—the handling of multiple jobs with an always declining force of volunteers. Now the proposed activity was more in the nature of that demanding the services of professional social workers.

With demobilization starting in 1919, the Red Cross actually had to increase its Camp Service staff that year to meet the requests of the Army and Navy. Hospital Service and Home Service demands rose sharply after November, 1918. The hospitalized and disabled veterans became a major responsibility of the Red Cross, and many of the able-bodied were helped to readjust to civilian life.

Wherever these activities were abundant, Red Cross chapters had little time or personnel for new programs. In those with no particular postwar activity, lassitude was the problem. Yet little by little the new health program managed to obtain a foothold.

Scattered chapters began various activities concerned with public health nursing, classes in home hygiene and sick care, nutrition and the organization of community health centers. Wherever the spark of interest flared, National Headquarters sent assistance from a newly created Department of Health. The Nursing Service, with a record of unbroken loyalty by its volunteer members, took up probably the most active challenge in the field of rural and semi-rural nursing. Family welfare work was encouraged through formation of a new Civilian Home Service, representing enlargement of the former Home Service for military personnel and their families, and subsequent assistance to families of veterans.

New ground was broken by the National Red Cross when it sponsored courses in social work in universities and colleges, and then helped to fill these classes by means of scholarships for public health nurses and social workers.

Great plans and grand ideas—these set a new pattern of Red Cross activities that were designed to keep alive the interest of chapters and to keep in training a host of volunteers. But did the public care? Or the chapters, either? As 1919 passed away month by month, the Central Committee began to wonder.

A few figures—dull as they often are—come alive in graphic fashion to illustrate this feeling as between the Red Cross and the public, and the National Red Cross and its chapters.

The total Red Cross began 1919 with total resources of $127,000,-000, of which the national treasury held $41,000,000 in money and $53,000,000 in supplies, and the chapters had $33,000,000. But the cost of the foreign program was so great that in 1919 a new fund drive was held.

The response to that drive was crushing. The subscribing members, who had exceeded 20,000,000 in 1918, dropped to under 9,000,000. And subscriptions, in response to a modest appeal of only $25,000,-000 compared with the wartime gifts, yielded only $15,000,000 despite a campaign led by an appeal from President Wilson himself.

Furthermore, when the National Red Cross found itself scraping the bottom of the barrel in its world-wide program, the chapters—many of them now securely wealthy—simply declined to contribute any of their funds.

Retrenchment was not only the order of the day; on it might rest very well the survival of the National Red Cross as against the alternative of an old-fashioned stand-by organization on the Barton-Boardman pattern. The debate that followed was bitter because within the leadership of the Red Cross itself there were many who thought the old way preferable and proper.

And then, in the logical nature of events, the whole question was confounded by the inevitable aftermath of criticism and questioning in high places of the very work that the Red Cross had done in World War I.

III

What the public feels it owns, it properly feels it has the right to criticize. And no criticism is more violent than inflamed reaction—often started from hidden sources for hidden motives—to situations in which the facts are buried in generalities.

In the fund campaign of 1919 the first charges of waste and mismanagement in the handling of wartime programs were made. Of course, for what comfort it may have been to the Red Cross, it was not alone. Similar charges were leveled at every other major organization, including the Y.M.C.A., whose overseas hostesses formed unofficially their own organization bitterly termed "the damned Y girls."

That the Red Cross "has charged the soldiers for supplies" flared into a burning issue. The moral behavior of nurses and social workers overseas became a favorite morsel of alley gossip. In the self-righteous aura of a period that brought Prohibition into being and banned the sales of cigarettes in many states, the Red Cross suddenly found itself pilloried for "destroying American youth" by free distribution of cigarettes to soldiers, which criticism made the giving seem worse than the other charge that it had sold cigarettes. The Russian relief program brought out two violent charges: that the Red Cross was reactionary and helping only the old order, and that it was contributing directly to Communism by feeding Russians.

Most charges of this nature finally die out as their palpable absurdity in over-all activity becomes apparent, and particularly when the organization under attack admits frankly that some individual somewhere has made a mistake that fits even the absurdity of the most extreme charge. However, criticism of the Red Cross now became more serious.

In February, 1920, Senator John Sherman of Illinois, addressing Congress, attacked the Red Cross for mismanagement and extravagance claiming that it used 40 per cent of its funds for salaries and traveling expenses. A substantial minority of newspapers took up the charges.

In 1921 the Hearst newspaper organization, through a series of articles in the New York *American,* attacked the Red Cross as a "cold-blooded, highly professionalized charity trust." It charged that the Red Cross was "taking over one after another the functions of our Government and using its delegated power to swell private incomes." Coincident with this "exposé," a resolution to investigate the Red Cross was introduced in the House of Representatives.

Such public airing of questions could not help but rub the raw edges of wounds opened by the internal controversy over future activities and procedure. John Skelton Williams, treasurer of the Red Cross, became the advocate of criticism within the organization; and the controversy finally reached such a peak that the Central Committee formed a committee under the direction of W. Frank Persons, former director of civilian relief, to conduct a self-examination.

The report of this committee was to become a landmark in the development of the Red Cross, not revolutionary in itself but as a guide to the long and painstaking reorganization of the Red Cross during the 1920s.

The Persons report suggested that the Red Cross realign itself as a domestic service organization. It suggested severe contraction of "overhead," which pleased the critics of Red Cross "extravagance," but gave no ground against those critics who would contract the services of the Red Cross.

In its most important definition of Red Cross posture, the Persons report suggested that the organization turn away from its wartime structure in which chapters acted as branches of an all-dominating National Red Cross, and maintain its national headquarters as a guiding, counseling and coordinating agency for chapter operations. To make this more evident, it suggested abolition of the very title of "general manager" of the National Red Cross.

There would be three vice chairmen responsible respectively for domestic operations, foreign operations, and finances, who, with the chairman, would head up a National Staff Council. All departments and bureaus were to be replaced by "services" headed by individuals who as additional members of the Council would advise it on questions of policy and activities.

These changes were made and, more important from the standpoint of public criticism, the national payroll of Red Cross employees was finally reduced to less than 3,000 by June of 1922, when operational costs fell to one-sixth of similar costs during the war.

On paper, much had been accomplished; most important the stemming of outside criticism. Internally the Red Cross was sick, even with encouragement given to many chapters by its new array of community services. The dispute over what the Red Cross should be in peacetime still remained an all-pervading issue.

But attention again was diverted by the injection of a new personality into the Red Cross, a tough, eloquent and vigorous man—and furthermore a chairman who laid one basis of criticism by serving without compensation.

Dr. Farrand accepted in October, 1921, the offer of the presidency of Cornell University. Judge John Barton Payne took over.

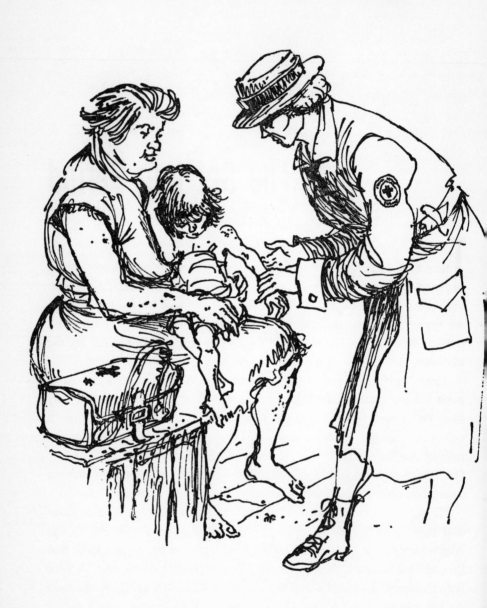

15

The Settling Period

THE YEAR 1922 was epochal in the Red Cross as an example of the organization's growing pains. It needed remarkable durability to survive the pulling and tugging in so many directions by its best friends. At times the now mellowing Headquarters might well have been termed Bedlam on the Potomac, with the bedlam multiplied by the idiosyncrasies of that erratic and headstrong genius, Judge Payne.

Judge Payne will long be remembered in Washington for a host of personal reasons, of which his chairmanship of the Red Cross is only one. He was a West Virginian who went to Chicago to become a celebrated lawyer, an art connoisseur and variously in wartime chairman of the United States Shipping Board and Secretary of the Interior. His first impression on the Red Cross was that of a penny-pinching executive given to boastful wearing of mail-order clothes.

He was a genius in organizational work but also was impetuous and capricious. Late one afternoon he issued an order abolishing the Nutrition Service of the Red Cross forthwith, on the assumption that this operation involved only running a cafeteria for employees. A bear for efficiency, he bombarded the chapters so lustily with memoranda on the virtue of economy that one harassed chairman finally wrote to National Headquarters a reply sufficiently pungent to be printed in the *Red Cross Courier:*

If he means that we do not have a lot of secretaries, officials and flunkies sitting around doing nothing but drawing their salaries and answering fool questions that he may write here and ask, and strictly observing all the red tape that can be hatched up— we are guilty. . . . All our organization work without pay.

While battling mightily for efficiency, Judge Payne for a time so forcefully backed a movement to cut down the number of professional aides in the social-service work of the Red Cross that James L. Feiser, a former general manager and later manager of the Southwest Division, resigned on a question of principle. But Judge Payne also was the type who could bring Feiser to a heart-to-heart conference, find a meeting of their minds, and bring back the seasoned expert to serve the Red Cross as a vice chairman for twenty more distinguished years.

Rough as the experience was on the Red Cross and its personnel, the year 1922 in particular possibly needed a Judge Payne. Decisions had to be made, vital decisions between the old Red Cross and the new—a knock-down struggle, however polite the words in which arguments were couched—between what was now the Boardman "old guard" and the new leadership that had come out of the war.

Years later Ernest Bicknell, who was in the middle of the Payne barrage, summed it up in two warm paragraphs:

During the war, we had, all of us, been busily expanding the Red Cross. Every day we took on new personnel, bought more things, watched things grow. It was an exhilarating experience. Everything was on the upgrade. Judge Payne came in, just in time to deflate the Red Cross. Constantly he had to let good men and women go. He had to simplify the organization. He had to reduce expenses. He had to be judge, jury and chief executioner. Nobody was happy about the situation.

Without heat, without resenting the inevitable criticism and complaints, the Judge did what was needed to be done. It was necessary not to throw the organization into a panic, not to allow the fear to grow up that the Red Cross was being wrecked. Through all this difficult and dangerous process, Judge Payne moved calmly, without rancor, without bias. How well he did, we all know today. He was a strong man in the right place. And those who once feared him as a stern, cold man, learned to know him as warm-hearted and genial, with a great sense of humor, a great love of children and a mind, like his office door, often open.

One wonders, with a smile, if Bicknell was able to maintain such an objective viewpoint at the time.

The big controversy developed over the Persons report, within a short time after its adoption by the Central Committee, was supposed to have settled many questions once and for all. Two viewpoints developed around the rather hazy terminology of the Red Cross charter itself, particularly with regard to "mitigating" and "preventing" the effects of disaster and suffering.

The *mitigators* were those who would have the Red Cross in the main stand by, quietly waiting for disasters and then coping with them after the fact. The *preventers* were those who foresaw for the Red Cross a future in which it would, at the broadest construction, build itself into a dominant force in all fields of social service. It was logical that the paid personnel of the Red Cross, many of them experts in the social-service field with vision enough to see the challenge, were ranged most generally on the side of the *preventers,* the followers of Persons, Feiser and others.

Nevertheless, the powerful prestige of the senior volunteers who had done so much to build the prewar Red Cross was present and it was vocal.

Heading the group of *mitigators* was Miss Boardman herself, strong, firm and unbending, re-established in all her prestige by the holding of two offices, those of secretary of the Red Cross and membership on the Executive Committee. Former President Taft and Robert W. de Forest, both vice presidents of the Red Cross in 1922, were ranged alongside her, and their most vocal spokesman was Harvey Gibson, wartime general manager. Potent names indeed. And their feelings about the Red Cross organization already had been summed up by Gibson in 1921, in a letter:

All the king's horses and all the king's men will never be able to make a dent in again getting it [the Red Cross] out of the hands of the thousands of professionals that are now eating up its endowments and its resources by taking millions of dollars in salaries in trying to find things for the Red Cross to do to keep the chapters going . . . and last and most important from their point of view, continuing jobs for them.

No such eloquently violent reply on behalf of the *preventers* appears in the records, but what was the Red Cross staff doing? Naturally, some of the personnel were fighting to retain their jobs, some were ambitious and some were stupid. Where in any organization do the exceptions not occur? Contrariwise, why was a social worker, whether Bicknell or a young college graduate, put on the payroll if not to think?

The debate is as old as organized social work, and as current today (although sometimes less apparent in such organizations) as it was in 1922.

It seems quite possible in retrospect that the Red Cross found its modern bearings, which bore such tremendous results in the great flood period of the 1950s, because of the moderate voice of Dr. Farrand, who now had stepped from the chairmanship to a post as more or less impartial arbiter.

The great debate on the issue came in the convention of chapters in 1922. At Red Cross conventions delegates do not pass on policy matters. They pass resolutions for consideration by the governing board, but may not make laws for the Red Cross. Their importance lies in the open forum provided by the convention system.

At this convention, Miss Boardman spoke in a manner that seemed to some of her hearers rather anomalous. The veteran leader, who more than anyone else had instituted chapter work for the purpose of building a living organization prior to 1917, now questioned whether the Red Cross had not "lost its bearings."

Dr. Farrand agreed, when he spoke in his turn, that the Red Cross must not become a "great organized charitable society," but he gave a renewed definition to its status as predominantly a great volunteer society necessarily trained and coordinated by professionals. There is, he said, "nothing more dangerous . . . than volunteer service unguided or unchecked or unadvised by expert knowledge."

The pattern pictured by Dr. Farrand was on a plane above such efforts as some chapters were making to collect and distribute old clothes to the poor, to displace other organized local charitable work, or actually to substitute Red Cross technical experts for officials of municipal and state organizations.

The conclusion was that the Red Cross could not be maintained for emergency work alone, unless there were continuing chapter activities to keep volunteers in touch with at least the rudiments of those things they must do in disasters.

When Miss Boardman became more critical of the Persons-Feiser-Farrand viewpoint, Judge Payne picked up his pen and notified her that in his view, rather than see her feelings prevail in the Red Cross, he would have it scrapped.

Before the year was out, the Central Committee ended the "great debate" with a new statement of policy:

Military welfare and disaster were to be the first concerns of the American Red Cross.

Chapters were to give priority to aid for disabled veterans and disaster preparedness.

Chapters must avoid duplication of the work of other agencies.

Promotion of public health should be a major undertaking, with continuance through trained workers of both the nursing program and the family welfare program.

Probably no one who voted for this program realized, after all the confusions of the years since 1918, that in it were embedded the foundation stones of the modern American National Red Cross.

But there is a wide river between policy and action, and often between statistics and reality. So perspective requires that the focus shift again back to the field, to the chapters.

II

From the statistical standpoint, and regardless of this qualification, the American Red Cross chapters after World War I constituted a truly national organization. Retrenchments there might be, shrinkage in income and membership and occasional policy disputes, but the Red Cross was big. It never again would be small or remotely comparable to its numerical or monetary strength prior to 1917. For all the foreseeable future its chapters would "cover every mile of the United States."

But what were some of the qualifications in the new era in which the Red Cross stood as a partially demobilized wartime force—whose sleeping strength could be called up in disasters (very rare) or mustered for ingenious community service (very spotty)?

The number of Red Cross enrolled and recognized chapters would never again drop below 3,500. In 1922 they totaled 3,627. In that same year membership, based on annual fund collections of a minimum of one dollar each, stood at 3,955,500. In 1925 this roll would reach the "bottom of the barrel" in the postwar depletion, with 3,012,000. How sad that total looked compared with wartime membership that had soared over 20,000,000. On the other side of the coin was the fact that at this lowest point after 1917 the Red Cross had more than 10 times the number of supporting members it had in December, 1916, when the figure was 286,461, and more than 133 times the total membership of 22,499 enrolled in December, 1915.

Such growth in chapters and membership was hardly failure, except for the concern about the retreat from the peak. But there were grave misgivings throughout the 1920s and 1930s concerning the highly diverse character and quality of the chapters and their operations in relationship to the new world in which they must make their mark.

In the main, the picture was one in which an optimistic National Headquarters pumped innumerable program suggestions into chapters, backing them up with personal visits by representatives of Headquarters, and hoped for the best. But it was disappointed with this best.

One optimistic Headquarters spokesman said, "The new program was centered in the community and stressed local interests and self-determination. It was so broad that every chapter, big or little, could find something of interest."

To help the chapters find something of interest the peacetime organization maintained three regional offices—Eastern, Midwestern and Pacific—and a staff of field representatives. But the field staff setup required almost as much paper work as many chapters. In some cases, field representatives had whole states as their "beats," and visits actually were apportioned on the basis of two a year to the more active chapters, one each to less active chapters, and none whatsoever to perhaps half of the chapters because there was nothing in them to warrant such visits.

Inevitably many of the chapters complained of lack of attention

from Headquarters, and the national staff complained of the difficulties
of handling its work with the limited resources available. Funds were
tight not only in Washington; most of the chapters were destitute
in so far as meeting the types of programs that National Headquarters
encouraged them to pursue.

It is also true that at this period—and it's not too far exaggerated
from the picture ever since—it was almost impossible to define what
constituted a Red Cross chapter; for nearly every one was an exception in some regard.

Some chapters were virtually satrapies within themselves, with large
conserved endowments, huge office buildings as headquarters and
whole regions under their control.

The Los Angeles Chapter covered an area 100 miles square, and
operated 49 branches out of its headquarters. Within the chapter's
geographical limits, as its potential support, lived a population greater
than the combined total residents of all the cities of Idaho.

The Chicago Chapter covered two and one-half counties, operated
some 60 branches and drew on a multimillion population.

The New York and Brooklyn, Philadelphia and Boston Chapters
were all "big business" with wealthy supporters and big budgets, as
was Washington, where Miss Mabel Boardman continued to hold
sway through two more decades.

To some of these, National Headquarters seemed a miserly source
of assistance; to others, as they remitted fifty cents from each local
contribution of whatever size from a dollar upward, it seemed a spend-
thrift sapping of the local contributions. And National Headquarters
was not always impressed by chapter size alone. One report pointed
out that a chapter in a city of more than 300,000 never could muster
more than 70 persons to attend its annual meetings.

At the other extreme were chapters that hardly knew their own
limits, such as Tucson, Arizona, covering 12,000 square miles with a
total population of only 93,000 persons, or Buford, South Carolina,
with fifteen islands within its jurisdiction. Some Red Cross field workers reported that they could not even find crossroads villages listed as
chapters on the rolls, let alone the local residents who might have
records.

In fact, the Red Cross travelers had many viewpoints. Miss Boardman toured the Southwest and West in 1925 and returned to report

that she was shocked by the "undignified and often wretchedly poor offices" which gave the Red Cross an inferior position and discouraged volunteers. These offices frequently were a room in a decrepit courthouse basement, in a garage, or even the drawer of a housewife's kitchen table.

Mutual understanding within the Red Cross still was in an evolutionary process. One disillusioned field worker wrote back: "These people do as they please, and the national organization can accept it or not." Another with more patience and understanding born of experience, reported: "After four and a half years in the field, the writer still gets an almost physical shock sometimes at the contrast when she arrives on the spot and compares the aspect of matters viewed from that angle with their aspect viewed from Headquarters. Probably quite a percentage of field staff will end up in the madhouse because of these frequent mental adjustments."

But there also were bright spots, epitomizing what the Red Cross could be in a community's life. Of one it was reported:

> No chapter in this territory is doing such sound work, and in no community could there be a finer Red Cross spirit developed solely by the fine chapter program that is being carried on conservatively but consistently by the chapter. The Board meets regularly and with almost perfect attendance, and every member of the chapter is interested in its program and progress . . . the joyous sort of spirit in the office, the Board members dropping in because they like being there, the volunteers having a good time at their work, and the fact that this chapter is reaching young and old, rich and poor, in the country and in the city, which seems to me the only way a chapter should be.

Gradually one big fact was being learned by the Red Cross. A chapter pretty generally reflects the type and spirit of the community where it is located. The Red Cross chapter can not be exclusive—either better than its community or worse—and neither can it be aloof.

The Red Cross volunteer is, as they were learning, seldom only a Red Cross volunteer. Community leaders, men and women, are leaders because they enjoy working for their community. If active, they usually are active in many ways. The leader of the Rotary Club will also be a leader in the Red Cross or other community welfare organizations.

The Red Cross leader is probably also a spark plug in the Parent-Teacher Association and the Y.M.C.A. If a community is lacking in enterprising individuals, there will be no Red Cross leadership or any other worth mentioning.

So why the carrying along of so many Red Cross chapters?

Even the weakest responds a little bit in time of need. Perhaps it raises a few dollars in the annual fund drive; its collections may be magnificent in a call to meet the demands of a national disaster. And should war come, as it came twice after the long frustrating experience of the 1920–30 decade, the roots for growth do exist.

For the long haul, despite the beefing and the complaints between National Headquarters and the chapters, there was an impressive program of constructive work going ahead, even though spotty in quality and widely varied in type. With all the qualifications, there was no state within which the Red Cross beacon was not kept lighted by a few signally outstanding regular Red Cross activities, in addition to disaster work ranging from flood and storm to the stark needs of whole populations caught up in the Great Depression.

However the Red Cross might fight over its own soul-searching, the public was getting its money's worth. The public proved this point by slow but consistent growth both in membership and contribution, rising after a small slump in the early 1930s to a total membership in mid-1941 of 9,190,474.

III

If the chapters are the components of the motor running the Red Cross machine, and the motor must idle a lot in peacetime, the batteries sparking this motor are natural disasters. Without natural disasters the Red Cross might, in a protracted period of peace and prosperity, be hard put to maintain itself in public interest; but more important, without the Red Cross what would the result of disasters be?

By the 1920s, and through the 1930s, the public was beginning to see in action a machine that cost the taxpayer nothing, and that on the whole could roll smoothly to the task of "helping people back on their feet."

Somewhere in the United States, on an average of more than twice a week over the twenty-year span from 1921 through 1940, Red Cross workers—chapter volunteers guided and assisted by a skeleton staff of "pros" from National Headquarters—swung into action in disasters. Statistically there were in that period 2,200 natural upheavals in the United States, seldom reappearing twice in the same place, that destroyed homes and ravaged human lives to a degree greater than could be handled exclusively by the local resources of the communities they struck.

How many persons were assisted with anything from shelter for a night and a hot meal to rebuilt houses, replanted crops or emergency funds to dress children and send them back to school, could not be recorded. But the measure of the help, in which the United States accepted this almost amorphous thing known as the Red Cross as its agent in humane activity, was recorded. And the total was almost an even $100,000,000 contributed in addition to the annual donations made in the fund drives.

Here was the high point of the Red Cross's public acceptance, and here was its greatest challenge, for in disaster rehabilitation lurk the worst of all public relations problems.

Who handles these problems, and faces the consequences? The professional staff, to be sure, but to a far greater degree the volunteers who staff the committees, make the awards and work with and in the communities.

Now and then a gifted person among the Red Cross volunteers sets down things that never could be gleaned from the official reports. A classic was written after the 1927 Mississippi flood by William Alexander Percy, Mississippi's "Mr. Will," in his classic book *Lanterns on the Levee,* published in 1941.

"Mr. Will" was the son of a Mississippi planter, who returned from service in France in World War I to write eloquently about his native South. In 1940 he set down his autobiography and adverted to his experience as chairman of the Red Cross Chapter, of Greenville, Mississippi, during the period when the state's river namesake submerged his rich delta section for four whole months. Of the aftermath of rehabilitation he said:

> I have noticed that if you offer people a chance to give, they are little less than angels; but if you afford them a chance to receive, they almost convince you somebody is right about the need for a hell. The shabby truth is that in June the Red Cross began

its campaign of rehabilitation, and people began to receive—food and clothing, of course, but in addition household goods, farms supplies and money.

Not only did the Red Cross do a magnificent job of giving, but I don't think there was a fraternal organization, or an organized charity in America that did not donate most prodigally. Particularly I recall the generosity of all Masons and the Christian Scientists. Our heroic people became mere people, they not only received, they grabbed. Everybody wanted what was coming to him and a little more. . . . It was a wretched period.

But wretched or not, each new disaster found its same response, and to such a degree that the Red Cross Central Committee was able to place its operations on a budgeted and businesslike basis. Out of the surplus carried over from World War I, a disaster reserve fund of $5,000,000 was set up. This provided working capital for relief wherever needed. If local, regional or national appeals were warranted by the need, the fund was restored from any surplus, which not often happened. Usually the fund was put back to par by appropriation from the receipts of the next general fund campaign.

The pattern of disaster relief changed in character but not in philosophy from the groundwork laid first by Miss Barton and developed under Miss Boardman's leadership. Only now the disasters were bigger—more people were hit by each one and the costs of things had risen prodigiously. And communications improved by wartime development made need more easily reported. No longer was any community out of touch with its own neighbors, or the United States compartmented into isolated cells.

And whether it was efficient or not in spots, the Red Cross was there, prepared in some degree, and more than that of any other organization, both to be on the job and reach out nationwide if necessary for assistance for the victims. And in this field it was completely accepted by those who wished to give, even though occasionally damned by the greedy, the confused and the ignorant among those it helped to rehabilitate.

As the disasters of the years marched past, the story renewed itself on every occasion, whether in the Florida hurricane, most devastating of its kind, in 1926; the Mississippi flood of 1927; the Caribbean hurricane of 1928; the great Ohio River resurgence in 1937; or the un-precedented hurricane that swept New York and New England in the late 1930s.

Each disaster bespoke its own challenge, and each required differing operations, but the Red Cross was there—to the degree that the statistics would be interminable.

These things people saw, and some remembered. Less evident was the growing list of volunteers who minded the daily chores of chapter work, enhanced the national programs, and were ready because of the rudimentary experience gained in work that bespoke no headlines.

During this period the chapter idea—even though not in all the chapters—was maturing, developing and flowering.

IV

Poor as they might appear in statistics, the chapters, a little here and a little there, were doing the things that perhaps will always be the prime function of the Red Cross: teaching, training and coordinating community skills.

The Public Health Nursing program launched with such fanfare right after World War I was a failure statistically, with not more than 1,152 chapters ever being counted as active in this field; but out of it grew an awareness in many states and cities that led to establishment of these very services as part of the public service.

It also acted as a program-builder, because its many branches provided a dozen other means of employing chapter talent. After all, it was sound policy that the Red Cross should not try to duplicate what others could or were willing to do. And if in its pioneering, as earlier in support of the fight against tuberculosis, it sparked mass interest in public health and public nursing, in sanitation and preventive medicine, it lost nothing in prestige with the passing on of these activities to other specialized and professional groups. It had enough to do, if the remainder were done well.

There was the Camp and Hospital Service for example, which in 1930 was still a major activity among disabled veterans, and the even larger Home Service for their families—involving everything from immediate relief of threatened destitution because of occurrences beyond a family's control to helpful work in filling out interminable government forms.

Most of this work gradually passed to the Veterans Administration, but it was the Red Cross that showed how to coordinate these activities, to use with minimum waste skilled persons in handling deep and serious human problems. This program, too, brought forth a lot of criticism, but the job had to be done.

The Home Service project sparked several hundred chapters to try another field called officially Civilian Home Service—practical aid for families and children who did not happen to be related to veterans but whose needs would be as great in the face of emergency. Judge Payne once called this activity "moonshine Home Service," but the chapters which pioneered it laughed off the irascible old boy's description and, where they felt the community could use this type of work, they did it. But Judge Payne's viewpoint carried a lot of weight, and chapter efforts often ran headlong into competition with other agencies that knew, or thought they knew, more about this type of work. The term has disappeared from the list of Red Cross activities, but across the country Red Cross chapters still cooperate substantially with sister organizations in the same sort of work.

In the meantime the Red Cross was hitting the jackpot of popular support through two services that dated from the recent but prewar past. Life Saving Service and First Aid Service were embodying hundreds of chapters in the main currents of interest in their communities.

Life Saving, as with so many successful ventures, saw the Red Cross chapter going out and working with other organizations, finding collaborators instead of creating competitors. And in a country taking more and more to the water, there was a popular response. Soon the Red Cross was the recognized organization to lead a vast project under the slogan: "Everybody a swimmer and every swimmer a lifesaver."

The "students" of the Red Cross units were themselves experts and appreciated what the work meant. Through the Red Cross life-saving institutes passed camp counselors, instructors for the Y.M.C.A. and Y.W.C.A., Boy Scout leaders, Red Cross chapter teachers and many other applicants. Today the Red Cross badge is the universal symbol of the trained life guard.

First Aid Service did not reach as many people directly but perhaps has saved far more lives. This course was offered through the chap-

ters, complete with manuals and trained instructors—soon the graduate students became the volunteer instructors—at a time when even
rudimentary first-aid work such as applying a tourniquet or giving a
specific simple antidote for poison was known to hardly anyone except
a doctor or trained nurse.

Through its courses the Red Cross opened the door for such training to all policemen and firemen. Like Life Saving, also taught to these
groups, the Red Cross seal of approval has become the accepted and
almost only standard, and through the years it has spread to factories,
labor unions and other groups wherever men or women face unexpected hazards in their daily lives.

More controversial was the development in this period of a formalized organization of Red Cross volunteers, cutting across and supporting all the services, but opening special doors of recognition to those
volunteers who would pledge themselves to specific responsibilities in
the services of their choice. This was the child of Miss Boardman
herself, a throwback to her earlier ideas of the Red Cross chapter as a
dedicated group of responsible and perhaps prosperous community
leaders.

She founded the Volunteer Service and became its chairman in
1923, and she headed it for seventeen years thereafter. The service
was born in controversy over the advisability of creating an elite corps
of volunteers, in contrast to the many practical volunteers who worked
when Red Cross needed them but had not the time or, in some cases,
the social acceptance for membership in the Volunteer Service of their
home chapter. That controversy has never quite died out, although
generally easier economic conditions have opened the doors for more
women desiring to do so to enroll.

Volunteer Service required from the start a pledge to devote eighteen working hours a year to the Red Cross, or an average of an hour
and a half per month. As reward for this enrollment the volunteer had
the privilege of wearing on duty or on such occasions as parades and
civic celebrations the uniform of the volunteer with a pin signifying
her special service—Administrative, Motor, Canteen, Nurses' Aide,
etc.

More important, in some chapters, acceptance became as treasured
as membership in a college club might be. It denoted, in an era of less
general prosperity, a certain degree of leisure not permitted to working

women or the heads of large and financially limited households; in too many cases it represented social acceptance by the tight little cliques of women who ran the Red Cross chapter as a sacred preserve just as they ran every other social movement in the community.

On the plus side, the rewards did attract a certain number of volunteers who otherwise might not have become interested in the Red Cross, and the fair conclusion is that such chapter activities as survived the humdrum of the 1920s and 1930s owed much of their continuity of effort to the recognized volunteers.

In any event, the Volunteer Service survived its patroness and lives today; and by the same token there are important leaders of the Red Cross movement, themselves volunteers, who consider the distinction between volunteer and paid worker to be one of the worst elements of the modern Red Cross organization.

16

The Challenge of the Depression—Public Agency or Political Stooge?

ONE OF THE HISTORIC problems of welfare agencies is that they suffer their worst depressions when the public, their clients, are well off. Then when hard times hit, the agencies are criticized because they, like their contributors, have not taken advantage of "prosperity" to build up their reserves.

That was how the depression caught the Red Cross. As the sequel, it then found itself boxed in a position where it had to fight off well-meant attempts to subsidize it with government appropriations that would have wrecked forever its character. The decisions it had to make were hard ones, and in retrospect a large part of the strength that preserved the Red Cross came from the increasingly irascible Judge Payne.

The question revolved around one point, whether the Red Cross—which to outsiders was big, unique and strong regardless of the internal debates that were eroding it—was a machine accountable to the public or to the government. In the end the public won, but as always there were vital changes in activity and outlook.

For the Red Cross, the Great Depression provided almost as many tests and challenges as war itself, but at the same time a great stimulation in the one simple fact that it gave the organization, from Washington to the remotest chapter, something tangible to do. Certainly without the stimulus of the work engaged in because of the depression there would have been far less experienced manpower among staff and volunteers to take up the problems that came with war in 1941. But in the meantime it collected bruises too.

The depression created an immediate problem for the Red Cross in matters of policy decision, and after policy was determined the question was money.

As a national relief agency it had built up precedents under a charter that authorized and required it to do certain things in time of war or national calamities. But the question was whether the withering of economic blight was a calamity in the same sense as a flood or hurricane. After all, there had been regional droughts almost every year, and dislocations or changing markets had created sweeping waves of unemployment in many sectors, particularly New England.

The money question was just as vexing. What would any program big enough to do any good cost? It would certainly run into many millions. The Red Cross was large as relief agencies were measured, but how big was *big* once it stepped into the pool?

Actually for such a machine it had pitifully small resources in 1929 —a little over $16,000,000 in available reserves at National Headquarters. It had spent, despite the retrenchments already noted, $10,-000,000 more than it had taken in during the decade after 1918. Its annual revenue had dropped to approximately $3,000,000 but the Red Cross still was spending $4,000,000, taking $1,000,000 a year from its reserves. Of course, the chapters had their own incomes, but in national disasters it is up to National Headquarters to find the money to foot the bills: the chapters provide only people except for the cost of such work as they undertake in their local areas on their own responsibility.

It was true that $1,000,000 of the $3,000,000 annual income out of which National Headquarters supported the national program came from invested capital, a kitty of money at which critics always have pointed a finger of question and asked, "How about all that money hoarded by the Red Cross?"

It never is quite understood that the principal of the Red Cross endowment funds can no more be touched by the Red Cross than a trust fund set up by a man to provide income for his family. These endowment funds, usually left by persons in legacies to the Red Cross, have the same strings attached—spend the interest, but if the capital is dissipated someone goes to jail.

For a while, in the debate over the Red Cross that flared up in Congress in the relief days, it looked as if everybody would be consigned to the dog house if not to jail, regardless of what was done or what was not done by it.

II

Most of us have forgotten at this writing that the Great Depression that hit industry, the cities and workers coincident with the stock market collapse in 1929 followed a drought in the previous summer that virtually eliminated all crops in the Southwest and great portions of the West. Furthermore, it came after years of declining prices. This calamity constituted poverty's ultimate blow to millions of formerly stable, prosperous and frugal persons.

Unlike the industrial depression that laid a creeping paralysis on job-holders, the drought was immediate and calamitous. As winter came in 1930 the United States faced for the first time the stark fact that millions of citizens simply had nothing to eat, and there was no place where they could borrow or beg the barest necessities for their families.

President Hoover, in his *pro forma* capacity as honorary president of the Red Cross, asked in August, 1930, that it stand ready to render such assistance as might be required as a result of the drought. The request was accepted as valid, despite serious doubts expressed in some quarters as to whether the drought itself came under the "disaster" relief authorization of the Red Cross charter. More important in retrospect, it may be cited that when President Hoover asked the Red Cross for potential relief he asked the *Red Cross* alone; not one or more of the numerous other welfare agencies in the United States.

Judge Payne responded by saying that the entire $5,000,000 disaster reserve would be used for that purpose, if necessary, but he and the remainder of the leadership began seriously to wonder how far $5,000,000 would go in the face of potential relief needs covering millions of persons. The remainder of the total $16,000,000 must be preserved as security for other work. Thereafter the Red Cross rolled with the calls upon it for several months.

First, money was spent for seed and supplies to assist farmers in putting in fall crops. But it was only a matter of weeks before the chapters in the affected areas began receiving streams of destitute persons for whom a crop months hence might mean ultimate recovery, but who must have clothes, food and fuel *now*.

The chapters picked up this burden where possible, since this was more a community responsibility than a national Red Cross operation, but soon Headquarters had to begin supplementing chapter resources. By the end of 1930 an unknown amount of chapter funds had been poured into this work, while National Headquarters had seen $1,000,-000 of its disaster reserves go out for the seed program and for chapter aid. And the surface of demand had hardly been scratched.

The whole thing turned into dramatic debate in January, 1931. On the sixth of that month, Judge Payne—who apparently was more vocal than thoughtful at the moment—said he thought the Red Cross could continue the necessary relief program through the winter without asking for additional funds, but he said he would "yell" if necessary. He "yelled" exactly one week later, and President Hoover thereupon issued an appeal for contributions to a special $10,000,000 Red Cross fund for drought relief.

This call for special contributions innocently precipitated the first crisis in which the Red Cross had to decide, once and for all, whether it would remain as it was or be sucked into the pond of government-subsidized and accordingly politically controlled agencies. This condition must be summarized far more briefly than its importance in the long picture warrants, but it was drama of a high order.

One must remember that in 1931 the dramatic political contest began to determine the federal government's responsibility for welfare work—the bitter fight between the negative attitude led by President Hoover and the Republican Party, who lost out in 1932 to the New Deal, with its positive stand for government relief.

Senator Joe T. Robinson, Democratic Majority Leader of the Senate in a Congress where his party controlled both Senate and House, introduced a measure to appropriate $25,000,000 to be given to the Red Cross "for the purpose of supplying food, medicine, medical aid, and other essentials to afford adequate relief in the present national emergency to persons otherwise unable to procure the same."

The Red Cross and the President protested against such action.

The immediate effect of this proposal was to put a damper on the Red Cross's appeal for contributions. The debate in Congress became so bitter that the *Literary Digest* commented that the Red Cross "may stumble out of the Washington cataclysm itself a refugee from disaster, and badly in need of the succor for which it is famous." To criticism by the Democratic leadership was added the oratorical attacking fire of Representative Fiorello H. LaGuardia, nominally a Republican who soon was to become the "reform" Mayor of New York, and of such radical publications as the *Nation*. On the other hand, as was to be expected, the *New York Times* and the Chicago *Tribune* supported the Red Cross position.

But it was clearly evident that Congress was in a mood to grant the appropriation anyway, and thereupon ensued a remarkable appearance by Judge Payne before the House Appropriations Committee. On January 28, Judge Payne testified as spokesman for the unanimous opinion of the Central Committee that the Red Cross did not desire the $25,000,000 in the form of an appropriation, and that *if the appropriation were voted the Red Cross would decline it*.

Judge Payne pointed out that his position was precisely that taken in World War I by Chairman Henry Davison of the War Council—still an active member of the Central Committee—and added, "All we pray for is that you let us alone and let us do the job."

This testimony killed the appropriating fever, and the public—at last shown clearly that the Red Cross belonged to the people, not to politicians—put the $10,000,000 drive over the top. Furthermore, a subsequent survey of 4,000 editorials in daily and weekly newspapers commenting on this debate showed that fully 90 per cent approved the Red Cross position.

How did the Red Cross do the job after refusing to become a tool of bureaucracy? A few figures tell a graphic story, in which it is well to remember that in the time of depression prices it was possible to provide the basic food for a family of four in drought-blighted Arkansas for a month at a total cost of $8.00.

Up to the time that spring crops were harvested, the Red Cross did plow $16,000,000 into this relief program, plus unknown amounts put into the same hopper by chapters. Aid was given to 2,500,000 persons in twenty-three states, or more than required assistance after the great Mississippi flood of 1927.

The job was handled by a peak roll of 2,000 paid employees, but the great bulk of the work was done by more than 37,000 chapter volunteers. And precedents were set, and lessons learned, that contributed many new wrinkles to future operations.

When the Red Cross spent this relief money, it purchased in so far as was possible relief supplies on the spot where they were to be used, so that the purchase of supplies in itself took business into distraught communities. As part of the food-supply program it introduced hot lunches into schools that eventually supplied these for 184,000 children, thus improving the diet of the children and teaching remote and backward school areas how to carry on this essential type of health program. In other communities the Red Cross, as part of the aid program, instituted popular teaching courses in canning and food conservation, plus many other innovations.

If some of this sounds a little on the side of excessive zeal, one must remember that the drought brought need to some areas that had lived apart from modern development of the most simple sort for a century and more.

Countless articles have been written as to how the drought-relief work done in the more backward areas in 1931 taught backwoods mothers how to feed their families a more varied diet, and one as easy to obtain or prepare as the traditional fatback, corn pone and greens. Very few have given sufficient credit to the teacher—the Red Cross representative working alongside many other willing but lesser-trained volunteers.

However, the Red Cross workers had not completed filling out their reports on drought relief before the organization was plunged by circumstances and the depression into an operation for which this seemed little more than rehearsal; and it again faced the necessity to decide on its posture in the face of demands upon it such as no leader prior to 1932 had experienced in the remotest degree.

III

The Red Cross had to face the issue that much of the political leadership that came to power with the New Deal in the election of 1932 opposed private welfare agencies of any sort, believed that government agencies could do a better job in the same field. With the full impact of the depression, the professional social worker, the planner of broad projects financed by large appropriations of tax funds, was having his first day in Washington.

The Red Cross was a nonparticipant but a focus of attention in a struggle between deeply convinced forces on either side, each conscious of new demands on welfare work such as had never before faced the United States.

The Red Cross must work through this era and save itself, if it were to be saved, by showing aptitudes and reasons for existence under circumstances more difficult than those imposed by war, because unlike war the depression found it operating with constantly shrinking resources. The Red Cross, spurred by its traditions, rolled up its sleeves and went to work.

To anticipate the narrative in a small degree, it may be recorded at this point that in 1934, after the Works Progress Administration had been appropriated billions of dollars to stem the tide of unemployment, its administrator, Harry Hopkins, leader of the bloc that had argued hardest for direct government aid, looked back and said: "Red Cross chapters throughout America were the first line of defense during those trying months before the states and the counties and finally the Federal Government put its funds at the disposal of the unemployed."

Hopkins was by then the most intimate confidante of President Roosevelt. His earlier experience had included five years on the staff of the Red Cross, from 1917 through 1922.

Actually the chapters decided the Red Cross policy on relief in 1931, when drought relief already was the cloak for supplying assistance to persons and families who had never worked near a farm. One report stated: "The situation locally is so overwhelming that no agency is standing on ceremony these days, but all are endeavoring to give relief as speedily as possible."

Early in 1932 a roundup showed that 1,800 chapters of the Red Cross, or more than half the total, were participating in community unemployment relief programs. Of these, 400 had already received financial assistance from the Washington organization.

Of course, the Red Cross was not alone. The Red Cross chapter acted as part of its community, which it was—one agency among many, but generally with larger outside resources because of the existence of the reserve funds in National Headquarters. But it was hiding its light under a bushel of halfhearted publicity, so much so that the manager of the Eastern Area cautioned Washington that, "We need to turn from our policy of silence and give all possible publicity to what we are doing." He and many others in the Red Cross considered this the best defense against those who would swallow up privately supported agencies by merging them into bureaucracies.

Among the activities, hardly admitted as yet by Washington, were works by chapters carrying the major burden of relief in their home cities, because the local residents able to contribute money trusted the good judgment and integrity of the Red Cross.

Outstanding in this work was Birmingham, Alabama, which in 1932 gave aid to an average 12,000 families a month and paid out wages in various work programs to 4,400 men. In its work projects it paid men $2.00 a day for three-day stints of work in public parks or in gardens growing vegetables for distribution to the needy. This chapter set up six food-distribution stores, and even supported a toy shop.

In the meantime, other chapters were just as active—assisting coal miners in Pennsylvania, lumberjacks in the Northwest, transient workers. The job was nationwide, and hence the response.

All told in 1932, Red Cross chapters put $7,500,000 of their own resources into these programs, including projects benefiting 2,000,000 of the unemployed. And while doing this job the leadership had to make another great decision.

Now it was President Hoover who asked not that the Red Cross accept a subsidy but that it take on a great responsibility for distribution of government aid. The federal government held in surplus storage 85,000,000 bushels of wheat and 844,000 bales of cotton, with a total value of $73,000,000. If this could be turned into flour, livestock feed, and cloth or clothing, it would constitute a vast relief project at no fresh cost to the government for the raw stock it already owned.

At no point was the Red Cross to have its own funds enriched, but the request asked for a type of service that only the Red Cross could give. Why? It was the only organization in America entirely outside of government, with 3,600 chapters plus 10,000 branches, able to muster up to 1,000,000 volunteers competently supervised by a skeleton trained staff, and its integrity was unquestioned. For this was an opera-

tion in which many unscrupulous persons could have made their for-
tunes.

The job handed to the Red Cross included the making of nonprofit
contracts for the manufacture and distribution of finished food and
goods, surveys to guide distribution, final distribution and ultimately
absolute accounting for the handling of the project. The Red Cross
accepted the assignment, and furthermore completed the whole operation in a matter of months. The results seem staggering even now.

There are 3,098 counties in the United States. Something from this
government hoard, in processed form, went into 3,081 of those counties, which was about as nationwide as a project could be. In shipping
alone, the statistics included 30,000 railroad cars of flour and 7,800
carloads of stock feed.

Ten million barrels of flour were distributed to 5,800,000 families.
More than 100,000,000 items of clothing were distributed, of which
60,000,000 were made on factory contracts and the remainder were
cut and sewed in chapters themselves. Many, practically all, other
relief agencies cooperated with the Red Cross in this program, but the
responsibility rested solely on the Red Cross.

Of the work, President Hoover said that the nation had developed
complete confidence in the "efficiency, ability and singlemindedness"
of the Red Cross.

Then for a while it appeared that this massive work might be the
swan song, if not the tombstone, of the Red Cross.

IV

When after 1932 the federal government took over the relief program
set up to alleviate the depression, the Red Cross—national and chapters alike—faced a self-searching period that had been postponed from
1931 only by reason of the emergency activity of its early depression
relief work. Now this was taken out of its hands.

Income for National Headquarters held at approximately $3,000,-
000 a year, but this seemed to be not only rock bottom but the peak
of expectancy. The chapters found themselves on a similar lean basis.
And yet the Red Cross must remain at a certain minimum level if it
were to be prepared to meet the traditional disaster calls upon it, to
work in communities as it had been doing—work heartily approved

by the communities themselves. But it could not expect the public to pay taxes on the one hand for public services supplied under the new order and contribute to private agencies in support of the same work.

The field of the Red Cross faced drastic contraction, back to disaster relief and rehabilitation, First Aid, Water Safety, and very little else. Furthermore, it must learn to live within its income.

By 1935, Hospital Service had been severely curtailed, and the services known as Home Hygiene and Care of the Sick had been combined with Public Health Nursing. Almost a third of the national personnel had been abolished and the remainder had taken cuts in salary.

By that time, the total payroll of National Headquarters had dropped to 693 persons, including the doctors, nurses, trained disaster workers and all the field workers cooperating with chapters. It was lean indeed for a nationwide organization, but at last the budget was balanced.

Ironically, it was at this time and largely owing to the depression that a new series of charges were leveled at the Red Cross—that it was the tool of wealthy persons, that it had discriminated between whites and Negroes in some of the unemployment relief program, that it was a bureaucracy.

Some of the criticism had reasons if not justification. Mistakes had been made by some chapters; in others there had been a feudal attitude. Other criticism was inspired by the political atmosphere in which some elements came forth to criticize any large work simply because it was large. And there was a distinct tinge, in this day of America's political innocence, of the keenly perverted effort of communism to upset American thought by attacking its most established institutions.

In this predicament two things contributed to perpetuating the Red Cross, if such oversimplification ever is possible.

The first was a resurgence of national disasters, such as the extraordinary flood of the Ohio River in 1937, devastating territory from Pittsburgh westward, and other ravages of this period already noted. Nothing ever has revived the Red Cross in public esteem like a series of disasters.

The other was a change in personal leadership, which seemed almost to have been contrived by the guardian angel of the Red Cross.

On January 24, 1935, Judge Payne died and thereby vacated the office of chairman of the Central Committee. In thirteen years he had carried the Red Cross through the long pull of postwar reorganization, had steered it through great operations despite the poverty of its tangible public support, and had defended it as heartily in the face of criticism as he had been ruthless internally in facing realities.

Judge Payne, however, was not an individual who ever could understand the revolutionary social changes wrought by the depression and its child, the New Deal. Neither could the leaders of the new political philosophy understand him. The result was an abyss of misapprehension between National Headquarters and the whole Administration, centering in the White House only a five-minute walk away. Perhaps, too, it was time for the Red Cross to have a quiet leadership, one that would permit the now seasoned professional staff headed by Vice Chairman Feiser to work out remaining problems and direct operations.

In any event this was what occurred.

Into the chairmanship stepped, at the invitation of the Central Committee, a gentleman of the old school, wealthy, relaxed, unambitious Admiral Cary T. Grayson. His background, or his personality, could not have been farther removed from that of Judge Payne. He was a notable member of one of Virginia's leading families, a wealthy horse-breeder, and professionally a doctor who had been chosen by former President Wilson as his personal physician—hence the title "Admiral."

More than that, he was a close friend of President Roosevelt. For three years, as chairman, he could find a friendly welcome at the White House alike for himself and the Red Cross, which the Administration would see in a new light. Otherwise, he was content to let the Red Cross run its course, and it did just that.

The Distant Roll of Drums

THERE WAS GRIM humor in the role thrust upon the Red Cross in 1938, and the circumstances in which its management and membership alike found themselves. The manner in which it weathered this new storm certainly was helped again by a change in leadership—transfer of the chairmanship from Admiral Grayson, whose agreeable custodianship was ended by death, to Norman H. Davis, banker and diplomat who had headed missions to disarmament conferences under Presidents Hoover and Roosevelt, and who had been a vice president of the Red Cross since 1920.

As the whirlwinds of international tensions preceding World War II spurted into being, President Roosevelt and the State Department thrust a new job on the Red Cross. They poked it into crannies of tension as a representative of American policy where for political reasons the official gates were slammed shut.

In China and in Spain the Red Cross was frankly used as an arm of foreign policy, even when its own leadership and the public to which it looked for support, as demonstrated through the chapters, were something less than enthusiastic. This was a new wrinkle and a touchy one that might have had quite a different culmination in the relationship between the Red Cross and the government had not total war finally ended the debate.

The reasons for the position of the Red Cross in the field of foreign aid are rooted both in its charter and in its very formation as a special ward of the government. While the Red Cross raises its own funds and runs its own collective shop, it is more sensitive than any other welfare agency to the government, which is a sort of perpetual foster parent and trustee.

Specifically the Red Cross cooperates with the armed forces and each year must submit to an audit of all of its expenditures by the Army. That is the law. Practice broadens the relationship to a far greater degree, in the same manner that family relationships are regulated in society without being always stipulated in writing.

In the first place the presidency of the Red Cross, traditionally held by the President of the United States, is more than honorary. No Red Cross leader has ever yet turned down a request from the White House, although Roosevelt did have a little difficulty in the case of China. Second, it would be unthinkable for the Red Cross to cross government foreign policy even if it wished; so when a request is made to bolster foreign policy the Red Cross does as it is requested.

Finally, the Red Cross exists as a part of the community in national affairs just as the chapter is a part of the local community where it is located. Agencies supported by public contributions must be responsive to their sponsors, and this has been interpreted to mean full and ready cooperation with whatever Washington administration is elected on behalf of its supporters.

The Red Cross never had, therefore, the right or the will to question such requests made by American Presidents, whether these came from Theodore Roosevelt, Woodrow Wilson, Herbert Hoover or Franklin D. Roosevelt. But in the field of foreign affairs it discovered some new aspects of old problems when it tried to gain public support for international ventures thrust upon it by the White House at a time when Americans as individuals were predominantly nationalistic in their thinking.

In 1938, after Japan had committed some of its most brutal strokes in conquering China, President Franklin Roosevelt wanted to make a gesture of sympathy toward China. However, he did not wish to antagonize Japan, with which the State Department was negotiating. He specifically asked the Red Cross to put on a drive for a special $1,000,000 fund for relief of Chinese civilians. The money was hardly a drop in the bucket in relation to the need if any real relief effort were to be attempted, but the sum might seem impressive as a political gesture pure and simple.

Acting against their better judgment, because they knew well the attitude of local communities, the Red Cross leaders launched the drive. How correct was their view was shown after two weeks when only $10,000 had been raised. By the end of March only $100,000 had been raised. Americans felt in 1938 that there were too many problems of graver importance at home, and the public attitude furthermore still nourished hope of neutrality in world affairs.

President Roosevelt wrote on April 6, 1938, a letter that stated tersely that the Red Cross should try harder to arouse the public, that the organization "can raise $1,000,000 for the Chinese civilian population if [the public] is asked in the right way."

The Central Committee bowed to the President's right to direct it, and put pressure behind the appeal. This action largely confirmed what the Central Committee had feared would be the result. Many large city chapters refused to join in the campaign. Reports from the field pictured New England as resenting this "political pressure." In the Midwest opposition to extension of Red Cross work to the Far East was clearly evident. The campaign closed its books with only $800,000.

Then there was an even greater fiasco when the President and the Department of State used the Red Cross as a pawn in Spain. Here the civil war that had begun in 1936 had caused the U.S. Government, for reasons of policy, to embargo all arms shipments from the United States to either side, Loyalists or Nationalists.

In retrospect it is easy to condemn, but some history students still resent the manner in which the Red Cross, backed by its loyal millions of members as a humanitarian agency, was used in Spain in a political effort as a cat's-paw. They hope the backfire has taught politicians a permanent lesson.

The history of the Red Cross to this point, even in the Russian fiasco after World War I, was an example of the American feeling that relief of suffering knows no politics. Now, under political pressure, the history shows from the Spanish records how sorry a mess can be created by playing politics with human misery.

From the time when General Francisco Franco, leading his Moorish legions but acting in the name of Catholic Spain, precipitated the Civil War, the Central Committee of the Red Cross acted precisely and properly in line with the traditions of the Red Cross. This action was based on clear recognition that Franco's revolution, closely supported by Hitler's forces and Mussolini's troops, had European-wide implications. It also knew that the Loyalists courted and received open support from Communist Russia.

There were, however, the inevitable cases of innocent civilians driven from homes, the aged and children without food or shelter. For them the American Red Cross began to prepare such assistance as possible through the International Red Cross Committee, but with strictly correct statement of fact and sentiment, as these existed in the United States.

Along with a contribution of $10,000 to the International Committee for Spanish relief, the American Red Cross sent this message: "The whole sentiment of the country is for keeping out of Europe, and in official and private circles the feeling is that we should not expose ourselves in any way that might involve us." In other words, the Red Cross could never separate itself either from the public feeling upon which its whole idea was built or from its government. All of which was perfectly correct.

It was the government alone that made the issue. The White House and the State Department soon embargoed all shipments of arms to either side, thus invoking a policy of complete neutrality, but then attempted to run around its own public policy by sending food supplies, in the name of humane action, to the Loyalists. In this plan it called upon the American Red Cross and the Friends Service Committee (Quakers) to make the gesture as a means of showing this country's opposition to Franco. The Red Cross was asked to assume responsibility for buying surplus wheat held by the Surplus Commodities Corporation (a government agency), milling it into flour, and delivering it to the Friends in Spain for distribution among the Loyalists.

The Red Cross did this job, using $75,000 of its own funds and lending further amounts to the Friends Service Committee. It well knew that while the flour undoubtedly was welcome, and it wished to aid refugees, the basic plot was one to give some form of political aid to the Loyalists without the government appearing to do so as an official action.

The political leadership then asked the Red Cross to launch a drive for $300,000 to enlarge this work, making the request right when the Chinese relief drive was proving itself to be a fiasco.

Then the Red Cross really came under fire, particularly from the Catholic Church and its American spokesmen who had adopted the Franco revolution as a church crusade. The Catholic press lambasted the Red Cross. Important Catholic support began to be withdrawn from it. The Hearst press interpreted the gesture as a means taken by the Administration to circumvent the arms embargo, which it was.

The many groups who sympathized with the Loyalists, both openly sincere and fringe groups inspired by Communist propaganda, took the side of the Red Cross until February, 1939, when the State Department wavered in its own fear of the mounting criticism. It ordered that one Red Cross shipment be diverted to the Franco Nationalists. Now the lid of criticism of the Red Cross blew both ways as vocal friends of the Loyalists in the United States took up the cudgels of criticism. It was charged that Franco had been sending flour to Germany and that this American aid only helped him thus to repay Hitler for his support.

The total failure of the project as a political gesture, and the damage done to the Red Cross, were unmistakably demonstrated when, in May, 1939, the Spanish Relief Fund drive, with a goal set at $300,000, had to be abandoned with collections of only $50,000.

II

But as the war drums sounded nearer in 1940 and 1941, the same public that had lost much respect for the Red Cross in 1938 and 1939 turned again to it, surprising most of all the Red Cross leadership and its principal publicity advisers.

Here is a historic note of contrast: (1) In 1940, when the Red Cross was preparing its annual appeal for public subscriptions, then held in the fall, spokesmen for the three major radio networks advised it to keep all reference to potential European war relief work out of its messages because of public antipathy; (2) Before 1941 ended, with direct involvement of the United States in World War II, the United States, still at peace remember, had given to the Red Cross such great contributions for that very purpose that supplies valued at more than $50,000,000 had been poured by the Red Cross alone into Europe and a surplus of gifts remained.

Again the Red Cross had to roll with the punch to adjust itself almost overnight to changing public attitudes. Happily it found itself not only supported by the public but no longer at odds with political leadership. But it also must be noted that if political feeling had changed, the Red Cross itself had accepted grave changes in its own ideas since World War I.

The Red Cross remained an agent of relief for distressed peoples, but no longer was there any thought that it would or could operate outside the general limits of American foreign policy. There was general acceptance of the fact that the word *American* in its title meant just that. The Nazis, the Fascists and the Communists—not the Red Cross—had changed the old concepts and the old order.

The status of nations at war had changed. Any thought of sending a "Mercy Ship" with token medical assistance to the armies of all belligerents, as had been done in 1914, was dead. Armies now marched with complete skilled medical attendance for their troops, on the battlefields at least. Furthermore, in totalitarian states there was no way of dividing the military and civilian groups. Finally, the time had passed forever when the American public would support a program of aid, or the Red Cross would sponsor assistance, to countries whose politics and actions were anathema to the United States. All this in addition to the total disinclination of the United States in 1939 to become involved in more foreign entanglements.

The humane considerations underlying the Red Cross idea, that of helping all civilians in trouble, seemed incongruous in a period that saw saturation bombing of undefended civilians in cities far from the battle area and the mobilization of national economies to the degree that every civilian actually was a soldier.

Former President Hoover dissented from this attitude and, as a Red Cross vice president, urged a great Red Cross relief program for countries overrun by Germany, but he was voted down. Such aid perforce would support Germany's own economy. In September of 1939 President Roosevelt suggested a similar relief program, as an aid to the morale of friendly countries. Norman Davis himself replied that the country would not support such a campaign.

As a compromise between good intentions and realities, the Red Cross in 1939 allocated $1,000,000 of current funds for potential relief work and announced it would receive contributions "for relief in any of the countries involved." The response was insignificant. This was the period of the "phony war."

Some funds were sent through the League of Red Cross Societies and the International Red Cross Committee to finance refugee help in France and German-occupied Poland, and Finland later was added to the list. On June 30, 1940, an aggregate of $2,662,000 had been provided by the American Red Cross in funds and supplies for these three countries. That was all at the moment, but by then the ruthless German smash-through of May, 1940, had ended the phony war. This development changed almost immediately the character, the work and the stature of the Red Cross in the public mind.

When the German conquerors stood on the western shores of Europe, from the North Sea to the southernmost ports of France, the United States stopped being neutral. The first means at hand for direct action was the Red Cross. In work that differed only in method it became again the advance agent of support to future allies as it had in 1916 and 1917.

Money in this case became the tangible symbol, and the Red Cross the agent. The Red Cross made the hard and ruthless decision that now, in mid-1940, it could no longer operate or send relief to any country occupied by the aggressors; not even to Poland or Finland. The American Red Cross would work only on the side of democracy, where and as the newly aroused American community wanted it to be.

What was the result that shocked and surprised even Washington?

On May 10, the date that Germany launched its crushing attack westward and southward through the Low Countries and France, Norman Davis telegraphed the chapters to launch a $10,000,000 European assistance drive. Ten days later the goal was increased to $20,000,000. Within eight weeks, a surprising record, the fund was oversubscribed.

In the meantime Congress, always sensitive to public feeling, caught the new spirit of public opinion and appropriated $50,000,000, not directly to the Red Cross, but for the purchase of supplies to be distributed by the Red Cross in accordance with the pattern used in the "depression program."

Suddenly the Red Cross, so recently broke, criticized and degraded by the Chinese and Spanish ventures, held $70,000,000 as trustee for relief work among, as the Congressional action stated, "refugee men, women and children who have been driven from their homes or otherwise rendered destitute by hostilities or invasion."

Now the whole operation was as frankly political as a town meeting at election time. But politics was accepted as being on the side of the angels. Again the Red Cross had become in fact the servant of its master, the American people.

While aid was withdrawn from the three small countries where it had been sent, a vital and more far-reaching decision was made. No attempt would be made to send relief supplies into France, Belgium or Holland, as much as American sympathy went out to the peoples of these countries.

In total war it had become the established practice for conquering armies to send back to their own homes everything that could be moved. Supplies sent to Occupied Europe, therefore, would only support the German and Italian war machines.

Instead, the heavy emphasis was laid on relief to England, through contributions to the British Red Cross or the Women's Voluntary Services for Civilian Defense. The money went into nurseries for bombed-out children, for hot meals in the bomb shelters and medical supplies and clothing for general distribution among victims of the blitz.

For a while, when southern France still remained unoccupied, supplies went to French refugees there, not much but as much as shipping could handle; and bits and pieces got to the British Middle East, even China.

But soon even the relief program, large as it appeared by comparison with attitudes of such recent memory, became dwarfed in Red Cross operations by challenges closer to home.

Defense preparations, beginning with the draft calls of 1940, began also to mobilize the Red Cross again into its traditional wartime role—now in greatly modified form but in modern dress even more formidable, because by now the Red Cross held a recognized monopoly of responsibility that had not existed in many fields in 1917.

III

In 1940 the Red Cross in effect held a contract with the Army and Navy which constituted the anomaly of a vacuum packed with dynamite. The "vacuum" was clear-cut recognition at last that in event of a future war it would be the only organization recognized as the agency of communication between civilians and the services; no longer would it be linked in cooperative work with the Y.M.C.A. or any other relief or fraternal organization. In other words, it would—and the leadership had been most energetic in getting this monopoly— have all the responsibility, and would have to shoulder all of the inevitable criticism.

In the end, it might be noted, the Red Cross did not have in practice the monopoly, but it most assuredly cornered all the criticism.

But there was the question of what the Red Cross was to do with the great prestige prize, in cooperation with the most highly developed military machine the United States was ever to muster.

Modern military development, even when it still existed only on paper and covered a few scattered forces in 1939, had the highest standards of medical and hospital care; so the older structure of Red Cross ambulance units and base hospitals had become outmoded. All service nurses as well as doctors now were commissioned officers in the Army and Navy; the Red Cross still maintained a recruiting roster but it neither enlisted nor supported nurses or doctors. Industrial production planned for military use was so vastly increased over the 1918 level that there seemed no possibility of any future need for 800,000 women industriously knitting, sewing and making bandages. Even recreation in ambitious scope figured in the military plans—on paper.

Faced with this changing world, the Red Cross as early as 1934 had set up a committee to study how it could be of service in case of another war. As late as the first half of 1940 this planning group foresaw only a very limited Red Cross role, primarily Home Service and Hospital Service, and possibly the procurement of some "comfort" supplies for camps and hospitals to assist the work of the Field Directors who would be assigned to them.

In the atmosphere of popular thought as it existed in the 1930s, it was impossible for the Red Cross to make any public display, either nationally or through the chapters, of preparations for emergency activities. Consequently, there could not be any of the publicity that would help to build up financial reserves.

In fact, while the Red Cross continued through 1941 to collect great sums for its operations overseas—great compared with its poverty domestic budget—it was running badly in the red, eating up its reserves, in order to do quietly those things that needed to be done in the United States. In 1940 there were reports that Chairman Davis was considering abolition of services to veterans of the 1917–18 war as an economy measure.

The fall of France changed all of this cautious attitude, but not immediately. Furthermore, France fell after the fund campaign had been set in 1940, leaving the Red Cross on the ragged edge of means when mobilization of the large Army was begun late in 1940, and yet unable at the time to make a special funds drive.

Remember that the Selective Training and Service Act was passed in September, 1940. Under its operation, the armed forces expanded in 1941 alone from 425,000 to 2,000,000 men. And now the Civil Defense program, on which secret planning had been started in 1939, became an active operation, with Red Cross participation running into fantastic commitments—training of 100,000 nurses' aides, training of nutrition aides and a first-aid program designed to reach 5 per cent of all persons in municipal governments, industrial establishments and large business corporations.

Here was work for the chapters, but a pressing financial load for the Red Cross. As 200 training camps were set up for the new civilian army, field staffs were assigned to each, to repeat the services performed in World War I. Recreation programs for military camps became a major demand on chapters adjacent to them. Finally, the Army admitted that it could not obtain from industrial producers more than 10 per cent of the surgical bandages called for in planning estimates. In one swoop, the Red Cross agreed to produce 40,000,000 dressings.

The chapters responded as always when the Red Cross has had a genuine job thrust upon it. The 3,700 chapters—now all alive and active—mustered some 2,000,000 volunteer workers in their programs.

The public, too, was beginning to show again that it realized the value of the Red Cross. Despite the fact that even the 1940–41 members-and-funds campaign had to be conducted "under wraps," the subscribing members totaled more than 9,190,000 persons, or almost twice the enrollment of only two years earlier. The Red Cross went into its new operating year with a potential deficit of $2,500,000 after allocation of all the surplus in the General Fund as well as all receipts from contributors in this drive.

Then a new worry related to money did arise, for the first time, involving the relationship of the Red Cross to other welfare agencies.

In this work the writer has no intention of delving into the pros and cons of various types of fund-raising, but this citation represents a milestone in the development of the Red Cross—it is the evidence of the stature of the organization, and of the people who had come to believe in it despite the lassitude and occasional political problems that so threatened its development in the years between the world wars.

In 1941 not everyone was blind to the possibility of involvement by the United States in war. The Red Cross chairman, Norman Davis, who had had probably more experience than any other individual in leading American delegations to "peace conferences," read the foreboding signs. In March, 1941, a special staff committee was created to consider plans either for a national defense campaign or a war fund campaign.

Working also in secret, lest the operation either create fears in the public mind or, worse, lead to charges by others that the Red Cross was warmongering, the Red Cross established a National Advisory Committee as a stand-by agency.

Advising from the background of his distinguished Red Cross service twenty years earlier was Eliot Wadsworth. Now, other and newer faces fitted into the more active roles, but with close echoes to 1917. Thomas W. Lamont accepted the chairmanship of the National Advisory Committee, which closely paralleled the older War Council; Lamont had grown up to a partnership in J. P. Morgan & Co., the same firm that had loaned Henry Davison to the Red Cross. S. Sloan Colt, president of the Bankers Trust Company, accepted the vice chairmanship.

Working with this "outside" committee on plans was a War Fund Campaign Committee, consisting of professionals on the Red Cross

staff. As planning progressed the two committees ran into differences
of opinion regarding the best method of seeking the larger contributions that the Red Cross already was needing badly. Mr. Lamont
recommended that the Red Cross stage, if war came, an immediate
appeal for $25,000,000 as a special supporting fund. The internal
staff thought such a campaign impractical and leaned toward the
opinion that the Red Cross should put all of its effort into a greatly
broadened regular annual appeal.

Meanwhile, outside of Red Cross circles there was a growing movement among community chests for planning one "wartime campaign"
in which the public would be asked to make one smashing contribution that would support all welfare activities "for the duration."
This position was understandable on the part of the local organizations. In time of war, when the public is inclined to give overwhelming
support to national welfare organizations, it ceases to regard in the
same light the smaller units.

Now, the Red Cross leadership felt that the movement by the community chests represented only another tack in their longtime effort
to unite local appeals with the national ones by big organizations, a
position most strongly opposed up to then by the Red Cross.

The debate became so bitter and the positions so irreconcilable that
the issue was referred directly to President Roosevelt. On June 6,
1941, he made a statement that has stood ever since as a forceful extension of the Red Cross charter:

> The American Red Cross occupies a unique place as a popu-
> larly supported yet semi-government agency, acting in accord-
> ance with the Treaty of Geneva and under a charter from the
> Congress. Its services to the armed forces, its responsibilities in
> time of disaster and its foreign relief require that it act promptly
> and fully in time of emergency. It must continue to be the agent
> of the popular will and the reliance of the government. It must
> have mobility and freedom of action. . . .
>
> I, therefore, heartily endorse the action of the Central Com-
> mittee of the Red Cross in maintaining freedom to conduct a
> Roll Call for its annual membership and freedom to launch a
> campaign for funds to meet needs in disaster and in time of na-
> tional emergency.

Freedom of action was established for the Red Cross beyond challenge. Chairman Davis decided to adopt the plan of the staff committee for the 1941 campaign, rather than to ask the public for a special fund. The Red Cross hoped for, but did not ask for, the sum of $25,000,000.

It raised somewhat less, but its membership did balloon to the point of 15,000,000.

18

1941–45—The Deluge

O N THE EVENING OF December 7, 1941, the busiest spot in the United States was the closely guarded White House in Washington. Yet one of the callers admitted that evening to a personal conference with the President was Norman Davis, chairman of the Red Cross.

Pearl Harbor had put the American Red Cross again into the perspective of its great original conception, although evolution had ironically robbed it of the opportunity or need to fill the role on the battlefields for which it had been founded exactly sixty years earlier.

While Davis talked with the President, coded cables brought immediate word of Red Cross activities on the job where war had first struck.

From Honolulu—In the blackout of the first tense night after the bombings a temporary Red Cross canteen served coffee and sandwiches to civilian defense workers. During the night a canteen with larger facilities, manned by volunteers on twelve-hour shifts, began operating in the basement of Iolani Palace. From there Motor Corps volunteers went out with meals to radio and telephone operators, and other persons who could not leave vital posts. There were forty Red Cross women driving through the blacked-out and wreckage-strewn area. Three thousand women and children were evacuated from ruined areas on that first night, with the last one bedded down elsewhere at 3:00 A.M. Surgical dressings and blood plasma from Red

Cross stores were sent in a constant stream of deliveries to hospitals where the terrible toll of wounded was taken. (Who wondered now about the fears of a year earlier as to whether the Red Cross would have a job to do in the event of war?)

From Manila, where the Philippine Red Cross then was a branch of the American Red Cross, leadership was taken in the evacuation of 80,000 persons from Manila. Ten emergency hospitals manned by volunteer doctors and nurses were established. When the Army exhausted a "six-months' supply" of surgical dressings in two days, the Red Cross provided what was needed. When the Japanese landed and General Douglas MacArthur moved the main American forces to Bataan, he asked the Philippine Red Cross, its members already doomed to eventual abandonment altogether, to find means to send away his wounded left in a hospital in Manila. On December 31, just three days before Manila fell, the little Red Cross ship *Mactan,* an inter-island steamer, got under way with 224 Army casualties from that hospital to miraculously reach Sydney, Australia, four weeks later. By that time the Philippine Red Cross existed only in name as the Japanese invaders burned, pillaged and smashed their way through the Philippines.

Yet despite that background, inexplicable as it seems at this writing, the American Red Cross felt even after Pearl Harbor that perhaps its place, its responsibilities, and above all public understanding of its role, were limited.

The Red Cross that had boldly raised more than $100,000,000 in its first fund campaign after the outbreak of World War I, when all hostilities were more than 3,000 miles removed from American lives or property, now was enmeshed in an attitude of fearful conservatism. Seeing its role as small, primarily that of messenger boy between the troops and civilians, it seemed to lose for a moment the grand conception of its being.

On December 12, 1941, with the usual endorsing announcement by the President of the United States, the Red Cross asked the public to contribute $50,000,000 to a war-service fund. It asked for a war that directly involved the United States in blood from its start only half the sum it asked in 1917, for a smaller war involving a much smaller and less opulent country.

The $50,000,000 was presumed sufficient to carry the Red Cross through its first year of war. A group of banking advisers had decided that "the general economic and tax situation" had dulled the public response to Red Cross appeals; that the public would feel that the government which collected the swollen taxes ought to take over. James K. McClintock, vice president in charge of finances, backed by Norman Davis but openly criticized by some of the professional staff of the Red Cross, had said before Pearl Harbor:

"We should 'throw out the window' any idea that the Red Cross can raise three hundred or four hundred million dollars . . . we should go out for fifty million dollars and be smart enough to make it do for our program."

Despite this lukewarm approach, reflected alike in national planning and in the chapters, the goal was exceeded.

Goals were progressively raised as the job given to the Red Cross expanded into a world-wide support welcomed by the armed forces, but hesitancy marked the whole series of campaigns. These were for $125,000,000 in 1943, and $200,000,000 each in 1944 and 1945. Every goal was oversubscribed; in the four years of the war the Red Cross was given by the American people a total of $666,510,000.

Afterward much was made, publicity-wise, of this total constituting "the greatest free-will offering in history." The public gave all that was asked, and considerably more. And in 1945, membership, representing all individuals who gave one dollar or more, totaled 36,645,000, or more than one-fourth of the total population of the country. What this meant was graphically stated in a report made late in 1945:

> No other single cause save that of the country itself has received contributions that approach such magnitude. The membership is greater than the votes cast by either of our political parties in the 1944 Presidential election or than the membership of any of our great religious faiths. In addition [the Red Cross] has some 19,900,000 junior members. Its 3,757 chapters and 5,785 branches reach into every hamlet and into the nooks and crannies of the most rural, desert or mountainous countries.

Then why this conservatism?

In retrospect, the answer is simple, and has been restated by a re-formed Red Cross itself many times. Actually, in World War II the structure of the Red Cross, from National Headquarters through the dominant chapters, was out-of-date. It rested on the assumption that social position and wealth were the criteria of leadership. The public—including the now great labor unions, the groups of middle-income families in communities, the masses making up the hard substance of the United States—had for the most part no voice or opportunity for leadership in the Red Cross.

By the time World War II started, the Red Cross actually was at the breaking point with organized labor, and community chests considered the Red Cross a predatory competitor for the public's gifts. In the midst of the war the Red Cross had to reach agreements equivalent to treaties with organized labor to head off competing war-service fund drives by the latter, and President Roosevelt had to intervene again in the Red Cross–community chest controversy by issuing an order (as president of the Red Cross) *forbidding* the Red Cross to participate in joint fund-raising campaigns.

The World War II job of the Red Cross, as even its severest critics concur, was done well and conscientiously. But it was done by a leadership so boxed in by precedent and circumstances that, while doing its job overseas and at the chapter level, it also had to fight a defensive action.

In the meantime, the leadership remained vested in the traditional groups of volunteers, whose job was made harder by tradition. Successive fund chairmen after Colt were Walter S. Gifford, Leon Fraser and Colby M. Chester. Harvey D. Gibson, who had been general manager and Commissioner to France in World War I, returned to Great Britain as Commissioner, from where he supervised all Red Cross operations in the European Theater.

Organizational training within the ranks of the Red Cross staff now paid off, as James L. Fieser was made vice chairman at large, the senior post then open to professional staff, and new vice chairmen were created for Junior Red Cross and Personnel Relations, Areas Offices and Chapter Service, Public Relations and other domestic services.

As unassigned volunteers, there came back actively into the picture Eliot Wadsworth and Cornelius N. Bliss, along with new and prominent faces such as George L. Harrison and Lloyd B. Wilson, Landon K. Thorne and Nelson Dean Jay.

On the fringes of the Red Cross, however, there came a new face, of the same social breed and very wealthy, but in an extraordinary job. This man was manager of the North Atlantic Area, where he worked through the war exactly as a staff executive with the sole difference that he received no pay check. He battled with fund-raising and procurement problems, and negotiated for endless hours with the leaders of groups excluded from Red Cross leadership. He learned a lot.

The individual was E. Roland Harriman, brother of Averell Harriman, wartime ambassador and future governor of New York. Roland Harriman was preparing for a unique place in Red Cross history. He had inherited his mother's great interest in the Red Cross, and now he would lead the Red Cross into a new concept of itself and reorganization to fit its place in modern American life.

II

Each progressive stage of World War II found the role of the Red Cross expanding far beyond any contemplation of it in prewar planning. Before the war was ended it was neck-deep in new ventures never even dreamed of prior to the outbreak of hostilities.

The work of the Red Cross throughout these four years seems, in the perspective of time, to have been overglamorized, exaggerated and misunderstood—sometimes maliciously criticized. But nothing can detract from the facts that it was good, it was necessary, and its response to need went far beyond any duty or obligation. There might be wrangles over policy, but there was no hesitation in "doing those things which ought to be done" and as much more as was requested by the military.

While the role of the Red Cross at the start of the war lacked the headline-making features of establishment of base hospitals and shipment of great numbers of medical personnel and canteen workers overseas, otherwise it must have looked to the middle-aged volunteers like a duplication of 1917–18.

Hospital Service and Home Service and Field Service, manned in many cases by persons entering their second war operation, sprang to life. In each case the demands far exceeded expectations of any advance planning. And chapters found themselves again immersed in the old tasks. Very few were out of striking distance of expanding camps or hospitals. The old need for bandages patiently rolled and

trimmed by hand arose again. To these activities were now added two
others that had hardly existed at all in the short and victorious march
of the troops overseas in 1918.

One was Blood Service. The others were the heart-rending and
questioning one called Prisoners of War and Next-of-Kin Service.

In World War I there had been no Blood Service, or even a definition of the term. In World War I there had been no American prisoners of war in this new sense of the word. In fact, only aged persons
with recollections of the Civil War could recall a time when many
thousands of Americans had been in military stockades or prisons
such as Andersonville.

But this war started with prisoners, from the day that Bataan fell,
and—owing to fortunate pilot operations prior to Pearl Harbor—it
started with the Blood Service, which cut the loss of life from wounds
and shock immeasurably compared with that of previous wars.

As the war progressed, there were added to these activities Club and
Canteen Services overseas, plus wide extension of financial assistance
to servicemen and their families. Yes, the Red Cross became busy
beyond its prewar imagination. But before broadening out the picture,
let's take a quick look at the one unique development of this war's
experience—*Blood*.

III

One statistic highlights the Blood story: In World War II the American Red Cross collected from 6,660,000 American volunteers 13,-
300,000 pints of blood for the armed services. Later it collected
961,000 units for the military during the Korean War, and millions of
donations have been collected during that period and since for civilians.
But such capabilities did not happen overnight.

Back in 1929, it is recorded, the Birmingham, Alabama, chapter
suggested as a Red Cross activity the establishment of a transfusion
service. The idea came to life in a pilot program in 1937 in Augusta,
Georgia, when that chapter recruited individuals for referral to the
University of Georgia Hospital, where they were typed and registered.
A dozen other chapters imitated this lead.

In 1940, there started in New York, a "Plasma for Britain" project
—the extraction of plasma from whole blood having become by then
an established practice. Plasma did not do the job as well as transfu-

sions of real blood, but it was far better than none at all, particularly in alleviating shock during the hours that might elapse between injuries or wounds and removal of patients to proper hospitals. The New York Chapter worked with the Blood Transfusion Betterment Association on this pilot project, and a few other chapters followed suit.

Before the end of 1940 the Red Cross approved in principle the establishment of a Red Cross Medical Health and Advisory Committee, and in January of 1941 accepted an invitation by the Army and Navy to go ahead with organization of Blood-Donor Services.

The fantastic build-up, and the public response to the blood program, is a shining beacon in American history. To say it mushroomed is an understatement. It is a record of fact that never was the Red Cross, as collecting agent from volunteers, short in meeting requests from the armed forces.

During World War II, General of the Army Dwight D. Eisenhower was moved to say: "If I could reach all America, there is one thing I would like to do—thank them for blood plasma and for whole blood. It has been a tremendous thing."

While the American people deserve the credit for contributing the blood, the Red Cross alone can claim credit for the organization and distribution—establishment of a whole new "industry" involving every phase of handling a commodity so perishable that perfect refrigeration in handling, transit and storage is imperative. National Headquarters organized and paid principally for the project out of its funds, but the chapters did the work.

Speaking of costs, the entire Red Cross expense for World War II blood was $15,870,000. Here again was the story of the volunteer providing mass help for work under the direction of and alongside the skilled professional.

Thirty-five of the largest Red Cross chapters became Army-Navy Blood Donor Centers with laboratories and facilities complete for all types of blood procurement and handling. From these radiated at the peak of operations 63 mobile units—self-contained collection centers on specially built trucks, manned by doctors, nurses and technicians— that made visits by pre-arrangement to smaller chapters, some 2,200 of them.

The blood program involved a paid staff of 2,285 doctors, nurses and technicians, and with them worked an estimated 25,000 volunteers when the program hit its full stride. There is no estimate of the time or money represented by cooperating groups, some 20,000 business firms and labor, religious, civic and other organizations who rounded up donors, provided space and facilities for blood-collection centers, and all the other details of such a cooperative movement.

What did this program mean at the other ends of the lines—the countless ends as fighting fanned out over the world? The answers are graphic; here are a few samples:

From a Navy surgeon's report from the Pacific: "Six thousand units of plasma went ashore at Tarawa, and 4,000 of them came back in the veins of wounded Marines. At least half of the seriously wounded owe their lives to plasma."

Report by the Surgeon General of the Navy: "Only one per cent of the Navy personnel wounded in the Pacific died, thanks in large part to plasma." (Author's note: In World War I approximately 5 per cent of the wounded died.)

Report by the Surgeon General of the Army: "Plasma ranked first as the foremost life-saver used by the Army Medical Corps in North Africa."

Down in New Guinea, one of the remotest war areas, the Army forces involved finally named a hard-contested hill "Plasma Ridge." And as one added note, when the invasion of Normandy finally occurred, plasma was dropped by parachute to evacuation hospitals on that bloody shore.

With galloping swiftness, scientific research developed in the blood field under the pressure of war. From liquid plasma came development of dried plasma that could be shipped more easily and swiftly and to more outlying stations. By the end of the war whole blood was being delivered and used for transfusions within the critical period of two weeks during which it could be preserved.

Equally important as the war usage was the foundation laid for subsequent peacetime development, both technologically and scientifically —the unlocking of the secrets of fibrinogen and other by-products that are writing their own chapters in other histories of great developments.

To keep this record free from charges of withholding of recorded information, it must be noted that one controversy that gravely shook the Red Cross arose over the "color line" in blood. By public demand, as registered with the military, blood was labeled as to race of the donor so that, to put it nicely, a recipient might receive blood from a member of his own race.

This caused a furious outcry by Negro leaders, who cited unanimous opinions among experts that there is no racial difference in blood.

Chairman Davis finally had to issue public statements to the effect that the Red Cross was following its mandate from the Army and Navy, that it was not the responsibility of the Red Cross "to try to settle racial controversies."

In retrospect it appears that the Red Cross could have taken no other course.

IV

Now to turn to *Prisoners of War*, in a brief description that cannot hope either to portray their plight or the gigantic efforts made to assist them, but only hint at it.

In this description it is recognized that time has healed most of the scars of war, but this cannot be used as an excuse to gloss over the downright savagery to which many American prisoners of war were exposed, particularly the thousands who fell into the hands of the Japanese.

Considering the other factors involved, the record indicates that prisoners in the hands of the Germans fared on the average as well as could be expected in a bitterly contested war; those in the hands of the Japanese were treated in a manner that always will be incomprehensible to the Western mind.

The Japanese cared nothing about their own men who were captured; they bothered as little about their own prisoners, seemed in fact intent on accentuating conditions that would obliterate them. And yet some few supplies for prisoners did get through to Japanese corrals. In this picture there is no definite black or white. In summary, none of the 115,000 American servicemen who fell alive into the enemy's hands had a very happy experience.

Treatment of prisoners of war has been a major provision of the Geneva Convention since its inception, with occasional attempts to modernize practices in the light of a presumed increase in general civilized practices. On paper the progressive program had looked good.

One Convention framed in 1899 was accepted by forty-three nations; the exceptions among major powers being Russia, which did not sign it at all, and Japan, which refused to ratify it. The Japanese government was equally disinterested in a modernization of this Convention in 1929. But in World War II, everything possible had to be tried.

In general the Convention regarding prisoners of war is an agreement that prisoners shall be humanely treated and properly housed and fed, that officers shall not be required to do manual labor, that neutral observers may observe and report on camp conditions and list prisoners, and that certain designated supplies may be forwarded to prisoners on both sides.

In all of this work the International Red Cross Committee is designated as the operating agency. Supplies for prisoners are the responsibility of their governments, but the various national Red Cross Societies do the collecting and forwarding. The same channels serve families of prisoners who may send, under the Convention, certain personal comforts in limited quantities. In World War II, total supplies valued at $168,000,000 went to our prisoners (nearly 200,000 tons). But of this great quantity only $3,000,000 worth could be sent to American prisoners in Japan.

The job of the American Red Cross was one of organization, collection and delivery, and finally the setting up of a production line for supply cartons in Philadelphia. But even so the cost to Red Cross contributors, representing fringe expense, approximated $6,000,000.

Here is a thumbnail sketch of what was done:

Operational and directing headquarters for the vast prisoner-of-war network, which included a total of 1,300,000 Allied prisoners of war, was at Geneva. This committee acted primarily as agent for two countries: Great Britain, which attempted to maintain its own prisoners as the United States was later to do; and this country. As we became involved in the war, America also sent great quantities of food to French, Yugoslavian, Belgian and Polish prisoners in Germany.

The basic food package for a prisoner in Europe was a little box 10 inches square and 4½ inches deep, complying with German postal regulations. Its weight could not exceed eleven pounds. These boxes were packed with supplies intended to supplement prison diets—a fair sample containing raisins, liver paté, soluble coffee, corned beef, sugar, dried milk, oleomargarine, biscuits, orange concentrate, cheese, canned salmon or tuna fish, chocolate bars, cigarettes and soap.

Various supplements could be sent by the Red Cross, including special invalid foods for sick or wounded men, medicine kits planned to meet the needs of men in groups of 100 for one month, vitamin pills, toilet articles and clothing. Clothes, toilet articles and comfort kits might occasionally be sent by relatives of the prisoners through the Red Cross.

Here was a problem of business organization and nationwide communication rather than welfare work. It tested the efficiency of the business management of the Red Cross. After a period in which the parcels of food were purchased from manufacturers, the Red Cross set up assembly plants, the first one in Philadelphia, where packing was done by volunteers.

In the meantime, vessels eventually totaling nine were purchased or chartered in the name of the International Red Cross Committee to ship the great quantities of materials.

It is a pleasant footnote to the war record that not one of these ships—sailing under full lights in blacked-out oceans and radioing their positions constantly—was ever deliberately attacked by the enemy in the course of 127 crossings of the Atlantic. Three were struck accidentally in aerial bombings in the Mediterranean, one being sunk.

Early in the war, prisoner-of-war supplies for Europe were unloaded in Lisbon, Portugal, and sent by rail to Geneva, Switzerland, from which point they entered Germany in truck convoys under the Red Cross flag. When European transport became clogged in 1944, arrangements were made for the supply ships to unload at Göteborg, Sweden, whence they were ferried behind German mine sweepers to Lübeck, Germany.

After the surrender of Germany, convoys of supplies were rushed across the borders from every direction, but up until then the movements were closely restricted.

The International Red Cross, fortunately operating from the neutral ground of Switzerland, mustered a small army of its own to do the prisoner-of-war job, a total of about 5,000 persons, mostly volunteers from neutral nations. These ranged from neutral bankers and businessmen in the occupied countries, who acted as inspectors of camps, to truck drivers and warehousemen, operators of a complex communications network and—as Germany began to fall apart—virtually a law-and-order brigade.

Strangely enough, in the light of past hates and fears engendered by the Nazi nightmare, the postwar roundup of prisoner reports gave the Germans a passable if poor reputation in general. Prisoners of war, except in isolated instances of human sadism, were treated as persons rather than animals by the Germans. There was no comparison between the manner in which the German Army treated its wards and that in which the Hitler legions treated their own fellow citizens in concentration camps.

True, food rations to prisoners were short, normally down to the 1,500 calories a day necessary as a minimum for health. Often as relief packages arrived the rations were cut proportionately. But that might be considered as normal, as well as the overcrowding and disorganization that came in the later months of the war.

On the better side, the International Red Cross was enabled by the German Army to collect and dispatch much accurate information about American prisoners, the state of their health, and other news, and to keep its files and those of our own government up-to-date as to the location of each, within the limits of human possibility. The food package or comfort article consigned to Private Smith, a prisoner, was delivered in most cases to Private Smith precisely where he was imprisoned.

True, the American prisoners captured in Europe were subjected to hardship, but those taken by the Japanese from the Philippines, from units that from time to time were lost in the Pacific, and the mounting hundreds of fliers who in an attacking war must, in forced landings, go into the hands of the enemy—those were in hell.

The Japanese refused even to name the location of many of their prison camps, scattered as they were through southeastern Asia, the Philippines, Java, Thailand and Burma. The Swiss Legation in Tokyo, acting for the Red Cross, was able to locate some of the camps in Japan, but very few. No neutral observers were allowed to see most of the compounds.

Repeatedly the International Red Cross negotiated to get supplies through to the prisoners, and even to learn who and where they were. A few supplies did get through, but so pitifully few. As one example, there is the report from a Red Cross worker in the Philippines, taken after the fall of Bataan and afterward transferred to a civilian internment camp at Santo Tomas.

After almost two years of detention, the group at Santo Tomas
received a shipment of food parcels, enough to provide four for each
person. These were the first and last ever received there. The prisoners
were receiving from the Japanese about one-fourth the minimum diet
required to sustain life. They organized their parcels, which included
food, small quantities of medicine and blood plasma, to last them for
a year. Under such discipline they survived, to report: "We rationed
out the supplies to last us a year and without that small supplement
to our diet, many would have died of starvation or malnutrition. . . .
In many cases we administered the blood plasma as a substitute for
food."

V

The single word *Recreation* chalked up in the Red Cross responsibilities for the armed forces in World War II turned into the biggest
project in the history of the Red Cross. Hardly noted in preliminary
planning prior to 1941, and its World War I pattern apparently superseded by the development of the Army's Special Services organization,
it became a bogey and finally a Red Cross triumph. But here again,
because of lack of imagination somewhere, all had to be learned the
hard way.

Or can plans be made for sudden transformation of what is basically a welfare organization into a staff of hotelkeepers, restaurateurs,
club operators and crews running hundreds of mobile restaurants?
The old saying, "You never know till you try," held good here a
thousand times over in the experience of 5,000 amateurs—the Red
Cross overseas staff. They tried, and they did.

Recreation work meant as many different types of activities as there
were theaters of operation. These were as different as locales where the
war was fought. Their facilities ran the gamut of the types and places
where Americans served the world over.

The Rainbow Corner Club in London served as many as 60,000
meals in twenty-four hours to GIs on leave, and its quarters featured
every facility of a fine hotel. But it was no more appreciated, or important to the individual GI, than a tent pitched on Guadalcanal and

furnished principally with a phonograph and a couple of writing tables. Or the station wagon converted into a creaky clubmobile that wheeled out into the desert to serve 3,000 doughnuts and hot coffee (accompanied by the smiles of American girls) to 1,500 sun-blackened and beaten men being hauled in a crowded French freight train away from the debacle of Kasserine Pass.

The "marching orders" for the Red Cross Recreational Services were fairly simple. Wherever the Army, Navy, Marines or Air Force operated, the Red Cross was expected to be. And that included clubmobiles on the Stilwell Road linking India and China, remote desert outposts and jungle islands. It included likewise hopping of the Mediterranean for the invasion of Italy and monumental work in following the liberating forces to Europe.

At home, operated by the chapters, it meant clubs, "day rooms," snack bars and all the recreation facilities that could be devised for troops in transit, and everywhere "on-post" clubs and "off-post" clubs in leave areas—all the way from Hawaii around the Southern Hemisphere through Australia to Egypt. It meant also the eventual operation of a string of motion-picture projectors, completely supplied with films for regular program changes, for a combined audience of more than 1,000,000 men a month.

As always, it meant in addition almost incalculable supplies of cigarettes, magazines, writing paper, sheets and towels, and furnishings and plumbing.

And it was not all rest area work, either. At Iwo Jima, the bloodbath volcanic island where 20,000 Americans were casualties in twenty-six days of fighting, a field director was with them; and eighty-nine Red Cross personnel landed on bloody Okinawa.

At no place was fighting so severe, either, that the home problems of the soldiers could be forgotten or put aside by field directors for another time. Family complications, financial problems and the vagaries of life follow men even into combat. So while the new "business" of recreation grew and grew like Topsy, the older business of military welfare service made ever increasing demands as the forces overseas grew.

One thing about its role the Red Cross particularly grew to dread. This was the always recurring requests by soldiers for emergency home leave because of some real or fancied—and in a few instances fabricated—crisis. It was written earlier how the Military Service and Home Service of the Red Cross worked from field director to home chapter to investigate and report back on such cases; not to recommend military action but to report the facts. This created in the end unfavorable public relations that the Red Cross never has been able to explain away.

One American who was a company officer first in China and then in Korea frankly described how the system worked from the Army standpoint as he saw and practiced it.

"When there was a favorable report and a man was getting what he wanted," he said, "I'd call him in and say, 'We're mighty glad to do this for you, old man.' But when we got the report that he was exaggerating or lying and that command upstairs had refused leave request, we'd say, 'Too bad, the Red Cross says you don't rate it.' It worked swell for us both ways."

To sum it up, in this overseas activity that nonplused Headquarters at home, and which amounted to a world-wide American Red Cross before the firing ceased in 1945, there came into being 1,800 recreational facilities overseas staffed by 5,000 Red Cross paid workers and about 140,000 volunteers. They operated more than 500 on-post clubs and 400 in leave areas. One group operated 75 rest homes for combat fliers alone.

Others served a peak of 190 snack bars and canteens at remote air strips, and teams of girls wheeled 300 mobile canteens into areas where military vehicles were the only other wheeled machines operating over the first highways ever seen by the natives.

VI

Who were the persons doing these things? The civilian men in green uniforms with Red Cross insignia that gave identity but no authority, and the Red Cross "girls" whose recognition too often in after years has consisted of sly jokes about their presumed conduct or imputations of snobbery.

It might be noted that in both the big wars and in Korea, they were individuals who did not have to be there. This is obviously true of the woman whose assignment might be one of the big plush clubs but more likely was a remote snack bar in the desert or on a jungle island. But it is equally true of the male field directors and their assistants.

The Red Cross policy is that this service must never be a shield for the slacker or the young man seeking sheltered duty. Such younger men as wore the Red Cross uniform—the same younger men who landed with troops at Iwo Jima (where one found a welcome box of ocarinas in his supplies), on Cape Gloucester, on Normandy Beach and a hundred other places—might well have held in good conscience civilian jobs back home. The older and slightly paunchy men who made up the bulk of the male Red Cross personnel were capable of passing a rather strict physical examination, but as often as not they already had long since passed the draft age, and their contemporaries in military uniform were securely kept out of harm's reach by military orders.

The Red Cross "girls" were women, not children, perhaps mostly anxious for adventure, but willing to take what went with it—all pledged to go where they were sent—and they were sent literally everywhere. This included even "over the Hump" into China, where one unit of three women with club equipment including a piano was sent in response to General Stilwell's urgent request for recreational assistance for his hard-pressed men at Chungking.

When the Stilwell Road was finally opened, eight clubmobiles plied its length, setting a record in one day by serving 15,000 snacks to the men there.

All little things, yes, but in the aggregate such big things.

Let the record also show what so often is forgotten or overlooked. Neither the American Red Cross as an organization nor the individuals in it decided where clubs or clubmobiles or recreation centers should be placed, or whether these should be exclusively for officers, or mixed clubs used by officers and men alike. The military authorities requested each facility and designated its type. From 1942 onward, the Red Cross had to sprint to keep up with requests; never was it in the position of trying to advance its own position.

And it was the military authority, not the Red Cross, that decreed two regulations that have been among the hardest things the Red Cross has had to try to live down since World War II.

One involves money and the other involves the "girls."

As for the money criticism, apparently the report will never die that the Red Cross "sold things"—coffee, doughnuts, cigarettes—that had been purchased with funds contributed at home in order that these might be distributed free to the troops overseas. There were cases where the Red Cross did, and here is the reason why:

Soon after American forces began arriving in large numbers in the British Isles, military officers reported that relations with the forces of our Allies—both the British and those from occupied countries who had reached Britain and were enrolled in foreign freedom armies— were badly hurt by the great disparity between the pay and benefits of Americans and those of other countries.

One recommendation was that the Red Cross be required to charge token prices for food and tobacco served at canteens. The recommendation became a military order. Thereafter, under orders from the government the Red Cross did charge for such things *at designated recreation centers in leave areas.* But *such charges were not made in combat areas.*

Since there also is a minority of human thought that always likes to retail harmful rumors, many other stories came in the wake of World War II. One instance was the report from the Pacific that soldiers had to pay for blood plasma administered to the wounded. That story apparently will never die, despite repeated publicity that it apparently was based on the authenticated fact that one soldier who had lost heavily shooting craps wrote to his family asking for money to pay his debts, using as an excuse the urgent need for funds to pay for "Red Cross blood."

As for the Red Cross girls, both their morals and their alleged snobbery came under fire. The facts are simple:

1. On the morals issue, it would be absurd to think that some thousands of healthy young women could be suddenly transported from routine lives in normal surroundings to foreign, adventuresome environments—often in places where men outnumbered them by thousands to one—without there being incidents of promiscuity and pregnancy.

There were such instances. No system of screening or physical or psychological examination has yet been devised to determine in advance all the moral and mental quirks of even the most highly selected individuals.

But such Red Cross incidents were so few—and the files on them are most complete—that anyone who regularly reads the articles on sex in the popular magazines, based on studies of normal persons in normal peacetime surroundings, would be amazed at their infrequency.

On the social side, it will be reiterated far into the indefinite future that the "girls" were snobbish and associated socially only with officers. And that is true, for the simple reason that they were so ordered. The Red Cross girl was rated as a civilian in uniform, under military discipline, and the military decreed that she live in her private life in combat areas under the same standards as those set for nurses, all of whom are commissioned officers.

A truer picture of the Red Cross girl is that of her work on duty, when there was no rank in the men for whom she cooked, or organized entertainment, or drove her clubmobile into outer wastes. These things, in this writer's view, shrink into insignificance the occasional picture of the individual assigned for a while to a glamorous city where there might be time or opportunity to put on civilian clothes and go dancing for an evening at a hotel with some officer.

And part of that truer picture is the grim fact which is hardly known—perhaps many critics do not want to know it—that far more than a handful of these Red Cross workers died for their service.

Who stops to remember, if he ever knew, that deaths alone among Red Cross workers defined strictly as killed on duty or died of "service-induced disabilities abroad or soon after return home," total for the four wars in the period of the American Red Cross 283 persons.

Furthermore, there are more names of women than of men on this role of casualties.

Here are the statistics in bald form:

SPANISH-AMERICAN WAR:
>One man killed, transporting medical supplies to El Caney, Cuba.

WORLD WAR I:

Total Red Cross personnel	194
Men	70
Women	124

>(94 nurses, 4 nurses' aides, 2 dieticians, 24 miscellaneous)

WORLD WAR II:

Total Red Cross personnel	86
Men	34
Red Cross girls	52

KOREAN WAR:

Total (both men)	2

Had there been Red Cross nurses in World War II, the figures would undoubtedly have been much larger. As it is, they need no elaboration. But there is one graphic comparison that speaks for itself.

In World Wars I and II, the United States armed forces included a total of 20,467,000 men and women, of whom 533,828 were killed or died in service, a proportion of less than three individuals per 100 enrolled.

In World Wars I and II, the Red Cross paid staff totaled 51,600 —all noncombatants—of whom 280 were killed or died as a result of that service, a proportion of five workers for each 1,000 enrolled.

VII

Here statistics cease. They defeat their own purpose, and besides there is no end to them because when the fighting ceased the Red Cross could not pack up and go home.

Far ahead, beyond the imagination of the most gifted political leaders, there was to stretch an interminable period of military occupation of foreign countries, and recurring crises that, after an initial demobilization, called for reinforcement of areas overseas.

The Red Cross job was to be as indefinite and as inconclusive as the military program in which it held the position of esteemed camp follower. And so it has remained to the time of this recording.

The principal change was that it was to become less glamorous and less exciting, but still stimulating after a fashion to those involved. And all in all, the job created a new tax on the ingenuity of the Red Cross, to do that which was asked of it, to do it with the least amount of criticism and, above all, to find the money after the fever of war-generous giving was past.

Furthermore, once the shooting stopped, the Red Cross found itself with another problem, that of defending itself from criticism for its omissions or commissions in the war, of living down the overselling job that too zealous supporters had done during the war, and a state of mind in veterans that threatened to give it a black eye impossible to heal.

Gradually the American Red Cross awakened to the plain fact that no one seemed to care or appreciate what it had done in the war. Instead of emerging with a pat on the back for coping with millions of unforeseen problems, it found many critics who charged that it had as an organization taken a free ride with the military. And the only vocal veterans were those with real or imagined gripes.

This created a confusion easy to understand, plus what amounted to a guilt complex, immediately after the end of hostilities, over the great surplus of war-collected funds still remaining on hand. Remember that in 1945 a drive had been conducted on the basis of expected protracted war, the invasion of Japan in 1946. The atom bombs dropped on Hiroshima and Nagasaki ended that.

And in the meantime, Norman Davis had died in 1944 and was succeeded by a new type of figure in the American Red Cross, who would head it for five years, both as its last chairman under the old organization and its first president under a new form.

The new leader was Basil O'Connor, former law partner of President Franklin D. Roosevelt, and chairman of the Infantile Paralysis Foundation. While his period of leadership was controversial at times, Chairman O'Connor initiated the civilian blood program and supported the democratization of the Red Cross. He also served without compensation.

19

Realism and Reconversion

AMONG THE NOTABLE casualties of World War II, and one that few mourned or sought to revive, was the "Old Order." Twice before, at the conclusion of wars, the Red Cross had changed its leadership, but in each case the New Guard was simply another group from the same social order. Now the structure was to change as well as the faces.

There is a sentimental and deeply impressive symbolism in the fact that more than half the adult population of the United States were contributing members of the American Red Cross at the close of World War II. It is equally impressive and unbelievable to recall now that no nonreligious organization had a more self-perpetuating leadership than the American Red Cross.

Now, while continuing to meet the needs of its time—without conscious calculation but as an evolution in line with modern political and social development—the American Red Cross changed its whole structure without missing a step in its operating progress. In one self-searching gesture it hurdled the revolutionary change from social-financial dictatorship to democratic organization.

Perhaps that is why it was able to meet the totally unanticipated need of the postwar world of the 1950s. Because the world in which the Red Cross was to work had changed also beyond any possibility of reconstruction to the older pattern.

The speed and relative painlessness with which these changes occurred was due in large part to the new concepts of welfare organizations developing in the public mind. For the Red Cross the action was partially a defensive one, because criticism was raining down upon it —the vicious and often petty criticism of the little minds who hunt for fleas on dogs because they are jealous of the dogs.

Of the criticisms, and the steps taken to counteract them, more a little later. The preparation to face the United States as a responsible and responsive modern organization must come first. Leadership in this realization of the need to act has not been lost in the misty fogs of the past; it is definitely placed. First, as spokesman for the modern American thought, was E. Roland Harriman, the banker and railroad man who had worked in the field alongside the Red Cross staff. Second, giving full support to the work even though it might overturn all of his prior ideas, was Chairman Basil O'Connor.

What was the Red Cross organization at the end of World War II, as it went into "reconversion to peace" in 1946?

It rested, first of all under the 1905 charter, upon an organization of sixty-five persons known as incorporators. These incorporators were self-perpetuating; when one dropped out or died, the remainder chose his or her successor.

The Central Committee so often referred to in this chronicle consisted of eighteen persons. Under the old charter it was the governing body of the Red Cross, holding "all powers of government, direction and management."

The incorporators chose six persons. The President of the United States named six members, of whom one was the chairman of the Red Cross and the others were ex officio from the Departments of State, War, Navy, Treasury and Justice.

Finally, six members of the Central Committee were chosen by the chapters, but unbelievable as it seems now there was no machinery by which the chapters elected their six members. It simply was provided that these places were to be filled at annual meetings of delegates of chapters held each December, not at the spring convention of the chapter delegates. Now, with 3,750 chapters, *any fifteen delegates from chapters* could constitute a quorum for election of the six members representing chapters on the Central Committee, and each person so chosen could hold this powerful prestige office for three years.

Usually, the Central Committee turned its authority over to an Executive Committee, or a smaller group of itself, consisting of only nine members. But any nine of the eighteen who happened to be present could act as the Executive Committee.

The upshot of the whole scheme was: (1) the five government officials appointed by the President of the United States, being busy members of the government, seldom attended any meetings, and some none whatsoever; (2) the six chapter delegates were residents of remote cities and only occasionally were even three of them available for emergency meetings; (3) the six incorporator members, consisting primarily of persons living in or near Washington, always held the controlling vote on policies, appropriations and major decisions. And not even the President could question or remove an incorporator.

It is small wonder that the Central Committee, facing a new crisis, accepted the advice of the group headed by Harriman and, with O'Connor's backing, took a long look at itself and the accessory string of titles built up for its own exclusive group. These titles themselves were confusing.

From time to time, there has been mention of Red Cross vice presidents. These were honorary, as was the presidency itself held by the U.S. President. On the other hand, the chairman was the chief executive officer, serving at the pleasure of the President but, as we have seen, appointed for life. None was ever removed from office. Confusion began at the level of the vice chairmen, because these were the working executives of the Red Cross, almost always paid officers and with direct responsibilities in fields of operation.

On March 4, 1946, Chairman O'Connor set up a twenty-seven-member Advisory Committee on Organization, with Harriman as chairman. The committee, with the exception of two members who never attended meetings, rendered a unanimous report on June 11, and by September 16 the Central Committee had amended the report in some details and accepted the whole program. The recommendations of the Red Cross for reforming itself were so obviously right that a new charter was adopted as law by Congress without debate in either the House or Senate. Thus the Red Cross, almost overnight in relationship to its age, achieved the three goals set for the 1946 study:

1. That the Red Cross will truly represent the nation that it serves.

2. That the governing organization will truly represent, and be responsive to, the entire membership of the Red Cross.

3. That the organization structure of the Red Cross will lend itself to the most effective possible handling of the programs and activities of the Red Cross.

The President of the United States became the honorary chairman, with the right to name the chairman and 8 members of a new Board of Directors, reflecting the enlargement of major Cabinet offices. The big change came in the selection of 42 other members of the Board. Of these, 30 were thereafter to be elected by chapters at the annual conventions, in successive blocks of 10, for three-year terms. Each slate of candidates also must represent various geographical areas. Finally, these 30, plus the President's 8, were to choose 12 members from among persons of national stature as members at large. These were to be representative of broad national interest. Appointees are divided among labor, the sciences, arts and professions.

At the same time the Red Cross went under administration of a president instead of a chairman, and the administrative officers became vice presidents, as in other corporations, headed by an executive vice president and general manager—a post filled then and still held in 1958 by a Red Cross professional veteran, James T. Nicholson.

One more change was made in 1954, when the affairs of the Red Cross finally were recognized as needing the full-time service of a president, separate from the position of chairman and "principal officer." With that revision the office of president, created in 1946, became again the chairmanship, and the Red Cross installed a full-time president.

The new operating head of the Red Cross became a full-time official without relationship to his own personal means. He was elected by the Board of Governors. As its first president under the new order Ellsworth Bunker, corporation executive and former Ambassador to Argentina, became president. When he resigned to accept the offer of the ambassadorship to India, he was succeeded by General Alfred M. Gruenther.

In the meantime, since 1950, when Basil O'Connor retired, the "new Red Cross," had been headed by two men.

General of the Army George C. Marshall served as president from

October 1, 1949 to December 1, 1950. Thereafter, the architect of the modern organization, E. Roland Harriman, was called to the leadership, first as president from December 1, 1950, until January 1, 1954, and until this writing as "Chairman of the Red Cross and its Principal Officer."

With the old order, particularly the female domination of the organization, long a thing of the past, these three men—O'Connor, Marshall and Harriman—have reconstructed the Red Cross in a manner incomprehensible to its former leaders. Some of the reconstruction has been due to new ideas of business administration. More is the result of a changed pattern of requirements in keeping with the stature of the Red Cross.

It became after World War II the "big" welfare organization. Never again could it become small in the new atmosphere in which it worked.

II

After World War I the Red Cross had virtually collapsed, as far as need for its activities was recognized in the public mind. No such shocking decline came in 1946. Despite the criticisms and the slanders, the public in general continued to support the Red Cross, to contribute generously to it and to expect its services.

Some of the postwar confidence undoubtedly was made possible by the wholesale reorganization, and such things as bringing spokesmen for the great labor unions, the American Federation of Labor and the Congress of Industrial Organizations, onto Board membership alongside other outstanding leaders, not only from finance and the law but from journalism, education and—most importantly—the chapters.

Much of the atmosphere of a surviving healthy organization surrounded the tremendous job thrust upon the Red Cross with demobilization.

Most of the mobile canteens were brought back from abroad, and the great majority of the overseas hotels and restaurants were closed. Within two years the national payroll was cut back by two-thirds. The Red Cross showed the public how it was retrenching. It cut expenditures of $133,000,000 in 1945–46 in half the next year, and down to $50,000,000 in 1947–48. But yet, small as these seemed, they still

were ten times those of the last year before World War II. They would
not drop any lower in the next decade, although no attempt would be
made for some years to collect as much as was spent.

Oddly enough, the leadership of the Red Cross again underesti-
mated the extent of public support. There were grave fears of the re-
percussions of the "GI gripes," of the effect of the peace-consciousness
on public giving, and in 1947 the added factors of more disagreements
with organized labor plus a renewal of feuding over fund-raising with
community chests. Yet the Red Cross came out with colors flying.

In 1946 the fund campaign was cut back to $100,000,000, to be
roughly divided equally between National Headquarters and the chapters. The drive yielded $118,000,000. A year later a "modest" cam-
paign for only $60,000,000 yielded almost $80,000,000.

But in the meantime the Red Cross was deliberately spending far
more from its national budget than it was collecting. Rightly or
wrongly, and knowing something of the demobilization and reconstruction demands which it faced, the leadership determined to dissi-
pate as constructively as possible a large part of the huge surplus left
over from the war drives. This amounted for the national organization
on July 1, 1945, to $181,800,000.

In the meantime, the pattern of postwar work by the Red Cross had
changed beyond recognition, as compared with the task thirty years
earlier.

III

No longer was the Red Cross involved in the humane and often deli-
cate operations incident to foreign civilian relief, except in most
limited cases. A new concept and new machinery had come into being
for this work. This now was a task for governments, and the machinery was provided by the United Nations Relief and Rehabilitation
Administration.

The task of the Red Cross in the two years after World War II was
primarily that of converting from foreign military operations to domestic demobilization work, and in some fields supplying help to a degree
greater than ever before. The statistics are staggering in retrospect,
and Red Cross personnel, such as survived the constant staff-cutting,
shifted from job to job in totally unrelated fields.

The force of thousands of canteen workers abroad practically disappeared by the middle of 1947 when the Army took over the service clubs and recreation centers. But by that time other large groups of Red Cross workers were in hospitals and Veterans Administration facilities in the United States.

At one time the Red Cross held the power of attorney for 1,400,000 veterans, representing their claims in the red tape necessary to return to civilian life with proper benefits. Three hundred Red Crossers, excluding clerical staff, were assigned to this work alone. From the chapters innumerable Gray Ladies, nurses' aides, Junior Red Cross and members of almost every other branch of volunteer activities, answered the call for entertainment and personal morale work issued by the Veterans Administration.

Some 65,000 war brides required and received unlimited help from chapters in settling in their new environment. Disabled veterans, dislocated dischargees, families of veterans and men still in service—in 1946 and 1947 these mounted to a total case load approximating 4,000,000.

While statistics fell into fractions compared with the work of the services in wartime, the Red Cross by no means suffered the contraction of earlier postwar eras. In 1946–47, with the country theoretically at peace, the Canteen Corps served more than 3,000,000 servicemen and veterans, the Motor Corps logged 8,000,000 miles in its assignments, nearly 60,000 home visits were made by social welfare aides in response to appeals for help, and nearly 13,000 nurses' aides were each month carrying out hospital assignments.

This work, plus sewing for displaced persons in Europe and the scores of other required or assumed chapter tasks, occupied 275,000 enrolled volunteers in 1947, *five times the 1939 total,* giving moreover *twenty-five times the number of hours,* plus an estimated additional 2,000,000 part-time volunteers who worked less regularly than those who were officially enrolled.

The number of contributors to the Red Cross—paying members— did drop from the wartime peak of more than 36,000,000 to about 18,000,000, where it held steady thereafter for some years. But that was still more than twice the 1940–41 total, prior to Pearl Harbor.

It was noted, too, that the size of the contribution was greater per member. The older days of soliciting dollar campaigns were gone.

Now larger donations were requested, although a dollar still did, as it does now, rate a membership card.

Back behind the adult membership was the new school organization, born in World War I and now a part of the program of almost two-thirds of the country's schools. This was the Junior Red Cross with, in 1947, more than 19,000,000 children attending classes carrying out recognized programs. Yes, America was Red Cross minded.

While reorganizing its Headquarters machinery, readjusting its finances to peacetime levels and lopping off surplus war staff, the Red Cross management paid considerable attention to what it was *doing* as well as the means available for doing it.

It took a long look at its peacetime services.

Under its charter responsibilities and obligations, Disaster stood at the head of the list.

First Aid, Water Safety and Accident Prevention were the bulwark of peacetime training programs to keep the chapters profitably occupied, hold community interest, and increase constantly the dividends of Red Cross work.

In the opposite direction, government agencies had made such strides in public health work that the Nursing Service and public health work almost ceased to be a requirement of privately supported welfare work. Red Cross nursing was hardly needed anywhere, and the nursing connection with the armed forces, already confined to recruiting in World War II, dissolved in 1947 with creation of a permanent Army and Navy Nurse Corps.

To replace these activities, more emphasis was placed on training of nurses for disaster work and the civil defense program. A nutrition program caught the interest of a large majority of chapters.

Finally, the blood program was converted, hesitantly and carefully at first, into a civilian operation.

Despite all these activities, however, the Red Cross gradually slipped away from its high wartime plateau, except for a resurgence of sporadic work during the Korean War, with chapter after chapter retreating into a state of relative inactivity.

In later years, as so often before, it was natural disaster relief work that again raised the Red Cross standard high in the public understanding.

IV

It is a matter of fantastic record that in the four years of total national preoccupation with World War II not a single disaster of note happened in the United States. Otherwise errant rivers remained docilely within their banks, tornadoes on the Great Plains and in the South gave only token demonstrations, and no great hurricanes barged out of their Atlantic breeding grounds to devastate eastern or southern shores.

True, there were small disasters, intensely important to the individuals involved, but from the standpoint of relief and rehabilitation requirements easily handled in the Red Cross tradition by small groups of persons and expenditures of money that were negligible in comparison with other activities.

In fact, after World War II there was evident concern within the Red Cross on two points: (1) How to keep alive the skills and training that would need to be mustered should great natural disasters strike again; and (2) How to prevent the mushrooming government agencies (likewise fighting for survival) from swamping the Red Cross role in this now traditional task. In the two years of 1945 and 1946, even with a more generous attitude in making grants than had marked prewar years because of the higher cost of all things, the Red Cross expended only $7,000,000 in its work in disasters. These averaged 300 a year, but none was a large commitment.

A Red Cross report in 1946 stated that "clouds are appearing on the disaster relief horizon," because "Government today is rendering a number of services to disaster sufferers that were rendered by Red Cross disaster relief 10, 15 or 20 years ago." This meant, the report added, that "the Red Cross should be on the alert at all times to check every force, every trend, every development, no matter how small, that will reduce the efficiency of disaster relief."

To some critics of the Red Cross such statements seem self-seeking. But the cold fact is—as this reporting member wrote—that government had not then and has not at this writing ever displaced the *disaster services* built up over three generations by the Red Cross, or found the means to provide out of ordinary appropriations the money to do the things the Red Cross does.

To explain the difference may seem like a splitting of hairs, but it hinges importantly on Harriman's explanation that in disaster work the Red Cross is primarily "people helping people." Government may now replace the roads, restore public services, reopen demolished schools and spend scores of millions on *things*. But the Red Cross is the agency through which funds go to rebuild and refurnish small houses, get little businesses going quickly, clothe children, and care for the elderly and helpless. The pattern has never changed, except in terms of dollars and wider application, from the time that Clara Barton started it.

As recently as 1955, in the time of the great New England flood, President Eisenhower flew to the scene to emphasize the importance of the Red Cross role; in that and many other instances, states in disaster emergencies have designated the Red Cross as the official agency to receive and dispense relief funds.

It hinges on the fact that, basically, the Red Cross is organized for guidance and communications; it has the people and generally the confidence of the public; and through its chapter organization it is everywhere.

Another important point is that the Red Cross, despite occasional lambasting from critics, does not exist in a special world of its own or live surrounded by a vacuum. Every Red Cross volunteer knows that he lives in a world of crosshatching organizations. Scratch a Red Cross volunteer and you will nearly always find another organization coating or two underneath his Red Cross coloring. Pick out the leading volunteers in other community services and likely as not they are board members of the Red Cross chapter.

The Red Cross has failed to make this clear. Leaders of too many chapters concentrate in their publicity on Red Cross exclusively, and not enough on their interwoven status in community service.

A Red Cross vice president, battling with this task of mutual understanding, once told the writer:

"How can you make the public understand that the Red Cross itself never gave anybody a nickel, or never withheld a dollar from any victim of disaster. We are distributing agents, awarding relief from funds the public has trusted to us for humane work. The Red Cross in disaster work is everybody, and especially it's the public agent that stays behind for months helping the rehabilitation work of people, not just staying there long enough to pass out coffee and sandwiches and have its picture taken."

As a footnote to this comment, in the years since World War II, eighty-five to ninety cents out of every dollar spent on disasters from Red Cross contributed funds have gone into the unpublicized job of rehabilitation, contrasted with the ten to fifteen cents of Red Cross money and the entirety of other organization relief funds spent during the immediate period of emergency.

In 1946, while the Red Cross leadership was so worried about its future role in disaster work, none could forecast how this would dramatically face the Red Cross with financial crises before a decade had run out.

+   +   +   +   +

20

Roll Call at 75

TEN YEARS AFTER the end of World War II the American Red Cross reached its seventy-fifth birthday, or what in other times would have been called a Diamond Jubilee, but it had neither the time nor the will to sit back and celebrate.

In the first place, the word "diamond" created a bad taste in the mouths of administrative and volunteer leaders who were hard-pressed to make ends meet, despite generous contributions, in the face of the constant service demands made on the Red Cross. In the second place, the Red Cross was too busy.

The uneasy peace that sat upon the world had turned the Red Cross into a duality of operations such as the organization never had faced before. It had to be both a military arm and a continuing peacetime welfare organization. Furthermore, the outlook was that this condition would continue into all of the foreseeable future.

The military program, carried on in proportion to the continued high state of United States mobilization and foreign troop assignments, was a burden far heavier than anyone had anticipated in 1945 or 1946. Services to the Armed Forces remained, in fact, the largest year-in-and-year-out commitment of the organization. In addition, disaster relief and rehabilitation, the second largest operation, spurted after a few routine years into a fantastic demand on the Red Cross and, in turn, upon the public, whom it must ask for special assistance.

Added to these commitments came new programs such as the blood program, converted from a military to a civilian operation, and cooperative work in the civilian defense program. And all the while the more standard older services of the Red Cross continued to grow far beyond the normal rate of increase in the population.

The facts of the record were that the United States gave more and more acceptance to the Red Cross programs, and in turn the Red Cross services involved a heavily rising rate of expenditures. Although in some periods the financial support given to the Red Cross fell short of the actual costs, the organization had come into a peacetime acceptance without comparison. Gone was the most heartbreaking aspect of the past, the forgetfulness of Americans in times of peace.

In 1956 the Red Cross rolls carried the names of more than 40,-000,000 members, about equally divided between adult and junior groups. And in that year, in response to both the regular membership campaigns and special appeals for extraordinary demands of disaster, the American people contributed approximately $100,000,000 to the Red Cross.

In the chapters of the Red Cross, 2,000,000 volunteers rendered various services, particularly for veterans and in disaster work on the spectacular side, that in hours were reckoned as the equivalent of full-time work by approximately 20,000 persons.

Supporting, training and handling the technical work of the Red Cross were approximately 14,300 salaried persons, in the United States and around the world, including about 4,400 on the payroll of the national organization and 9,900 scattered through more than 2,300 chapters.

In the remaining 1,400 chapters, volunteers performed all chapter activities.

What were these persons doing? How had the peacetime Red Cross grown so large? They were doing substantially what had been done down through the years, but better and more completely than earlier— people helping people. Roscoe Drummond, of the New York *Herald Tribune,* summed it up in a special article by terming the Red Cross "the trustee of the nation's humanity."

Yet, while the Red Cross seemed large, and its outlay of $100,000,-000 a year seemed huge when set off by itself, the wonder was that this organization—largest of the welfare agencies and unique in its responsibilities for military and disaster relief work—was yet only a dot on the page of the total welfare outlay by the people of the United States, to which the public contributed about four billion dollars each year.

Let's take a quick look at some summaries of the Red Cross in action as 1956 closed its seventy-fifth year—facts drawn from the audited report for the fiscal year running from July 1, 1956 to June 30, 1957.

II

There is a message center operated in Washington by the Red Cross that averages a message a minute around the clock around the year. There are few areas in the world outside the Iron Curtain from which the messages do not come, or to which they are not addressed. This is the link of communications between the men in the armed forces overseas and their home communities, the private and confidential link communicating their problems, the family questions, and the reports of solutions outside of military channels.

Here is the means by which the serviceman in Korea whose wife may be expecting a baby, or another whose father has died, may have his immediate questions answered and his pressing problems, in so far as possible, resolved.

There is no point in the world where a Red Cross staff man is not in touch with military units, and no place in the United States so remote that a Red Cross chapter does not get into touch with it in answer to such messages. This is the result of organization on a two-way street. Abroad there are at this writing more than 600 Red Cross field staff members serving with the troops; in the United States every chapter, no matter how small, is geared to handle, as well as humanly possible, through Home Service, this phase of military work.

And that is only one detail of the job for the armed forces which the Red Cross workers have learned to do. They counsel and guide in personal problems, and comfort the sick and injured. In cases of distress, the Red Cross loans the GI emergency tide-over funds, and while loans are expected to be repaid the loans sometimes—very often —have become gifts.

The "uneasy peace" days of 1958 aroused echoes of war work in

the Red Cross routine as it followed the military to scenes of crisis in
Lebanon and Formosa.

A Red Cross field director landed with the first detachments of
soldiers and marines at Beirut, flying down from Wiesbaden, Germany. Within a few days he was joined by half a dozen others, forti-
fied with 20,000 pounds of supplies flown in by Air Force cargo
planes. What kind of supplies? Writing paper, cigarettes, towels, razor
blades, candy (all luxuries when the military moves in a hurry) and,
according to a *Stars and Stripes* story the most popular item of all—
pocket sewing kits known the world round as "The Housewife."

Then came the Formosan crisis in September, with renewed calls
upon the Red Cross, most simply described by this fragment of a dispatch to the *New York Times* of September 22, 1958:

> They [the American reinforcements] came with such speed
> that some not only forgot their razors but were plunged into the
> unsuspected depths of domestic difficulty by neglecting to adjust
> their personal pay records.
>
> As a result many soldiers have suddenly found themselves on
> some remote base in Taiwan without personal articles and with
> no post exchange in sight. Also, they came to realize that their
> wives in Japan, the Philippines and elsewhere were likewise
> stranded without rent money, since the Defense Department does
> not dispense wages in the absence of properly validated docu-
> ments.
>
> A large number of these men appealed to the nearest Red
> Cross station for help. As a result the Red Cross itself has had to
> expand its Taiwan complement in a hurry. A Tokyo Red Cross
> officer flew here so suddenly that he forgot his own pocket comb.

In the military hospitals Red Cross workers carry forward medically
approved programs of entertainment, recreation, crafts and hobbies,
which is largely the field of the volunteer. In fact, with deployment of
great forces overseas, in many areas the Red Cross volunteers in this
work are themselves the wives of servicemen assigned to the installations.

In sum, such activities so easily and briefly noted represent a job that
in itself would require a world-wide organization if the Red Cross did

nothing else. In its seventy-fifth year of American service, three fantastic totals were recorded by the Red Cross in its Services to the Armed Forces:

1. 144,000 members of the armed forces, veterans, and their families *were served each month* in chapters;
2. 98,000 members of the armed forces *were served each month* in military hospitals and installations here and overseas;
3. 8,200 volunteers *worked each month* in Home Service to help members of the armed forces, veterans, and their families.

More than half of the total payroll of the National Headquarters of the American Red Cross—including 127 in Washington, 1,721 around the country and 623 abroad—were assigned to the military job, and almost a third of all the money spent by the national and chapter organizations went to support it.

But money is not the only gauge of the size of this job that a decade earlier would have seemed unbelievable in a world at peace. Almost 45,000 volunteers racked up over 4,000,000 hours of work in more than 750 military and veterans' hospitals and installations.

The old glamor days of the overseas' clubs and rambling clubmobiles were almost things of the past, although a few clubmobiles were still maintained in Korea and there were a few recreation facilities for able-bodied servicemen adjacent to isolated military posts in France and Morocco.

Now the Services to the Armed Forces were an inspiring but hard, routine day-to-day task. Without it, the serviceman, particularly overseas, would be far closer to a cipher in military regulations, enmeshed even in his leisure as well as his personal life in red tape. In his problems and his personal affairs, the Red Cross was an important link to his individual security as a citizen.

III

Two areas of speculation in which man has never been able to make definite predictions are proverbial: one is horse racing and the other is the weather. In disaster relief, therefore, the Red Cross always has had to study averages and plan accordingly.

As a prudent speculator it has followed for many years the processes used by companies that write insurance against death, fire and other hazards. The Red Cross first appropriates an annual sum in its budget to cover disaster commitments; second, after World War II it set aside the unused portions of these annual appropriations as a Disaster Reserve; third, when an extraordinary disaster beyond available resources occurs, it launches a special appeal for additional funds, just as a mutual insurance association might assess its members to meet deficiencies.

The system worked well until nature turned in 1955 from normal capriciousness to wild behavior in a totally unexpected manner that bore no relationship to the pattern of great disasters of the past. In 1955, and for the following two years, the disaster pattern took on new aspects while amply retaining the normal features of the old. Hurricanes occurred with unprecedented violence in areas far from their established courses, floods ravaged areas untouched by excessive high water in the country's history, tornadoes turned from "twisters" that damaged localized and isolated areas into major devastators of large communities. In Europe an eruption against communism in Hungary caused dislocations and special relief needs that themselves were new in American Red Cross experience.

To put the comparison simply, this work can record, at its completion early in 1958, a contrast that in less than three years had completely changed the financial situation of the Red Cross:

Disaster costs in 1955, 1956 and 1957 were so great that, despite special drives that netted $22,102,297 in contributions over and above the annual fund campaigns, the Red Cross closed the two fiscal years ended June 30, 1957, with expenditures from National Headquarters exceeding receipts by approximately $17,000,000.

The last cent of the cash reserve funds remaining from the surplus of the World War collections, plus other reserves built up in succeeding years, was gone.

In issuing the 1957 financial statement, Chairman Harriman and General Alfred M. Gruenther, president of the Red Cross, said:

A hundred million dollars was received by the Red Cross during the year in membership fees and fund campaign contributions, in disaster contributions, and in income for other special purposes. Yet because disaster relief over the past two years cost about $50,000,000, the organization ended its fiscal year on June 30, 1957, with its reserves practically exhausted.

This was the accounting of the Red Cross just before the period when the recession of 1957 ended what had been for most public and private organizations an era of unprecedented prosperity. But there was another side to the picture, and it was good. By maintaining its pledged services, putting relief of human suffering above worries over financial reserves, and plunging ahead with confidence, the Red Cross appeared to have gained far more in public understanding and approval than it had held in any other peacetime era.

The Disaster Program of the Red Cross was changed very little in tone from fifty years ago; it just happened that there were more disasters, more persons affected, and more costly damages to be rectified in the limited manner that relief and rehabilitation are given. The word "limited" is used deliberately.

The Red Cross found out long ago that it cannot replace all losses. In *relief*, it helps to rally facilities for shelter and feeding of all persons immediately affected. In *rehabilitation*, its rule is to help the helpless without other places to turn, to get back on their feet, just to—but not beyond—the point where they can begin to rebuild their lives. In extreme cases up to $5,000 has been spent for the benefit of individual families, but these are rare, despite misconceptions to the contrary. No loans are made and no repayment of gifts expected or requested.

Since its founding the American Red Cross has spent $246,000,000 on disaster work in the United States and $46,000,000 in foreign countries.

Thanks largely to the stimulus of volunteer training for civil defense work—the added glamour that spurred such training—the Red Cross human resources for disaster work reached a new peak of effectiveness among volunteers by the mid-1950s.

Whether a cyclone wiped out a Kansas community, hurricanes tore through the Gulf states, or floods ravaged northeastern or far northwestern areas where residents had only heard of such occurrences far away on the Mississippi or Ohio Rivers, Red Cross workers were ready. Added to their own instructions in manuals and by skeleton national field staffs were their own newly developed skills in mass feeding and care.

When the tasks of rehabilitation, principally the restoration of damaged homes, were undertaken, there were new groups of volunteers consisting of bankers, businessmen, contractors and real estate specialists ready to assume, as realistic local Red Cross committees, the tasks of awarding grants in aid that in earlier days had fallen to Red Cross staff personnel.

This one development alone took from the professional staff the onerous job of saying "no" in many cases, with consequent damning criticism of the Red Cross, as Percy noted in "Lanterns on the Levee." Furthermore, the new practice saved money. Outsiders could be more realistic, and better informed about local conditions, than the Red Cross social worker could know or dare to be.

These are the reasons why the American Red Cross, even when spending scores of millions on disaster operations, does it with a paid staff smaller than the number of persons employed in single units of supermarkets. In 1956 all disaster work was supervised nationally by 94 persons, and at the peak in 1957 this total grew to only 137.

This meant that in two years in which there were 583 disaster relief operations the Red Cross national organization maintained on its payroll an average of one person for each five disasters, or one paid expert for each half million dollars of money spent on emergency relief and rehabilitation.

Lest disaster work be lost in a statistical maze of dollars, let four facts be recorded for 1957 as the human side of this picture:

In that one year 593 chapters in 44 states answered calls for disaster relief:

Giving emergency mass care to 311,000 persons;
Plus long-range recovery assistance to 88,000 families;
With the assistance of 82,000 volunteers.

IV

The number of lives saved by the Red Cross blood program, both in its pioneering work and in day-to-day operation is incalculable. Any guesswork is liable to either exaggeration or underestimation. But it has contributed in peacetime to as great a development in humane assistance as it did to revolutionizing the techniques of war.

These statements are factual. And yet this program has generated controversies that seem inconceivable in a modern society. The Red Cross has had to fight its way through arguments and criticisms comparable only to the aftermath of the wartime program for the armed services. These criticisms have not come from blood donors or blood recipients, but from outside critics whose charges have ranged from "busybody" to competition with other agencies.

As one result, the Red Cross blood program is not truly national. Chapters participating in it generally are located east of the Rocky Mountains, and it is spotty in many areas. In large cities such as New York it is accepted by some hospitals and medical groups, but not by others.

One result has been—and is likely to continue—that on frequent occasions the desperate family told that only blood transfusions will save a member, or the family's physician, find themselves denied access to Red Cross *free blood,* never by the Red Cross or its chapters but by local practices and regulations.

Another headache which caused the Red Cross to consider occasionally the desperate step of stopping the blood program altogether has been the matter of criticism about "charges for blood." Yet the Red Cross has never charged for blood. Here are the simple facts, if the record will help to explain this situation:

Red Cross blood is free, given freely by donors and handled as a charge paid from funds of National Headquarters and chapters. In recent years the hospitals and clinics drawing upon the Red Cross blood banks have paid the small cost of the special containers in which it is packed. Hospitals using this blood do make regular charges for administering it. In too many cases, patients have not understood that their bills in connection with blood transfusions of Red Cross supplies have been exclusively for *service,* not for the blood itself.

Yet despite this continuing battle for understanding, the blood program has become a miracle of organization and, under Red Cross development, a service that it would be difficult to duplicate otherwise.

At this writing the Red Cross blood program is operating in fifty regions with the cooperation of 1,440 chapters. And this program is supplying 40 per cent of all blood used in civilian hospitals, in addition to "blood fractions" for clinical use and for study by scientists.

When one writes that the Red Cross is supplying blood, it means that as an agency of understanding volunteers, it has collected in a single year approximately 2,200,000 individual blood donations, and distributed this blood to civilian or federal hospitals in every state for treatment of patients. More than 118,000 volunteers made it possible to carry out this program at a cost of less than six dollars per unit collected, or a very small fraction of the commercial payments recipients otherwise had to pay for blood from professional donors.

But mere distribution of blood for normal infusion into patients, important as it was, may have been, for the long run, the minor part of the picture. New and great developments were coming out of the blood program.

Take fibrinogen as a prime example. This derivative from blood is credited with great value in controlling hemorrhage resulting from certain complications in childbirth. It was isolated in research by scientists cooperating in the blood program. However, it was scarce and hard to extract. In fact, announcement of its availability for clinical use was withheld for a long time lest false hopes be shattered.

In 1957 fibrinogen was no longer an optimistic mirage because new techniques developed through pilot investigations contracted for by the Red Cross with the State of Michigan Department of Health Laboratories found a key to its processing.

This was only one dramatic development. Another was the supplying of blood in ever widening practice for use in the miraculous heart-lung machines used to send oxygenated blood through the bodies of patients, while surgeons perform operations in hearts temporarily diverted from their normal action.

The Red Cross distributed substantial quantities of serum albumin and gamma globulin, other blood "fractions," whose Latin names are usually meaningless to laymen, unless acute need has made the products vital to lifesaving.

The cumulative distribution had in mid-1958 a current commercial value of more than $57,000,000.

And all the while the Red Cross was supplying serum albumin for stockpiling by the Federal Civilian Defense Administration and continuing its planning for national emergency operations.

In this work there were few headlines, but rewarding dividends for those who knew the meaning of the programs in terms of human life.

V

There are few persons who will not recall having seen on Red Cross posters the traditional "Red Cross nurse," symbolized by the scarlet-lined blue cape. Yet so many Americans consider the figure as a memorial tribute to the time when Red Cross nurses served with the Army as a professional civilian group.

The symbolism is there certainly, but the Red Cross nurse is today very real and active, at the very peak of the trained and professional volunteers ready to drop their income-earning jobs to answer disaster calls and meanwhile contributing their time to almost world-wide chapter training programs.

The enrollment of nurses as volunteers in the Red Cross exceeds at this writing the total of 50,000. They are the teachers and leaders in the training of the volunteer nurses' aides on whom hospitals have come to depend and who are an integral part of the civil defense program. They conduct weekly classes in programs descriptively named "Care of the Sick and Injured," and "Mother and Baby Care."

The volunteer Red Cross nurse is frequently on hand in the school health programs, and in Salk vaccine immunization projects.

When survivors of a maritime disaster are landed at a port, Red Cross nurses meet them (as in the case of thirty-two mustered to assist the victims of the *Andrea Doria* disaster), and they do the anonymous job of attending large public functions where help is miraculously available if someone becomes ill or an accident occurs.

To name some high lights of the work done by volunteer nurses in the seventy-fifth anniversary year of the American Red Cross:

2,300 nurses accepted assignments in 30 major disaster operations;

129 assignments were made for polio nursing;

4,300 gave their time to attend disaster training conferences.

No, the Red Cross nurse has not been relegated to legend.

VI

It is fundamental in human nature that much attention is given to individuals who do spectacular things—a proper tribute to courage, ingenuity or skill—but the forgotten individual in human society is the teacher whose training enabled the hero to be a hero.

In this field the Red Cross must always accept the anonymous role of the teacher, and yet fight for at least enough recognition to gain public support and the dollars to continue. The Red Cross as an organization never rescues a person from drowning, but the chances are 99 out of 100 that the lifesaver who makes a rescue has taken the course required to earn a Red Cross lifesaver's certificate.

In 1957, when our population was three times its size in 1912, drownings totaled only one-third of the figure for the earlier year. The motor patrols on the highways that respond to accident calls usually are policemen or firemen, but their first-aid training has been given by a Red Cross expert.

At a time when 85,000,000 Americans have come to some form of participation in sports on or in the water, water safety as a Red Cross program has become an established part of the American pattern of life. We are a water-wealthy country and since World War II have burgeoned into a water-play country. This does not mean just at seaside resorts or around notable lakes. For example, there is a favorite riddle often asked of water-safety students: What State has the longest shoreline of banks bordering waterways? The answer is Oklahoma.

There is human value indeed in the fact that in the last recorded year nearly 2,500,000 certificates were awarded in Red Cross classes to persons completing training courses in first aid, water safety and home nursing; that 172,000 volunteers in almost 3,000 chapters were needed to give the courses and that 108,000 Red Cross volunteers gave chapter services and manned safety services on the highways alone.

VII

On the evening of July 19, 1958, National Headquarters of the American Red Cross issued a news story containing this announcement:

"General Alfred M. Gruenther, president of the American Red Cross, expressed the organization's official pleasure today that the Red Cross had been able to arrange for the release of the nine U.S. servicemen detained in East Germany since June 7."

This carefully correct language marked another milestone through the years in which the Red Cross, as a world-wide association, is able to cross otherwise blocked national boundaries in carrying out its humane errands—always, of course, with the advice and consent of our government when the American Red Cross is involved.

In this case, the nine men had been forced down by bad weather that blew their helicopter into East Germany. Why they were detained by the Communist government (as others had been similarly detained) is at this writing inexplicable, but in any event the normal and civilized means of communication by governments were shut off by the Iron Curtain. Yet when the government authorized the Red Cross in Washington to open negotiations, Dr. Werner Ludwig, president of the East German Red Cross, was permitted, and was willing, to negotiate with our Red Cross.

The first meeting was held June 27. Starting in July, an American Red Cross representative took parcels and mail daily to East Berlin, for delivery to the prisoners and was permitted to carry messages out for them. Final arrangements for their release were made on July 16 and 17.

Ordinarily, in the highly organized and complex modern world, the Red Cross of one country helps that of another by sending contributions in money or supplies. In the postwar years this was the usual form of sisterly society aid given by the American Red Cross as various disasters struck around the world. Likewise, at the time of more spectacular disasters in the United States large contributions have come from other lands, including Russia.

There are, at this writing, approximately eighty national Red Cross Societies, including highly organized and efficient ones in such Iron Curtain countries as the Soviet Union itself and East Germany. These differ in some degree, however, from the American Red Cross, usually —as also is the case in some western European countries—in that often they receive government subsidies and in effect are hired for such duties as hospital operation, clinical work or ambulance service.

In October, 1956, there occurred a mustering without precedent of the Red Cross societies of the free world to respond to the catastrophe that struck civilians in Hungary as a result of the abortive revolution finally suppressed by Russian troops. In this work, fifty-two Red Cross societies participated, definitely establishing the line of separation existing between the Red Cross as it lives in the hearts and minds of free people, who rushed to help, and the Red Cross as it is directed by Communist political masters.

The Hungarian revolution and subsequent massacre resulted in chaos within Hungary and the flight of thousands of refugees into Austria. Of these, some thousands were admitted to the United States by government action, flown in military planes from Europe to Camp Kilmer, New Jersey.

Here was an historic example of the American Red Cross being on the job as one among many members of the International League of Red Cross Societies. Furthermore, it was a notable case in which only a fraction of the costs was paid by Americans.

The Hungarian refugee program cost in its first year approximately $30,000,000 in supplies and service. From the United States went $5,-000,000, substantially the amount contributed for this special cause by individuals; it was not charged against Red Cross general funds.

At the peak of the refugee operations, forty-four camps for escapees were being operated in Austria. For a while motor convoys traveling under Red Cross flags were able to carry food and medicines for distribution by Red Cross representatives exclusively to the aged, the ill, and children in Budapest.

Of the forty-four camps, six were operated by American Red Cross workers. And when the dazed refugees came to Camp Kilmer as a stopover in their resettlement,108 Red Cross staff workers and 1,630 volunteers from surrounding chapters took care of them.

VIII

When the Junior Red Cross was conceived in World War I as a means of inculcating patriotic concepts in school children, a seed was planted that blossomed into a fantastic national program.

While not in all schools, the Junior Red Cross forty years later had 67,300 elementary schools enrolled and 36,100 others in which pupils participated in programs without enrollment.

The enrolled schools account for the 20,000,000 or more Junior Red Cross members—a fraternity within the adult group with its own small dues, its own segregation of funds and its own international program. Here is the area in which, under the guidance of teachers who themselves are Red Cross volunteers, children receive aid and instruction in the highly civilized training of "people helping people." The pennies and dimes of the enrolled juniors amount to a working fund of approximately a quarter million dollars a year.

What do they do? They are truly the "junior" Red Cross.

Homebound and hospitalized children regularly receive surprise visits and gifts from the juniors in their communities, and 400,000 gift boxes, packed by American children, went to children in other lands as a neighborly gesture in 1956. In the name of the Junior Red Cross, 100 chests—each complete with equipment and supplies for a classroom—were sent to South Korea.

After the outpouring of refugees from Hungary in 1956 and 1957, American youth spoke through gifts to the helpless victims of that event. Here is one example:

One day before Christmas, 1956, a truck bumped down the snow-covered highway skirting Salzburg, Austria, and swung through the gates of Camp Siezenheim, a onetime military post turned into a center to house Hungarian refugees pouring across the Austro-Hungarian frontier.

Siezenheim was the first stop on a Christmas mission that was to take this truck ranging from one end of Austria to the other to bring some measure of holiday happiness to the bewildered children who had fled to a new world with their parents.

Nicknamed the "Toymobile," the truck was packed with dolls, games, rocking horses and other precious items that were to bring shouts of delight from many a youngster who had feared St. Nicholas would never find him.

The Toymobile was only one example among many Junior Red Cross ventures that lightened the lot of the Hungarian youngsters caught up in a situation they could not control, and which few could comprehend. In all, American juniors furnished supplies valued at $155,200 for distribution to these young people.

Paintings from classroom work, and "correspondence books" made up of letters written by the children, go in constant rounds between American and foreign schools, so that children may learn to communicate with each other in their own terms.

As rewards, and for development of leaders in the lower teen-age brackets, the Red Cross has sent junior members to overseas training centers in Japan, Germany, England and the Netherlands, and received juniors for comparable studies in the United States.

In the last recorded year ice was broken for even more advanced development of Junior Red Cross leadership. An international study center was established at Hood College, in Maryland. At this center, during the summer holiday, fifty-nine American Junior Red Cross members chosen by selection from widely scattered chapters met with young persons from eleven foreign Red Cross Societies to discuss in their own terms the problems of living together and working together in the modern world.

IX

Truly, after seventy-five years, the Red Cross is "many things to many people."

Yet, after wading through the years of development, sampling the mountains of statistics, and peering alike at the highlights and the depressed periods, one may ask, "What is the Red Cross in the life of modern America? Is it truly vital?"

That is a valid question in an era of all-embracing government activity, of streamlined scientific development and a general attitude of acceptance of public welfare as the responsibility of tax-supported agencies.

One answer certainly lies in the stability and virility of the Red Cross as it exists well past the middle of the twentieth century. Another lies in the character of its support, both by money contributions and by people as volunteers. And that answer is found in the community rather than in Washington or its regional branches.

There was a time when the Red Cross volunteer fitted one of two categories: either he was an individual of wealth and community leadership by family or environment who adopted the Red Cross as a cause; or he was one of the mass who rallied to help when called upon in time of emergency or war but then went back to his or her (usually her) own responsibilities.

Today that picture has changed, and the change is permanent. There are many manifestations of this change.

For one thing, about 20 per cent of the financial support of the Red Cross comes from industries and businesses of all sizes that support it because these business leaders see it earning its keep in community service. They realize the continuing need for a national organization that ties together rather than competes with thousands of other agencies.

The Red Cross volunteer today is the typical community worker and leader—the individual willing to give countless hours to the business of human relations as well as to personal services. No longer could the Red Cross be called by its severest critic a "sewing circle." There are a few communities where the chapter still is the stronghold of a hereditary or self-appointed group. But these are becoming rare. The Red Cross Chapter Board of Directors in a typical city is made up of businessmen, bankers, real estate agents and storekeepers and their wives. Seldom is such a board a self-perpetuating group. In more and more communities special efforts are made to bring in what once were called minority groups, with the realization that no one is a minority as a citizen-individual.

There are big jobs and big responsibilities in the Red Cross, and people big in experience must fill them.

It may even be a healthy thing that the Red Cross has had to use its available cash reserves, and that its endowments yield such a small fraction of the income necessary to do its job that it could not in the foreseeable future survive without regular appeals for public support. This keeps the Red Cross lean and trim. It helps to prevent the development of sluggish self-satisfaction and the temptation to perpetuate itself simply for organization's sake.

The Red Cross undeniably does have problems in justifying itself, its costs, and the services that are so blended with the community life of America that they are taken for granted. No longer does it stand out, as in the days when service groups could be counted on the fingers of one hand. The Red Cross is not spectacular; in fact, its role of leader rather than monopolist has encouraged development of many other groups who sometimes appear to be its competitors in appeals for public support.

Never have Americans been asked to support so many types of welfare work or special study groups. In the roll of organizations with their own merits, and far more spectacular achievements, the foundations engaged in specific health research—heart, cancer, mental health, *et cetera ad infinitum*—are better known to many individuals than is the Red Cross.

What is seldom seen is the cooperation the Red Cross is able to give to these organizations, without fanfare, simply because it is what it is.

This assistance takes form in a thousand ways, from the provision of blood for research work to the members of the Motor Corps who regularly drive the cars that carry crippled children on outings. Red Cross chapters frequently have the only permanently organized head-quarters available for special help to community organizations.

More important, it seems clear now that the Red Cross stands as a foremost example of the fact that, in a humane, civilized society, government never can do everything, radical opinion to the contrary. Americans are determined in their desire to help themselves and others, as individuals, as free people.

The Red Cross as we know it was born because of recognition of that fact in the American Amendment adopted so long ago. It will stand just as long, and only as long, as this is the American attitude.

There was more than rhetoric in the words written by Red Cross Volunteer Number One, Chairman E. Roland Harriman, at the lowest ebb of the Red Cross's financial picture after the drains of service in 1956:

"The Red Cross enters the new year with spirit and determination and remains steadfast in its concern for the nation's well being. With God's help and faith in the future, the Red Cross will carry on."

And so it is.

IN APPRECIATION

One who attempts to summarize the history of an organization as diverse, widespread and multi-faceted as the Red Cross obviously undertakes a job beyond the scope of any individual. Proper research, or even the attempt to place events and developments in perspective, requires the assistance and guidance of many others.

For research assistance, a deep bow to the Historical Section of the Red Cross, and to Dr. Foster Rhea Dulles, professor of history at the University of Ohio, who undertook after World War II the task of preparing for the Red Cross a definitive and highly detailed history of its work. Assisted by as many as forty persons in these researches, Dr. Dulles produced a monumental documented story of the Red Cross. For the serious researcher this work is unparalleled, and no attempt has been made to duplicate it.

Rechecking of the facts set down in this work was meticulously done by Clyde E. Buckingham and Miss Olivette Suttles, of the Red Cross staff.

Otherwise this *Compact History,* financed entirely by the publisher, is a look at the Red Cross and its place as an American expression of awareness of man's responsibility to his neighbor, in peacetime and in war.

In organization and writing of this work the author is also indebted to many persons other than those who can be named here. For four years Chairman Harriman has extended his confidence and cooperation, including the privilege of attending many meetings of the Board of Governors, visits to all the regional offices (Alexandria, Virginia; St. Louis, Missouri; Atlanta, Georgia; and San Francisco, California) and to many chapters.

Likewise confidence and friendly cooperation have been extended by the two presidents of the Red Cross in recent years, Ambassador Ellsworth Bunker and General Alfred M. Gruenther.

Ramone S. Eaton, vice president of the Red Cross, under whose jurisdiction are responsibilities for public information and fund-raising, and educational relations, among others, has been a constant collaborator in studies, together with his principal assistant, Harry Martin, director of the Office of Public Information.

Linking the records of the past with personal recollections have been many others: notably James T. Nicholson, retired executive vice president; Fred Winfrey, recently retired senior vice president; John E. Wilson, vice president; and DeWitt Smith, recently retired vice president.

Among the governors to whom special indebtedness is felt for assistance and guidance in learning something of the Red Cross from the viewpoint of the longtime volunteer must be included Miss Margaret Hickey, public affairs editor of the *Ladies Home Journal;* John Sinclair, president of the National Industrial Conference Board and recent chairman of the New York Chapter; Joseph R. Stewart, attorney, of Kansas City, Missouri; Cornelius T. Dalton, of the Louisville (Kentucky) *Courier-Journal and Times;* and W. Croft Jennings, attorney, of Columbia, South Carolina.

Appendices

APPENDIX A

THE JOB OF THE RED CROSS

The American Red Cross is a nationwide voluntary organization through which all people may serve in the American tradition of neighbor helping neighbor.

Organized under the Congress and directed by a board broadly representative of the people and the government, the work of the Red Cross is performed by over two million volunteers and a small staff, serving across the nation and overseas.

Under federal laws and regulations, the Red Cross provides emergency relief for disaster victims and needed assistance in restoring them to normal living, gives personal assistance to men of the military services as a volunteer auxiliary between members of the armed forces and their families, fulfills America's obligations under certain international treaties and, along with seventy-nine other Red Cross societies, conducts an international relief program.

To perform these and other functions designed to prevent or alleviate suffering caused by family, community, national, or international emergencies, the Red Cross carries on a total of ten service programs. The Red Cross is a membership organization deriving its support from over forty million adult and junior members.

APPENDIX B

HISTORICAL TABLE OF THE HEADS OF THE AMERICAN RED CROSS

TITULAR HEAD OF RED CROSS

NAME	DATES	TITLE OF RED CROSS POSITION
Clara Barton	June 9, 1881– May 14, 1904	President
(Interim Period)	June 16, 1904– January 16, 1905	

Mrs. John Logan served as Acting President, May 14–June 16, 1904. On the latter date, William K. Van Reypen was named by Senatorial Committee developing the reorganization to head Red Cross until a new charter could be secured from Congress.

NAME	DATES	TITLE OF RED CROSS POSITION
William Howard Taft	February 8, 1905– December 4, 1906	President, Board of Incorporators
	December 4, 1906– March 19, 1913	President

Former President Taft resigns March 19, 1913, in order to establish precedent that the President of the United States should also be president of Red Cross (now Honorary Chairman). This was agreed to by President Wilson, and the precedent has been followed by each President since then.

NAME	DATES	TITLE OF RED CROSS POSITION
Woodrow Wilson	March 19, 1913– March 4, 1921	Honorary President

PRINCIPAL OFFICER OF RED CROSS

NAME	DATES	TITLE OF RED CROSS POSITION
Clara Barton	June 9, 1881 January 26, 1895 December 11, 1901 December 9, 1902– May 14, 1904	Chief Executive Officer President, Board of Directors General Executive Manager Chairman, Executive Committee
William K. Van Reypen	January 16, 1905– February 13, 1906	Chairman of Central Committee
Robert M. O'Reilly	February 13, 1906– December 4, 1906	Chairman of Central Committee
George W. Davis	December 4, 1906– October 28, 1915	Chairman of Central Committee
William Howard Taft	October 28, 1915– January 7, 1919	Chairman of Central Committee

Former President Taft accepted chairmanship on condition that he be given assistance of a younger man to act as actual head of Red Cross. ELIOT WADSWORTH was elected Executive Vice President Sept. 1, 1916. Mr. Taft referred to himself as "nominal chairman" and Mr. Wadsworth as actual manager of Red Cross.

WAR COUNCIL. May 10, 1917–March 1, 1919

HENRY P. DAVISON, Chairman. With our entrance into World War I, President Wilson appointed a council of nationally known financial leaders to conduct the greatly expanded wartime program. The Central Committee "confirmed the decisions of this council." Mr. Wadsworth was a member of both groups. At the conclusion of the war, the Central Committee again assumed direct control of policy and operation.

Livingston Farrand	January 15, 1919– October 15, 1921	Chairman of Central Committee (Presidential letter of appointment gives "Executive Officer")
John Barton Payne	October 15, 1921– January 24, 1935	Chairman of Central Committee (and "Executive Head of Corporation")
Cary T. Grayson	February 8, 1935– February 15, 1938	Chairman of Central Committee (and "Executive Head of Corporation")
Norman H. Davis	April 12, 1938– July 2, 1944	Chairman of Central Committee (and "Executive Head of Corporation")
Basil O'Connor	July 13, 1944 May 8, 1947– October 1, 1949	Chairman of Central Committee President (of the Corporation)
George C. Marshall	October 1, 1949– December 1, 1950	President
E. Roland Harriman	December 1, 1950 January 1, 1954–	President Chairman of Red Cross (and of Board of Governors) and its "Principal Officer"

Warren G. Harding	Honorary President	March 4, 1921– August 2, 1923
Calvin Coolidge	Honorary President	August 2, 1923– March 4, 1929
Herbert Clark Hoover	Honorary President	March 4, 1929– March 4, 1933
Franklin Delano Roosevelt	Honorary President	March 4, 1933– April 12, 1945
Harry S. Truman	Honorary President Honorary Chairman	April 12, 1945– May 8, 1947– January 20, 1953
Dwight D. Eisenhower	Honorary Chairman	Janury 20, 1953–

President of the Corporation (Chief Executive Officer) now elected by Board of Governors:

Ellsworth Bunker, January 1, 1954– December 31, 1956

Alfred M. Gruenther, January 1, 1957–

APPENDIX C

VOLUNTEERS THROUGH THEIR RED CROSS TYPIFY THE GREAT HEART OF AMERICA

1881–1955

Red Cross, The Story Of Warm-Hearted Volunteers

The story of the American Red Cross from its very beginning is a story of warm-hearted volunteers bringing together their skilled hands, their time and their energies in services as varied as human needs. Chairman Harriman, himself a volunteer, has said, "In many people doing what any one of us would do for a neighbor lies the thoroughly human story of the Red Cross."

The multitudes of Red Cross volunteers come from every walk of life and give joint expression to the great human impulse to help those in need. Their continued, generous, loyal, and dedicated participation makes real the fulfillment of the charter obligations of the American Red Cross, and gives to the organization a decisive endorsement and a clear continuance of the mandate that Red Cross services must be available whenever and wherever they are needed. The estimated hours served by volunteers from 1917 through 1955 are the equivalent of a staff of 50,000 full-time workers serving continuously during these 39 years. These volunteers serve as officers, committee members, and consultants, at national, area, and chapter levels; as instructors of Red Cross training courses in health and safety services; as Junior Red Cross teacher-sponsors; at first-aid stations, with detachments, and mobile units; in blood collection programs; as speakers and fund campaign workers; as Service Groups workers, and in numerous other capacities essential in policy-making, administration, and operation of the organization.

Volunteers and paid staff alike respond in larger numbers during war years. The highest count of volunteers serving during a single year was the 8,200,000 active during 1918–19, the last year of World War I. The next highest count was the 7,500,000 serving during 1944–45, the last year of World War II. During each World War the same average number of volunteers, some 4,000,000 served each year. Since 1917–18, an annual average of more than 1,500,000 volunteers have served each year—a count which is more than 150 times the average count of total paid workers on duty each year.

Conspicuous among the volunteers working in various capacities is the average of nearly 882,000, who have served so generously each year since 1917–18 in the Service Groups activities. The volunteer hours given by these workers were first reported in 1932–33. Since then more than 1,128,000,000 volunteer hours have been given by this segment of workers in service to members of the armed forces, veterans, disaster victims, and various other fellow Americans. These total hours constitute the equivalent of approximately 65 times the number of hours that have transpired since the birth of Christ. During each year of this period, these Service Groups volunteers have given an average of 50,000,000 hours of service, or more than three times the hours spent by the average count of total paid workers serving Red Cross each year.

Some Of These Volunteers Provide
Service Groups Activities

Among Red Cross volunteers, described by General George C. Marshall as "the life blood of the American Red Cross," is that group of workers performing the Service Groups activities. These organized services are currently known as Arts and Skills, Canteen, Entertainment and Supply, Gray Lady, Motor, Production, Social Welfare Aide, Staff Aide, and Volunteer Nurse's Aide. Discontinued services include Braille, Canteen Aide, and Dietitian's Aide. During World War I, as many as 8,000,000 volunteers performed these activities in a single year, most of them engaged in production. The peak annual count participating in World War II was 4,000,000 during 1942–43, a major portion of them also engaged in production activities.

Statistics tell a very incomplete story of the incalculable services performed by these workers; however, figures do serve to a limited degree to highlight the measure of volunteer participation recorded for Service Groups workers. The resumé of such participation is as follows, according to the chronological sequence of the organization on a national scale of the various Service Groups.

(Organized 1916)

PRODUCTION SERVICE was organized initially, under the direction of the Women's Bureau, to make surgical dressings, hospital garments, and clothing for war victims in other countries during World War I. Upon request of the Army and Navy, the group also make supplementary comfort supplies for servicemen. The year of peak activity was 1942–43, when more than 3,500,000 gave a grand total of 220,000,000 hours of service.

As an average each year, more than 728,000 workers have given over 37,-000,000 hours. Since World War I, these volunteers have produced 3,000,000,-000 surgical dressings, thousands of them complicated sewed dressings, such as T-binders, face masks, and scultetus binders; also 160,000,000 knitted and sewed garments, among them more than 10,000,000 sweaters for American and Allied servicemen during World War I and World War II. Kit bags containing comfort articles for servicemen here and overseas totaled 17,000,000 during both World Wars.

The estimated grand total value of chapter production during World War I and World War II amounted to approximately $200,000,000. Production volunteers during other than war years are busily engaged in peacetime production activities in keeping with local and national needs.

(Organized 1917)

CANTEEN SERVICE. Few Red Cross services have done more to boost the morale of the disaster victim and the man in uniform than the Canteen Service. During late 1917 khaki-clad women and girls, engaged in one of the most familiar of all Red Cross activities on the home front, were busy handing out cups of coffee, sandwiches, doughnuts, chocolate bars, and cigarettes. Some

55,000 women were taking part in this work when World War I ended, and during the two-year period had made a grand total of 40,000,000 servings.

Total servings to date approximate 185,000,000, including 121,000,000 during World War II. As an average each year, more than 21,000 volunteer canteen workers have provided canteen services and have given to their tasks, since 1932, over 33,000,000 volunteer hours, or an annual average of 1,500,000 hours. The year of peak activity was 1942–43, when nearly 106,000 canteen workers gave 5,400,000 hours of volunteer service.

(Organized 1918)

MOTOR SERVICE. Workers drive their own cars, or chapter-owned cars, in providing transportation essential in the performance of Red Cross activities, such as services to hospitalized servicemen and veterans and their families; to ablebodied servicemen and their families; to patients of free clinics and children's and other civilian hospitals on medical visits and outings; in providing disaster relief; in the collection and distribution of blood; and in numerous other chapter activities.

As an average each year, 11,000 volunteer workers spend a total of 1,700,000 hours while driving some 10,000,000 miles. During the 1942–43 year of peak activity 45,000 Motor Service volunteers gave more than 6,500,000 hours of service.

GRAY LADY SERVICE. This group was originally organized as the Hospital and Recreation Corps to provide Red Cross services in the convalescent quarters of military hospitals. These volunteers now provide friendly, personal, and recreational services to hospitalized servicemen and veterans, to patients in civilian hospitals, to the aged, and to children in homes and institutions; and in numerous ways help the more or less disabled persons to live as fully and happily as possible.

During 1944–45, the year of peak activity, some 50,000 Gray Ladies gave 6,400,000 volunteer hours of service. As an annual average 19,000 volunteers spend 2,100,000 hours providing the individual and group services given by these workers.

VOLUNTEER NURSE'S AIDE SERVICE. Once known as health aides, this group does just what their current name suggests—they assist nurses by performing authorized services in Veterans Administration and military hospitals, clinics, public health agencies, civilian hospitals, community agencies, and blood donor centers.

Emergencies of war and disaster increase the need for these trained volunteers who during the 1944–45 year of peak activity numbered more than 110,000 and gave some 15,000,000 hours of service. These volunteers, since 1932, have served a grand total of 54,000,000 hours. This is equivalent to 18,500 persons working 8 hours per day throughout an entire year. As an average, more than 17,000 volunteer nurse's aides give 2,300,000 hours of service each year.

(Organized 1921)

BRAILLE CORPS. Once organized as a national program, the activities of braille transcription continued through 1942, at which time technological and commercial developments reduced the general need for this highly specialized volunteer service. During the 21 years of national activity, an average of 1,600 volunteers spent 87,000 hours each year transcribing braille. During this period, they transcribed a grand total of 6,000,000 pages for benefit of the blind.

(Organized 1922)

In this year, three Services were organized nationally to meet needs for additional volunteer assistance in the conduct of Red Cross chapter programs in the communities, at Veterans Administration and military hospitals, and at military installations.

ADMINISTRATION SERVICE was organized to assume responsibility for the direction of the expanding program of specialized volunteer services. An annual average of 8,000 volunteers have spent well over 1,000,000 hours performing such administrative tasks.

SOCIAL WELFARE AIDE SERVICE, formerly Home Service Corps, has brought together a group of workers able and interested in performing family welfare services, through chapter Home Service, mainly to servicemen, veterans, and their dependents. As many as 16,000 such volunteers have in a single year given over 2,000,000 hours providing these family welfare services. The annual average shows 7,500 workers giving 773,000 hours to these community assignments.

STAFF AIDE SERVICE, previously Staff Assistance Corps, has given invaluable assistance through a multiplicity of office assignments in virtually every phase of the Red Cross program. Their secretarial abilities and business training equip them to provide able assistance particularly during such emergency periods as war and disaster. Typical of their fine response is the fact that an average of 23,000 workers give 2,000,000 volunteer hours each year assisting in the chapters and in the communities upon assignment by the chapters. In 1943–44, the year of peak activity, these volunteers numbered more than 128,000 and gave more than 8,000,000 hours of service, equivalent to the full time spent in a year by a paid staff numbering 5,000.

(Organized 1942–1947)

During this period, the vastly increased number of hospitalized servicemen and veterans created new and pressing demands for Red Cross services. To meet certain of these needs, largely in those fields handicapped through wartime emergencies by the shortage of professional paid personnel, Red Cross provided volunteer assistance through the national organization of two new Volunteer Service Groups—CANTEEN AIDES, organized in 1942, and DIETITIAN'S AIDES, in 1943. After relatively few years, with the decline of wartime emergencies, both Services were discontinued.

Also during this period, two other Services were given revised functions and new titles: ARTS AND SKILLS in 1944, and ENTERTAINMENT AND INSTRUCTION in 1947. The latter Service was further reorganized in 1952 and given its current title of ENTERTAINMENT AND SUPPLY SERVICE. In the main, volunteers in these Services provided such recreational and instructional supplies and services to hospitalized servicemen and veterans as were not immediately available to them through government-financed channels. In recent years, these services have been extended, along with other Red Cross services, to the aged, the handicapped, children in homes, institutions, and hospitals, and patients in civilian hospitals, including mental hospitals.

Workers in Arts and Skills Service and in Entertainment and Supply Service have given since their respective organizations a combined grand total of nearly 9,000,000 hours of service. The volunteers giving these services each year average 3,400 in Arts and Skills Service and 38,000 in Entertainment and Supply Service.

Volunteers Meet Spectacular Needs
for Red Cross Service

Worthy of special mention are the occasions when Red Cross volunteers respond, with outstanding services, in areas of great need. A spectacular example of an occasional need is that which, during World War II, created the prisoner-of-war-packaging project. This service was given by volunteers in 5 selected centers during the years 1942–45. Throughout this period a grand total of nearly 2,000,000 hours was given by an annual average of 13,500 volunteers, in the Brooklyn, Chicago, New York, Philadelphia, and St. Louis chapters, who meticuously filled, in assembly-line fashion, more than 27,000,000 prisoner-of-war packages for American and Allied prisoners in Europe and the Far East.

The more common spectacular need is during a disaster emergency. Obviously the stress of the emergency makes quite insignificant any effort to count the volunteers who respond in large numbers when disaster strikes. The record, therefore, of these selfless volunteers—some working the uncommon stretch of 48 hours without rest or sleep; others continuing for 72 hours with no thought of self, reluctant to stop or to give way to replacements—is written only in the memories of the persons they helped. The trained Red Cross specialists in charge of disaster relief operations agree that "When disaster strikes the problem is not that of getting volunteers to work but is that of getting volunteers to stop working."

So it is that since 1881, endless individual records of heroism, self sacrifice, and untiring service of volunteers continue to tell the great humanitarian story of the American Red Cross. Volunteers through their Red Cross typify the great heart of America.

Index

Index

THE AUTHOR AND HIS BOOK

CHARLES HURD, *author, journalist and public relations consultant, was born on May 11, 1903, in Tonkawa, Oklahoma. He received his boyhood education from tutors and was an extension student at Northwestern University, Evanston, Ill., from 1918 to 1923. He began his writing career during his college years as a full-time reporter for* The Associated Press *in Chicago and then in New York City. He became an associate editor of* Liberty *magazine in 1926 and left three years later to join the staff of* The New York Times *in their Washington bureau. Until 1949 he remained there, having served as White House correspondent at various times and having been a London correspondent specializing in international politics during 1937 and 1938. He has since been actively engaged in the public relations field doing industrial promotion work through his own firm, Charles Hurd Associates. He was also a news commentator and has contributed to many magazines including* Life, Reader's Digest, *and* American Magazine, *wrote a regular feature on personalities for* Redbook, *and has had material published in anthologies. His books are* The White House (*Harper, 1940*); The Veterans Program (*Whittlesey House, 1946*); and* Washington Cavalcade (*Dutton, 1948*). He was married to the former Eleanor Branson of Washington, D.C., in 1934, and they make their home in New York City.*

THE COMPACT HISTORY OF THE AMERICAN RED CROSS (*Hawthorn, 1959*) *was designed by Sidney Feinberg, completely manufactured by American Book–Stratford Press, Inc., and illustrated by Gil Walker. The body type was set on the Linotype in Times Roman, originally designed for use by* The Times *of London.*

A HAWTHORN BOOK